Also by Peter Navarro:

THE COMING CHINA WARS
Where They Will Be Fought, How They Can Be Won

DEATH BY CHINA
Confronting the Dragon—A Global Call to Action

CROUCHING TIGER
What China's Militarism Means for the World

IN TRUMP TIME

IN TRUMP TIME

A JOURNAL OF AMERICA'S PLAGUE YEAR

PETER NAVARRO

Assistant to the President and Director of the Office of Trade and Manufacturing Policy

Defense Production Act Policy Coordinator for Trump Administration

To "a helluva broad," Evelyn Littlejohn.

May she rest in peace.

Cover design by Timothy Shaner

Jacket and endpaper photography: Official White House photos courtesy of Peter Navarro

All Seasons Press
6800 Gulfport Blvd. Suite 201-355
St. Petersburg, FL 33707

First Edition: October 2021

Interior design by Timothy Shaner

Library of Congress Cataloging-in-Publication Data has been applied for.

ISBNs: 978-1-7374785-0-8 (hardcover), 978-1-7374785-1-5 (ebook)

Printed in Canada

10 9 8 7 6 5 4 3 2 1

Trump Time *phrasal noun, idiom*
/trʌmp/ /taɪm/

1. To implement a government policy or action as quickly as possible
   Example: A vaccine to fight the deadly virus from Communist China was developed in Trump Time.
2. The age of the presidency of Donald Trump
   Example: America's economy was unusually strong during Trump Time.

It's the day before the New Hampshire primary, and the Boss is up in the Granite State trolling the Democrats. The West Wing feels a bit to me like the ballroom on the *Titanic* as the coronavirus spreads. There's no question in my mind that this is going to hit hard. It's going to go on for a long time. It will be an existential threat both to the country and to the administration if it's not handled properly.

—*Peter Navarro, journal entry,*
February 10, 2020

CONTENTS

CONTENTS

IN TRUMP TIME

PROLOGUE

A *RASHOMON* ELECTION

It's human to lie. Most of the time we can't even be honest with ourselves.

—Akira Kurosawa, *Rashomon*

Conventional media wisdom has it that Donald Trump lost the 2020 presidential election because of two simple mistakes. When bad luck and trouble hit America in the form of a deadly virus from Communist China, he failed to manage the pandemic properly. This put a low, hard ceiling on the president's approval rating.

The media also claimed America's first Twitter president made a daily habit of alienating just about everybody outside his core deplorables base. So, in a political climate where Americans were already way over their emotional pandemic edge, it was sayonara to suburban soccer moms, adios to Hispanics, and bye-bye birdcage to anyone with their own personal pronouns.

Yet, this kind of CNN, paint-by-the-Never-Trump-numbers quickly falls apart when measured against the stunning closeness of a race that pre-election pollsters billed as a Biden landslide. It is precisely this photo-finish reality of the 2020 election that must lead us to examine a more complex set of reasons that might account for the outcome.

Of those who might conduct such an inquiry, I can modestly lay claim to a unique vantage point within the White House and often within the Oval Office itself. From these twin perches, I was able to see some things better than most and other things that might otherwise never have seen the light of day.

It is also true that you can literally count on three fingers the number of senior White House advisors who were with the president for the entire journey—from the winning 2016 campaign all the way to the end. On those three fingers are illegal immigration czar Stephen Miller, tweetmeister Dan Scavino, and yours truly—assistant to the president and director of the White House Office of Trade and Manufacturing Policy.

That I survived five long and tumultuous years at the president's side is, in and of itself, an unlikely outcome. The deadpool on Peter Navarro when I first entered the White House was that I was an ivory tower rube unschooled in the ways of the Washington swamp who would last less than a month and be the first to go. Yet somehow, despite a surfeit of powerful enemies, I outlasted all who were out to get me.

In seeking a more textured view of history, my promise to you is this: I will hold nothing back and speak only the truth as I have seen it, at times as an active participant, at times simply as an observer.

In support of this promise I will rely heavily on a *pour mémoire* journal that I began keeping early in the administration on a daily basis. As a key witness to what I knew would be one of the most important historical periods of our time, I wanted to get that history exactly right. And the deeper I got into the fight, I also wanted accountability.

History—and the American people—deserve no less. So, as that great tower of a man I used to call the Boss might say, "Let's go!"

ONE

THE SKINNY DEAL, EAST WING, RED, WHITE, AND BLUES

We are facing an implacable enemy whose avowed objective is world domination by whatever means and at whatever cost. There are no rules in such a game. Hitherto acceptable norms of human conduct do not apply.

—The Doolittle Report, 1954[1]

January 15, 2020, would be an unseasonably warm day in Washington, DC. It would also turn out to be both the beginning of the end of Donald J. Trump's presidency and America's Third Day of Infamy.

On this fateful day, President Trump is surrounded on a stage in the East Wing of the White House by a high-ranking delegation of Chinese Communist Party officials, several members of his own trade team, and a Brutus who will betray this American Caesar almost exactly a year later, Vice President Michael Richard Pence. The president is on this stage to co-sign with Chinese vice premier Liu He in what is being billed, at least on the American side, as a "historic" phase one trade deal.[2]

At this seemingly triumphant time for Donald Trump's America, a second term for the greatest jobs president, trade negotiator, and populist economic nationalist in White House history appears a near certainty. One key reason: on the growth-inducing policy wings of tax cuts, deregulation, strategic domination of the energy sector, increased defense spending, and a parade of new trade agreements, America's forty-fifth president has built the strongest American economy in the last fifty years.

In this vibrant Trump economy, the Dow Jones Industrial Average is moving rapidly toward breaking the 30,000 barrier.[3] The unemployment rate has fallen to an astonishing 3.5 percent. And Blacks, Hispanics, and women—three key demographics critical for a 2020 victory—are all enjoying record low unemployment rates.[4]

Best of all, politically, real wages are rising disproportionately for lower-income workers,[5] and those benefitting include many of the very same factory workers who have been so important to tipping the scales for the president across the Rust Belt and its Blue Wall states in the 2016 election. It had been these Trump Democrats who had told their union bosses to go pound sand when they had been urged to vote for Crooked Hillary.

Said I on more than one occasion in the media when broadcasting these impressive statistics:

Every American who wants a job in the Trump economy can find a job. And every American who wants to search for a better job has ample opportunities to do so.[6]

It isn't just the economy that's going well for President Trump. On immigration policy, his border wall is going up at the rate of about a mile a day, to the delight of his rock solid and red meat base.[7] Under the threat of tariffs, the Mexican government has deployed 15,000 troops to help secure the border.[8]

Under similar Trump pressure, the Northern Triangle governments of Guatemala, Honduras, and El Salvador are likewise playing Trump *beisbol*, allowing US Customs and Border officials to send illegal aliens right back to the Northern Triangle through so-called safe third country agreements. As a result, and after a massive spike in illegal immigration in May 2019,[9] illegal immigration is trending dramatically down and border security is looking up.[10]

On foreign policy, the news is equally good. POTUS's good cop–bad cop bromance with "Rocket Man" Kim Jong-un has led to at least the temporary grounding of North Korea's budding missile arsenal and the cessation of Kim's underground nuclear bomb testing.

Confounding his Globalist critics, the president has also demonstrated friendly working relationships with world leaders ranging from progressives such as France's Emmanuel Macron and Canada's Justin Trudeau and pragmatists like Germany's Angela Merkel and Japan's Shinzo Abe, to brutal authoritarians like China's Xi Jinping, Russia's Vladimir Putin, and Turkey's Recep Erdoğan.

And nowhere around the world is America engaged in any major shooting wars. No George Bush Middle East shock and awe followed by Dick Cheney chaos and confusion. No disastrous Barack Obama Libyan and Syrian debacles.[11] Not even a Clintonian "wag the dog" bombing of Serbia.[12]

In fact, the only really intense battles President Trump had waged on the foreign policy front had been with a seemingly endless supply of endless war political appointees. These included most prominently National Security Advisor H. R. McMaster and his successor, John Bolton; Secretary of State Rex Tillerson; Chief of Staff John Kelly; and the Pentagon's Jim "Mad Dog" Mattis.[13]

All of these president's men thought they knew better than the man who had actually gotten elected by the American people. None of them wanted to end any of the endless wars that Trump's predecessors had bogged America down in and dearly cost American lives. And each of these disloyalists had regularly ignored or violated the presidential chain of command—right up to the day each got fired.

On the wings of these robust domestic and foreign policy achievements, the President's Gallup Poll job approval rating has soared to a personal high of 49 percent.[14] His handling of the economy has skyrocketed to 63 percent.[15] His foreign affairs rating is up from 33 percent in November of 2017 to a personal best of 47 percent.[16] And numerous political handicappers in January 2020 put the odds of a Trump reelection at well over 50 percent.[17]

What will happen in America's plague year following this January high-water mark will, however, mark the greatest turn of events in modern presidential election history.

ALWAYS A TIGHT RACE

To be clear here, and unlike other key senior administration officials—most dangerously the Wall Street wing of Treasury secretary Steve Mnuchin and National Economic Council director Larry Kudlow—I never thought a victory in 2020 would ever be a landslide, no matter how strong the economy got, no matter how high the stock market rose, no matter how rosy the polls looked.

That the 2020 presidential race would always be close was a matter of sheer math and starkly simple statistics. Every Republican candidate in this modern era always starts out on Election Day far behind in the Electoral College count. That's because the Left Coast of California, Oregon, and Washington together with New York and Illinois would rather vote for a Democrat corpse than a live Republican—and together, these deepest shades of blue states account for almost 50 percent of the electoral college votes a candidate needs to win the presidency.

I also always remembered what too many of my White House colleagues would too easily forget: that the thinnest of thin 2016 margin of victory across the Blue Wall states of Michigan, Pennsylvania, and Wisconsin was equivalent[18] to a football crowd at the Rose Bowl spread over three states and 150,000 square miles.[19]

If just those three Blue Wall states with their forty-six Electoral College votes had held like a true wall for the Democrats, rather than crumbled under the weight of Trump's populist economic nationalism, candidate Trump's apparent "landslide" Electoral College victory of 304 votes to Hillary Clinton's 227[20] would have given way to a decisive Clinton beatdown.

Of course, all of these thoughts about our 2020 election prospects were far from my mind as I sat to the right of the stage with other White House senior staff watching the spectacle—in my mind, the debacle—of the signing of what had come to be derisively known as the Skinny Deal.

The short version of the Skinny Deal story goes something like this.

SUDDEN ZEN VERSUS DRAGON IN A POT

Candidate Trump had promised in 2016 to put a swift end to China's economic aggression through the imposition of hefty tariffs.[21] Such economic aggression came in the form of what

I had dubbed China's Seven Deadly Sins during an August 4, 2019, *Fox News Sunday* slugfest with Chris Wallace.[22]

These sins, which speak directly to the predatory structure of Communist China's protectionist and mercantilist economy, include:

1. Widespread cyber hacking to steal America's business information and trade secrets.
2. A relentlessly sophisticated government-sponsored campaign of intellectual property theft that cost American businesses and workers about a half a trillion dollars a year.
3. Forced technology transfer by American companies in exchange for access to China's markets.
4. The dumping below-cost of a myriad of products into American markets at the expense of American jobs and factories.
5. Deep-pocketed, predatory-pricing State-Owned Enterprises that destroy American industries and seize global market share.
6. A "beggar thy neighbor" currency manipulation that subsidizes Chinese exports and suppresses American exports to China while ballooning the US trade deficit. And finally
7. Communist China's relentless annual slaughter of tens of thousands of Americans through its flooding of our communities—often our poorest, working-class communities—with deadly fentanyl and other opioids.[23]

By the time President Trump took office in January of 2017, he had identified two broad strategies to deal with China's Seven Deadly Sins. He could go full "Sudden Zen" with immediate across-the-board tariffs in fulfillment of his campaign promise. Alternatively, he could embark on a far more subtle and perilous route that I would label our "Dragon in a Pot" strategy.

You know the derivative story here. Toss a frog into a pot of cold water and slowly turn up the heat. The frog never tries to jump out and eventually gets boiled alive. The strategic analogue here was to slowly implement the Trump tariffs over more and more Chinese products at higher and higher levels until one of two things happened. Either the US economy effectively decoupled from the parasite of China **or** the Chinese Dragon eventually kowtowed and signed a truly Trumpian agreement that would fully, finally, and forevermore put an end to all of its Seven Deadly Sins against American workers and the American people.

My crystal-clear preference was for Sudden Zen tariffs. After writing a trilogy of books about China's economic aggression and quest for military dominance—*The Coming China Wars* in 2006,[24] *Death by China* in 2011,[25] and *Crouching Tiger* in 2015[26]—I was utterly convinced that trying to get a workable deal with the Chinese Communist Party in the absence of tough tariffs would simply suck us down yet another endless series of empty "all talk, no walk" Hank Paulson–style summits and useless dialogues like those that had plagued previous clueless and spineless administrations dating back to the original too clever by half China dupe, Henry Kissinger.

There was also the demonstrably sociopathic nature of the communist regime itself to consider in the strategic calculus. If history has taught us anything, it is that the Chinese Communist Party **never** fully abides by *any* major agreement.

The most glaring poster child of such bad faith was also one of the more recent in US-China relations. In 2015, on a beautiful September 25 day—the forecast was "sunny with a 100% chance of lies"—China's president-cum-dictator Xi Jinping solemnly promised Barack Obama in the White House Rose Garden that China would both stop hacking American computers and cease militarizing the South China Sea.[27] Of course, both of these Communist promises have long since been shredded.

So, my strong view was to keep what I regarded as candidate Trump's most sacred promise of the campaign and immediately slap on the full Sudden Zen China tariffs. The problem I had in pushing this position was, however, this: I was a one-man China hawk band totally without power or allies in a White House filled with a symphony of Wall Street transactionalists and China dove appeasers.

A FLYING DUTCHMAN ON INAUGURATION DAY

Now at this point you must ask, just how on Trump's good earth did all these bad personnel show up in a White House with a commander in chief who had campaigned as an uber China hawk? It all started with what Steve Bannon has called the "Original Sin" of the administration:[28] a populist economic nationalist president would immediately enter into a power-sharing arrangement with a traditional Republican establishment that loathed much of what the upstart Trump stood for and had campaigned on—from fair trade and secure borders to an end to endless wars.

That power sharing began as soon as POTUS turned over the keys of the chief of staff's office during the transition to Republican National Chairman Reince Priebus—and I would be one of the very first Trump loyalists that Priebus's deputy chief of staff Katie Walsh would try to send straight to Original Sin hell.

Indeed, by the time Inauguration Day rolled around, I had gone from working in the campaign penthouse as the top economic and trade advisor at Trump Tower straight to the West Wing outhouse—otherwise known as the Eisenhower Executive Office Building.

The EEOB is just thirty yards across the street from the White House, but it's a hundred miles away from the West Wing's notoriously cramped halls and corridors of power. And my comedownance had come brutally the very first time I walked onto the White House grounds on Inauguration Day.

On that cold bucket of water day, I had found myself unceremoniously stripped of the rank of assistant to the president that I had been promised. That demotion would mean no walk-in privileges to the Oval Office and therefore a de facto isolation from the president. I would also be banned from senior staff meetings, where all the inner workings of the White House and our policy agendas would be revealed.

Walsh also stripped me of much of the support staff I had recruited—making me quite literally a one-man band. I was even left like the Flying Dutchman without an office for most of the first month of the administration and worked standing up with my laptop like a ghost in the hallways.

While Katie Walsh, and later John Kelly, knew that the Boss would never tolerate my firing, they thought that if they could humiliate me enough, I would simply quit and go back home to California with my tail between my legs. Walsh and the globalists in the West Wing she was carrying water for were wrong on that count, as they were wrong on so much else. It was on more than one night I thought, *Screw them. Stay the course.*

Walsh, by the way, lasted barely two months and got fired for leaking.[29] Karma is truly a schadenfreude bitch.

THE DUMBEST SMART GUY I'VE EVER MET

Her slings and arrows notwithstanding, Katie Walsh would turn out to be the least of my worries within the West Wing. My far bigger problem was in fending off multiple knife attacks from a coalition of the aforementioned Wall Street transactionalists who viewed Communist China more as a capitalist piggy bank than an existential threat. They saw me—the Harvard guy and one true populist economic nationalist other than Steve Bannon—as their only real obstacle to reining in the president's tough on China, pro-tariff policies.

Foremost among these Wall Street transactionalists were the National Economic Council director and former Goldman Sachs kingpin Gary Cohn and the aforementioned Mnuchin. Cohn was ideologically opposed to the president's trade policy, he particularly detested tariffs, and during his tenure at Goldman Sachs, Cohn never saw an American job he didn't want to offshore in the profane name of supply chain efficiencies.

My most enduring image of Cohn is that of him loading up his massive monogrammed golf bag into a White House limousine in the dead-ass middle of a working week so he could go try to break a hundred at a nearby country club. It would have been hilarious if it weren't on the taxpayer's dime.

For his part, the Yalie capitalist Mnuchin, another Goldman Sachs alum, had raised and made millions from Communist China prior to joining the administration,[30] and he had his jaundiced, pieces of silver, Judas Iscariot eye on making billions more. But there was also this: this second coming of Neville Chamberlain, contrary to all facts, logic, and every classified briefing Mnuchin ever sat through, simply did not believe that the authoritarian and dictatorial People's Republic of Communist Concentration Camp

China posed any economic or military threat to the United States whatsoever. And human rights? Let the Uighurs and Tibetans eat cake.

So, between me and Mnuchin, it was Mars and Venus from the get-go. I saw him as the dumbest smart guy I'd ever met. He saw me as an inconvenient bump on the road to making billions in Beijing.

A SIMPLE ACT OF FRIENDSHIP GOES AWRY

Beyond Gary Cohn and Steve Mnuchin, I also had to contend, quite oddly, with the slings and arrows of the Department of Commerce secretary, Wilbur Ross. I say "oddly" because Wilbur and I had been brothers-in-arms during the campaign, co-authoring numerous articles and reports together and taking turns debating Clinton campaign surrogates like Austan Goolsbee and Gene Sperling.[31]

When Wilbur was crestfallen because he hadn't gotten the Treasury secretary job, which went to Mnuchin, I sat consolingly with him in his Manhattan office suite. As dusk turned into a brilliantly lit New York skyline, I convinced this Wall Street legend that he should take the Commerce job and turn it from a Cabinet backwater into a juggernaut of trade policy.

This simple act of heartfelt friendship would, however, turn out to be one of the biggest mistakes of my life, as Wilbur, with his transactionalist Wall Street DNA, quickly joined the transactionalist camp.

MORNING AT MAR-A-LAGO

With Sudden Zen tariffs taken off the table by the transactionalists, that left the default strategy of the Chinese Dragon in a Pot. In pursuit of that strategy, and within months of taking office, President Trump invited China's president Xi Jinping to Trump's palatial Mar-a-Lago resort in Palm Beach, Florida. This glitzy, two-day April 6 and 7 summit would officially kick off what would become a long and winding road to the Skinny Deal that the president was about to sign in the East Wing.

Along this more than one-thousand-day march,[32] the president had conducted a quintessentially Trumpian negotiation. He would juxtapose praise-laden bromance talk about his alleged "good friend" Xi against a brutal series of gut punches in the form of progressive layers and levels of tariffs on Chinese products.

As the president ratcheted up this pressure, he would use me to send appropriate Churchillian signals of strength—Bannon called me the "default option" if talks failed. Meanwhile, to reassure financial markets, the Boss would let Munich Mnuchin, Cohn, and, later, Cohn's successor Larry Kudlow wave their Neville Chamberlain-Lord Halifax appeasement flags.

It was an absolutely genius Trump strategy that allowed us to progressively increase tariffs while growing support among the American people for our Tough on China policy. That public support steadily grew because we only ever raised tariffs after the Chinese were clearly seen to be acting in bad faith.

It was an absolutely genius Trump strategy, that is, right up until to the very bad day it was not. That bad day came in a harsh reality check on May 3, 2019. That's when China's chief negotiator, Vice Premier Liu He, backed out of what had been a very firm handshake deal[33]—a deal that would have been the biggest and most important not just in American history, but also in global economic history.

Lest you think that might be a bit of Trumpian, Sean Spicy hyperbole, think again. This original full monty China deal was a nearly 150-page Trump masterpiece. It would have forced the Chinese Communist Party to cease committing its Seven Deadly Sins and thereby fundamentally restructure and transform Communist China's protectionist and mercantilist economy into a model of free, fair, and capitalist international trade.

With such a deal, this would have been Communist China's own version of the Soviet Union's Perestroika moment. *Both* the U.S. and Chinese economies would have rocked. And the global economy would have rocked and rolled with us.

Of course, once the Chinese side walked away from that handshake deal, President Trump could have, and should have, doubled down on his tariff strategy and decoupled through blanket steep tariffs across the Chinese economy. And he should have held that hard, red line—the only kind of line the Chinese Communist Party understands—until such time as Xi Jinping sent his grim band of apparatchiks back to the bargaining table on their collective knees ready to sign the full Seven Deadly Sins deal.

Instead of this peace through strength gambit, however, the same coterie of Panda-hugging transactionalists within the West Wing who had blocked Sudden Zen would immediately begin secretly collaborating with a small but powerful cabal of billionaires to move the president to the Skinny Deal he was about to grudgingly sign on this fateful January day in the East Wing.

I say "grudgingly" here because the president's big smile notwithstanding, he was steamed not just at Xi Jinping and the Chinese Communist Party for, in Wall Street lingo, successfully **retrading** the original handshake deal. The Boss was equally peeved at the relentless lobbying of a billionaires' cabal that had, in effect, anointed itself as the president's de facto China Appeaser Kitchen Cabinet.

OF SHEEP AND JACKALS

Just who are these billionaires? As I sit in the East Wing this fateful January 15 day, I can look right into their dollar-green eyes. They are sitting centerstage in prime seats like vultures and wolves ready to applaud the Skinny Deal—and then go right back home on their chartered jets to check their bank balances and corporate income statements.

This billionaire group includes most recognizably the casino moneybags of Sheldon Adelson and Steve Wynn. Wynn, with a net worth of several billion dollars, created Las Vegas strip landmarks like Treasure Island, the Bellagio, and Wynn Las Vegas. With a net worth more than ten times that of Wynn,[34] Adelson had earned the distinction of being the single largest political donor in America to federal campaigns.[35]

While both Adelson and Wynn had made their original dough and bones in Vegas, each had also made a very big bet on massive casino operations in China's Macao. If the US-China relationship fractured, their Macao holdings would likely be first hostages and eventually collateral damage. Accordingly, these casino moneybags have a huge vested interest in seeing a Skinny Deal consummated—and the fate of the American nation and its workers and businesses under siege from China's Seven Deadly Sins be damned.

Two other key members of this billionaires cabal are a pair of Wall Street jackals who have played key supporting roles in moving millions of American jobs offshore to China: Steve Schwarzman, the chairman and CEO of the notoriously globalist Blackstone Group, and Larry Fink, the CEO of BlackRock, the largest money manager in the world and the biggest cheerleader and propagandist on the street for investing in Communist China.

Here, one can be assured that when Schwarzman or Fink have trouble sleeping at night, it was not because of any anxiety over inconvenient Chinese Communist truths like the jack-booted asphyxiation of democracy in Hong Kong, People's Liberation Army war drums in the South China Sea and Taiwan Strait, concentration camps in the Xinjiang and Tibetan gulags; China's nuclear-tipped aid to rogue Iranian and North Korean regimes, or any of the Chinese intercontinental ballistic missiles now aimed at Seattle, Chicago, and New York.

What really is driving the Skinny Deal for Schwarzman, Fink, and their broader Wall Street pack is a provision that will open up Chinese markets for American credit card and insurance companies and other financial services. Of course, this narrowly targeted opening of the Chinese market for Wall Street's elites was *never* a key objective of the original Seven Deadly Sins deal, and I had repeatedly warned against the inclusion of this Wall Street perk in any Skinny Deal.

Such a provision provides additional latticework for offshoring American jobs. And that further entrenches Wall Street money in China, where jackals like Schwarzman and Fink then become even more vested in advocating Chinese Communist Party interests.

AMERICA'S THIRD DAY OF INFAMY

As I watch this spectacle from a front row seat along the right flank of the stage, I am consumed by an almost primordial fear. I'm literally sweating in an otherwise cool room, and it is a cold and nervous sweat.

My fear is rooted in what will all too soon become an all too prescient prediction. Wrote I in my 2006 book, *The Coming China Wars*, China, as "the world's prime breeding ground for new and exotic" viruses, might well spark "a pandemic in which tens of millions of people may die."[36]

In light of this 2006 prediction, my antenna had gone up on full alert a few days earlier as news began to trickle out from Wuhan, China, of a mysterious virus rampaging through this massive city.

Now, as I sit in the East Wing amidst a packed crowd and a broad ring of TV cameras beaming this historic event to the world, and as I scan the eyes of China's poker-faced diplomats, I can't help asking myself these questions:

- What do these Communists know about what is going on in Wuhan that we don't?
- Is there significant human-to-human transmission of this new emerging virus and therefore the possibility of a global pandemic?
- Have any of these Chinese diplomats been exposed to the virus, and if so, are they possibly contagious?
- And if that possibility even remotely exists, why are these disease vectors and possible assassins here breaking bread with us, smiling, and shaking not just the hands of US trade team members like myself, but also the hands of both the American president and vice president?

Most darkly, I even wonder if this virus might be some sort of bioweapon explicitly designed to attack an ascendent America now firmly led by the first president in history to challenge the economic aggression of the Chinese Communist Party. Knowing this implacable enemy as I do and knowing there are no rules in the game of world domination they are playing, I cannot not rule this out.

America's first Cordell Hull moment had come darkly on December 5, 1941. As Japanese diplomats arrived at the US State Department to talk peace with Secretary of State Hull, Admiral Isoroku Yamamoto was moving an aircraft carrier strike group in for the Pearl Harbor kill.

With the benefit of hindsight—and a mountain of additional evidence—we now know that what the world was watching in the East Wing on January 15, 2020, was Washington, DC's second Cordell Hull moment[37] and America's Third Day of Infamy—with 9/11 occupying the clear second infamous position.

Looking back on this fateful Third Day of Infamy, I now see it as Pearl Harbor and the Twin Towers all rolled up into one massive biological Chernobyl. For even as China's vice premier was smiling and signing a trade deal with President Trump, China's President Xi Jinping was busy back in Beijing orchestrating a series of heinous actions that would ensure that a novel and deadly coronavirus almost certainly spawned in a Wuhan bioweapons lab would mushroom into a global pandemic.[38]

In the broadest of strokes, consider these two questions:

Which day of infamy will turn out to be worse historically—the one propagated by Imperial Japan in 1941 or the one spawned by the Chinese Communist Party in 2020?

And why did the American media so wrongly blame President Trump for a deadly pandemic that the Chinese Communist Party should have rightly and righteously been held accountable for—perhaps along with, ironically, Dr. Anthony Fauci?

In seeking answers to these questions, I will offer what I believe to be the definitive insider's account of America's plague year.

This is a tale that will be full of as much sound and fury as historical significance. It will ultimately even involve a bizarre political twist on the most famous play in football history—the Green Bay Sweep.

Over the course of these pages, from your front row seat in the White House, you will see that there is much to get to the bottom of—from what happened on January 15, 2020, November 3, 2020, and January 6, 2021 to what likely went so very, very wrong at Anthony Fauci's bureaucratic empire and in a Wuhan bioweapons lab.

TWO

FEAR, LOATHING, AND SAINT FAUCI IN THE SITUATION ROOM

This [virus] is not a major threat to the people of the United States and this is not something that the citizens of the United States right now should be worried about.
—Anthony Fauci, January 21, 2020[1]

Travel bans don't work.
—Anthony Fauci, January 28, 2020[2]

The overall clinical consequences of Covid-19 may ultimately be more akin to those of a severe seasonal influenza.
—Anthony Fauci, March 26, 2020[3]

Thus misspoke Dr. Anthony Stephen Fauci. Over and over and over again.

Consider this: Dr. Fauci is an eighty-year-old bureaucrat who graduated from medical school in 1966 and went to work for the federal government two years later. At that time, if a doctor wanted to separate blood plasma, he used a hand-cranked metal centrifuge. This is akin to using a washboard for cleaning clothes prior to the debut of the electric washing machine in 1908.

We can at least credit Fauci for his longevity. But also consider that he consistently gave the US president and the American public a seemingly unending stream of confusing and contradictory advice about a coronavirus from China that, as it has turned out, he himself may well have helped spawn.

My first experience with Fauci would be in the White House Situation Room on January 28, 2020. It was the first of many confrontations with an individual who would do more damage to this nation, President Trump, and the world than anyone else this side of the Bat Lady of Wuhan.

"Situation Room" is really a misnomer. Rather than a single room, it is, instead, a 5,525-square-foot complex that occupies much of the bottom floor of the West Wing. It was created by President Kennedy after the failure of the April 1961 Bay of Pigs invasion. Kennedy wanted a crisis management center with a more centralized space for intergovernment coordination, particularly across intelligence agencies.

Harry Truman's beloved bowling alley, built in 1947, would be swiftly razed to make way for Kennedy's Situation Room. It very quickly came in handy during the Cuban Missile Crisis.

After JFK, Lyndon B. Johnson made the Situation Room his command center for the Vietnam War. And Jimmy Carter spent long days and nights tilting at the Iranian hostage windmills that would cost him a second presidential term.

In the modern era, it was also in the Situation Room that Barack Obama, in a windbreaker and polo shirt, watched the killing of Osama bin Laden and Donald Trump, in a suit and tie, monitored the joint op that took out the world's number one terrorist, Abu Bakr al-Baghdadi.[4] That Delta Force–Army Ranger operation was inspiringly named in honor of Kayla Mueller, a young American humanitarian worker who had been captured, tortured, raped, and murdered by Baghdadi and his gang.[5]

On January 27, 2020, the Sit Room began a new chapter of its storied history as the War Room for many of the deliberations of the soon-to-be-formed White House Coronavirus Task Force. The night before, the forty-fifth president of the United States had assigned me a task he believed was essential to saving hundreds of thousands, perhaps millions, of American lives. Said the Boss, "I'm taking down all flights coming into the US from China. It'll rattle the markets and Biden and the Left will hit me hard. But this virus looks like it might be bad, and we need to do it. So get that Task Force behind me. Be tough. You're my tough guy."

Thought I after that conversation, *POTUS is seeing the pandemic chess board exactly right—we urgently need that travel ban.*

Troubling smoke signals had come just four days earlier from satellite images of China's Hubei province. Its major city, Wuhan, a rival in size to New York, had caught viral fire, and Wuhan's crematoria were burning so many corpses that brown smoke was darkening the skies.[6] More than 5 million Wuhanians fled the plague city, with many taking the virus along to spread to the rest of the world.[7]

For weeks prior, I had been talking about the dangers of the virus with Steve Bannon and one of Steve's friends and backers, the Chinese expat billionaire and CCP opponent Miles Guo. Miles, along with experts such as Dr. Steven Hatfill, were warning us that the trouble in China was not just on the way. The virus was likely already here precisely *because of* the lack of travel restrictions.

Guo, on the basis of intelligence he had gotten from behind enemy lines, did not rule out the possibility that this was a Chinese attack. It might be aimed at anything from snuffing out democracy in Hong Kong to derailing the reelection of President Trump.

For his part, Bannon, ever ahead of the curve, had started a new podcast called *War Room: Pandemic* just two days earlier. The hapless World Health Organization would not officially declare the pandemic until March 11.

A SIT ROOM GAGGLE OF GLOBALISTS

As I walked to my Sit Room seat at the middle of the table, a quick scan of the participants for this pow wow indicated that my mission for the president might not be easy. To my immediate right was Secretary of State Mike Pompeo's second in command, Stephen Biegun.

As a top Ford Motor Company executive, Biegun had been Ford's "offshorer in chief" to China. He was as notorious for his Globalist views as for his tendency to ignore the chain of command that ran up to the far more hawkish Pompeo. He was especially reluctant to offend the Chinese with a travel ban.

Twenty feet away to my left and at the head of the table was the White House Coronavirus Task Force chair and acting chief of staff, Mick Mulvaney. Going up against Mick would likely not be pretty. With Mulvaney, it never was.

Part of Mulvaney's antipathy toward me was simply his own Never Trump ideological antipathy toward two of my key remits. I was the Boss's point guy in the White House on tariffs to defend our domestic industries and on "Buy American" rules for government procurement. Mick loathed both.

Next to Mulvaney at the head of the Sit Room table was Matt Pottinger, the deputy to National Security Advisor Robert O'Brien. Pottinger, known as "the Boy Scout" around the

West Wing, was a firm "yes" for the POTUS travel ban; it was he who had initially gotten me a prime seat at the table.

Yet Pottinger's voice likely wouldn't carry much weight with Mulvaney. In fact, Mulvaney gave Matt even more grief than he gave me.

Pottinger's "sin" in Mulvaney's eyes had been to take the deputy position at the National Security Council when Robert O'Brien had replaced John Bolton as national security advisor in September 2019. Mick had tried to strongarm O'Brien into putting a Mulvaney puppet in as O'Brien's deputy. However, Robert would have none of that; Matt got the job and did a helluva job at that.

Besides Biegun, Mulvaney, and Pottinger, there were across the table from me at the ten and eleven o'clock positions Health and Human Services secretary Alex Azar and the director of the Centers for Disease Control and Prevention (CDC), Dr. Robert Redfield.

The avuncular Redfield—the spitting image of Orville Redenbacher—would soon make one of the worst mistakes of the pandemic by bungling the liftoff for virus testing. We would lose precious weeks while Redfield fiddled and the CDC burned with incompetence.

Of course, the last person in the Sit Room worth mentioning was sitting right across the table from me at high noon. It was a position that would, as it turned out, have no small amount of symbolism.

This small man with round glasses had a grin or a smirk on his face—I couldn't tell which. It was none other than Dr. Anthony Fauci. When I looked into his eyes, he promptly averted his gaze, and I thought to myself, *This could be trouble.*

And trouble it was. Within minutes of Mulvaney calling the meeting to order, I immediately got into a heated argument with Fauci over whether to ban all travel from China. As I'm sparring with him and thinking about all of the bodies being burned in Wuhan, I'm thinking to myself like Butch might say to Sundance, *Who **is** this guy?*

My clash with Fauci started with a comment from him that echoed several comments he had made a few days earlier. In a radio interview with WABC's John Catsimatidis on January 26, Fauci had described the Wuhan virus as "a very, very low risk to the United States."[8] *Oh, really?* thought I when I heard that clip.

In the Sit Room, Fauci echoed that sentiment; and my sharp retort was that even if there were a low risk, there would likely be a very high cost associated with what in his view was an unlikely pandemic. In that case, clearly the best decision would *still* be a travel ban—better safe than sorry.

In response, Fauci, in his thick Brooklyn accent, tacked toward a different argument. The exchange went something like this:

FAUCI: I've studied travel restrictions many, many times, and travel restrictions don't work.

NAVARRO: You mean to tell me if China is sending us over twenty thousand passengers a day into airports like Kennedy, O'Hare, and LAX, some of whom may have escaped from the Ground Zero of Wuhan, that there is no risk that some of these passengers will seed and spread the virus?

FAUCI: In my experience, travel restrictions don't work.

NAVARRO: Again, let me ask you this simple question. If twenty thousand passengers a day are flying into the United States from China, wouldn't it be prudent to pull down those flights to eliminate the possibility that at least some of those passengers may be infected with the virus?

FAUCI: In my experience, travel restrictions don't work.

Of course, that made about as much sense to me as a conversation with Flaubert's parrot. As for the CDC's Redfield, his opposition to the travel ban seemed simply in support of his colleague Fauci. I've seen sheep exhibit more leadership than Redfield did that day—and I would have to wait more than a year (until *after* the presidential election) for him to exhibit any kind of courage.

FAUCI'S FIRST BLOOD: THE AIDS EPIDEMIC

If you get the idea that I don't care for Fauci, you are reading my lack of subtlety correctly. Fauci would do enormous damage to the president's election prospects by constantly and gratuitously contradicting him.

He would do even more damage to the American public with his conflicting public statements. Those statements sowed both confusion and mistrust, even as his actions—and often inaction—cost American lives.

Whether it was needlessly delaying the approval of the Trump vaccine or blocking the use of safe and effective therapeutics such as hydroxychloroquine, Fauci's go-to Angel of Death argument was always the same: "There simply isn't enough data." As Yogi Berra might have said, it was déjà vu all over again.

During the AIDS epidemic in the 1980s, Fauci had sung the very same "there's not enough data" song to block approval of a suite of drugs proving to be quite effective at preventing a pneumonia that was the leading cause of death among AIDS patients. In his 1990 book, *Good Intentions: How Big Business and the Medical Establishment Are Corrupting the Fight Against AIDS*, Bruce Nussbaum recalled a critical 1987 meeting between the AIDS activist Michael Callen and Fauci—then the closest thing in America we had to an AIDS Czar:[9]

> Callen told Fauci that there was plenty of evidence from community doctors that it was possible to prevent the onset of . . . pneumonia by prophylaxing with a new drug, aerosol pentamidine, or with an older drug, sold as Bactrim or Septra. Fauci nearly shouted, "I can't do that. I can't issue these kinds of guidelines. . . ." "Why not?" shot back Callen. "There's no data," Fauci practically screamed."[10]

It should be the screams of the gay men who literally suffocated in their own phlegm that we should remember here. Sean Strub, the author of *Body Counts: A Memoir of Politics, Sex, AIDS, and Survival*, tabulated Fauci's blood on his hands contribution to the AIDS body count at "nearly 17,000."[11]

Beyond that AIDS-era carnage and Fauci's partisan involvement in delaying the Trump vaccine and blocking FDA approval of the use of hydroxychloroquine to combat covid-19, there is also Fauci's deeply ironic role in sparking the pandemic itself. It was Fauci who went behind the back of the Trump White House in 2017 to lift the ban on dangerous "gain-of-function" experiments. [12] It was Fauci's agency at the National Institutes of Health that helped fund and orchestrate such gain-of-function experiments at a bioweapons lab in Wuhan, China[13] where the pandemic almost certainly originated. And it was Fauci who, as we now know from a trove of Fauci emails,[14] was being told as early as January 31, 2020, that the virus was likely genetically engineered.[15]

Yet Fauci kept *all* of that information from President Trump and the White House Coronavirus Task Force and hundreds of thousands of Americans likely died as a result. But let's not get too far ahead of our story . . .

FROM CONSENSUS TO CHAOS IN A FLASH

With everybody's cards now on the Situation Room table and discord clearly in the air, Mick Mulvaney, the Task Force chair, inexplicably proclaimed, "I guess we have a consensus. The group does not support the travel ban."

To which I replied in a nanosecond and in no uncertain terms, "Mick. There is absolutely no consensus in this room."

At that point, the hitherto silent Pottinger finally chimed in, "Chief Mulvaney. The National Security Council is also supportive of the travel ban."

With that, Mick threw up his hands, and the meeting adjourned in chaos. More resolute than dejected, I quickly left the Sit Room and headed home to ponder my options; I hated to let POTUS down. *The next morning, I would pen a memo to the Task Force that would turn out to be one of the most consequential documents of the pandemic.*

The story behind that lifesaving memo, which would turn the recalcitrant Task Force on a dime, actually started in the late 1970s in a Harvard classroom. There I had a life-changing experience while attending a lecture by Professor Richard Caves. Caves was not only a premier scholar; he was also one of the most dynamic speakers I have ever watched and listened to.*

* Dick Caves left this world on November 22, 2019, and may he rest in peace.

It was that lecture by Professor Caves that inspired me to pursue a doctorate in economics at Harvard, with a special focus on industrial organization and the related subfield of Strategic Game Theory. I would rely on my Strategic Game Theory training to build POTUS's case for the China travel ban.

At zero dark thirty on January 29, this game theoretic approach hit me like an "Oh, duh" clap of the hand to the forehead. After a quick breakfast, I jumped onto my bike in the dark, freezing morning and headed in to the sweatshop.

For the next six hours, I worked feverishly on a memo that I, in homage to Martin Luther, intended to at least figuratively nail to the door of the Situation Room for the next Task Force meeting that afternoon. I worked so hard on that memo I skipped one of the most important events of Donald Trump's presidency, an 11:00 a.m. ceremony on the South Lawn celebrating the passage of the United States–Mexico–Canada Agreement (USMCA).

At that ceremony, my front-row seat was conspicuously empty when the Boss gave me a shout-out of thanks for helping him to keep his promise to renegotiate NAFTA. My view, however, was that it was far more important to focus on the task at hand than to burn time in pomp and circumstance.

This attitude had served me well throughout my tenure at the White House, and I owe a debt of gratitude here to an official named Narciso Campos in the Mexican Ministry of Finance with whom I had engaged early on in the NAFTA renegotiations before Robert Lighthizer was confirmed as United States Trade Representative and assumed the chief trade negotiator role.

Narciso had served as chief of staff to Mexico's Secretary of Foreign Affairs, Luis Videgaray—the real brains behind the NAFTA deal on the Mexican side—and Narciso had confided in me about how you could either spend your time in government in ceremonies and at cocktail parties, or you could actually get some things done. He always chose the latter, and I took his advice once I got to the White House.

By noon I had finished my game theory memo and sent it over to the National Security Council staff for distribution. In my email to the NSC, I gave *clear* instructions that the memo be immediately distributed to the *full* list of all those involved in the Task Force. That is, it should be sent not just to the principals but also to their deputies and analysts down the line. I wanted to paper the crap out of everybody on a distribution list that approached a hundred people.

My thinking was that with a distribution list so wide, *it would be impossible for Mulvaney, Fauci, or anyone in between to cover their asses if they continued to oppose the ban.* The large distribution list, coupled with my dire predictions in the memo if the travel ban weren't promptly approved, virtually guaranteed a leak if the opposition to the ban continued.

Here's an excerpt—and the money shot—from that memo. You will see that what Strategic Game Theory enables you to do is to find the so-called dominant strategy based on the facts in evidence and the probabilities associated with possible outcomes. In this case, all you need is a greater than 1 percent chance that a pandemic will hit, and the president's travel ban will be the dominant strategy. Here is how the memo presented the case that more than a half a million Americans might die without a China travel ban:

> In light of the rapid spread of the Chinese coronavirus, game theory is instructive in assessing the need for swift containment and mitigation measures.

In a game-theoretic framework, we confront two stylized choices: Aggressive Containment versus No Containment. We also face two stylized outcomes: A relatively modest "seasonal flu–like" outcome with relatively low rates of transmission and mortality versus a more deadly "pandemic flu" such as witnessed with the Asian, Hong Kong, Spanish, and Swine Flus.

Costs estimates [noted in the matrix below] range from zero in the Seasonal Flu/No Containment outcome to $3.8 trillion in the Pandemic/No Containment outcome. These cost estimates account for both the loss of economic activity and human life and are derived from a recent [White House Council of Economic Advisers] study.

	SEASONAL FLU SCENARIO	PANDEMIC SCENARIO
Aggressive Containment [Travel Ban]	–$2.9 Billion	–$34.6 Billion
No Containment [No Travel Ban]	0	–$3.8 Trillion

From this cost matrix, one can compute the "expected value" of each possible outcome from assumed probabilities. As soon as the probability of the Pandemic outcome rises above roughly 1%, the dominant strategy is aggressive containment [that is, the travel ban]. This is because the costs of a No Containment/Pandemic scenario are so staggering, including the possible loss of as many as half a million American lives.[16]

My memo indeed had its intended effect. It hit the Task Force like a crisp Floyd Mayweather jab to quickly bloody some noses. That afternoon, the Task Force turned 180 degrees and provided a full-throated endorsement of the president's China travel ban.

Too bad I wasn't able to see the Task Force's change of heart and vote that day—and the reason for why that was so was bitterly funny. When I had gone to the Situation Room to attend the meeting, I had been informed by the receptionist that I was *not* on the list of participants. Not for the main conference room. Not even for the overflow room where the meeting was being telecast to the lower-echelon staff.

That interception right at the door, particularly of an assistant to the president who normally has free run of the place, was highly unusual. But I quickly figured out that the receptionist had been specifically instructed to block and tackle me. What my banishment was, of course—and it would be permanent—was Mick Mulvaney's revenge.

But I still think I got the better end of the deal. With no seat at the Task Force table, I did not waste endless hours at daily meetings that were generally less interesting than watching grass grow. Instead, I used the time to draft a series of Action, Action, Action memos that I would unrelentingly pepper and pound the Task Force with.

Those missives often prodded the Task Force members to move on items they otherwise would not have. Sometimes the pen is mightier than a seat at the table.

BOB WOODWARD GOT IT DEAD WRONG

As a coda to that meeting, I note for the record that in his book *Rage*, the Never Trumper Bob Woodward got the slice of history I have just shared with you dead wrong. To wit: to take the credit away from President Trump for one of the most important and consequential decisions of his presidency,

Woodward spun in *Rage* the alternate-universe fiction that it was Fauci, Azar, and Mulvaney who had ultimately convinced the president to ban flights from China.[17]

Au contraire, mon muckraker. As this account of the January 28 meeting in the Situation Room and my January 29 memo illustrates, Woodward more than twisted the truth. At least in my experience, Woodward is nothing more than a propagandist who intentionally shades the truth to advance his pro-Left agenda.

As a final thought on this episode, if there are any young folks reading this book who have their sights or hearts set on working in Washington, my one piece of advice is to *always* do what you must to follow your conscience and your heart.

THREE

THE WHITE HOUSE VIRUS DENIER COUNCIL AND TASK FORCE OF DOOM

The Task Force is not moving anywhere near fast enough on just about everything—vaccines, facemasks, clinical trials. I talk to [Secretary Alex] Azar at [the Department of Health and Human Services] and light a fire under him. . . . Russ Vought, the OMB Director, is fairly dismissive of giving money to HHS and sees them as spendthrifts. I emphasize the seriousness of the crisis and promise him a granular budget by Tuesday.

—Peter Navarro, journal entry, February 16, 2020

It's the Nevada caucus today. I talk to [Acting Chief of Staff Mick] Mulvaney in his office and he's sick as a dog after coming back from Great Britain. I do not rule out that he has the coronavirus. I tell him we may face an election future in which there won't be any traveling to rallies. . . . That will not play to our advantage.

—Peter Navarro, journal entry, February 22, 2020

The coronavirus is spiraling out of control. The stock market has its fastest correction in history. . . . We are not running against the Democrats. We are running against the virus.

—Peter Navarro, journal entry, February 27, 2020

With his announcement of the China travel ban on January 31, President Trump got off to the strongest possible start battling the pandemic. He hit a pitch-perfect tone as a wartime president ready to make courageous decisions in a time of great national crisis.

But it's not how you start; it's how you finish. And the Boss was surrounded by a group of advisers who would discount the potential lethality of the virus and the high probability that we were headed for a deadly pandemic.

BAD PERSONNEL IS BAD POLICY

Here I want to be clear about the criticisms I am about to levy. Donald Trump ran as a Populist Economic Nationalist in 2016, speaking directly to American voters. During the Republican primary, he vanquished every single one of his seventeen Republican opponents. And that November, he prevailed over the presumed Clinton succession.

After that victory, President Trump found himself in a difficult position when it came to staffing the White House, the cabinet, and a myriad of federal agencies. Most of the people in the Republican Party most experienced in government were not Trump Populists and Loyalists but rather Traditional Republican Globalists.

Far too many of those Globalists found their way into key positions in the Trump administration. When a deadly virus emerged from Communist China, President Trump's limited personnel options would come home to roost.

I got my first glimpse of this problem shortly after 9:00 a.m. on February 3 in the West Wing at our weekly senior staff meeting. There, in the Roosevelt Room, I watched as the director of the National Economic Council, Larry Kudlow, told the assembled throng of twenty or so staffers, "This

China thing is no worse than the flu. Don't worry about it. We've got it under control."

That was very bad news. With Kudlow telling the president, "Don't worry, be happy," it would be all the more difficult to get the White House moving into high pandemic-fighting gear.

Over the course of the next several months, Kudlow's de facto National Council of Virus Deniers would be populated most prominently by Acting Chief of Staff Mick Mulvaney, Treasury secretary Steve Mnuchin, and Vice President Mike Pence's chief of staff, Marc Short. Those high-ranking officials did tremendous damage by propagating two falsehoods that would cut against the grains of both common sense and science.

The first falsehood was that we had the virus under control. The second was that the pandemic posed little or no threat to the American public.

According to the virus deniers, we were overreacting to a disease that was no worse than the flu. Of course, that fantasy quickly ran into the brick-wall reality of a virus that would kill more than six hundred thousand Americans in a little more than a year.

In contrast, over the last ten years, annual flu deaths have ranged from a low of around twelve thousand in the 2011–2012 season to a high of sixty-one thousand in 2017–2018.[1] I'll take the flu anytime.

THE FOLLY OF A PAST-TENSE PANDEMIC

From the get-go, Larry Kudlow in particular kept saying imprudent stuff in the media. Just consider this early January 29, 2020, exchange with anchor David Asman on Fox Business:

ASMAN: How much are you expecting this virus to affect the American economy?

KUDLOW: Very little. . . . Minimal impact. . . . The Chinese have got the virus. This is not going to have any major impact on the United States. . . . This is a Chinese pandemic.[2]

Of course, that was the very same day I sent my Paul Revere memo to the White House Coronavirus Task Force warning about the possibility of a global pandemic that could kill millions of Americans and cost our economy trillions of dollars.

A little more than a month later, on March 6, Kudlow would double down on his virus denial with CNBC's Carl Quintanilla, opining that the virus "looks relatively contained" and "the vast majority of Americans are not at risk for this virus."[3] He also played the "no worse than the ordinary flu" card while urging Americans to "stay at work."[4]

With comments like those, Kudlow, with his high TV profile, did more than any other single senior administration official to propagate the misperception in the public's mind that we in the White House had not a clue about what we were doing. In fact, the opposite was true.

By the way, Larry's worst moment in fanning the flame of public perception that the White House was woefully out of touch with the misery being inflicted upon the American people came at the Republican National Convention. By video, Larry spoke to a world audience about the pandemic *in the past tense*—as if it were gone, dead, buried, and back in China.

That was at a time, mind you, when the death toll was more than one thousand Americans a day with no end in sight, and Kudlow was rightly roasted for that inanity across the media dial, from MSNBC's *Morning Joe* and Vox to ABC News.[5] The funniest of the roasts was in *The Atlantic*, where Russell Berman noted, "If the pandemic were truly in the past, however, Kudlow would have been delivering that message to a packed, roaring crowd at the Spectrum Center in Charlotte, North Carolina."[6]

Instead, he was opining from his rustic Connecticut mansion, "a talking head surrounded by bookshelves in the comfort of a home that is not safe to leave."[7]

At least Treasury secretary Steve Mnuchin mostly kept his mouth shut on the subject of the pandemic when he was on television. Instead, he caused his virus denial damage only in our private Oval Office Trade Team meetings with the Boss.

Like Acting Chief of Staff Mulvaney, Mnuchin was big on joking about how the "kung flu" was no worse than the regular flu and nothing to worry about. In truth, I don't believe Mnuchin really believed that nonsense. Rather, his joking about the kung flu was likely far more Machiavellian.

To Mnuchin, all that mattered was keeping the Phase One trade deal with China intact. If POTUS believed that the virus was deadly and blamed China for the plague, he might blow up the trade deal. So in the Oval Office, Mnuchin always downplayed the threat from the virus.

MASKLESS IN SEATTLE

Though Larry Kudlow was the White House's most public face of the "don't worry, it's only the flu" crowd and Mnuchin was its Machiavelli, the vice president's chief of staff, Marc Short, was its Godzilla.

As a virus denier—and a key player on the White House Coronavirus Task Force for Pence—Short literally wore his indifference on his face for all to see. He adamantly refused to wear a mask. Just wouldn't do it. No way, no how.

Early in the pandemic, Short would commit one of the most foolhardy acts of hubris ever witnessed in the West Wing: he engineered a March 5 trip by the vice president to visit the nation's first virus hot zone in Washington state.

Now, I know it's common for the president or vice president to visit disaster areas and show support for the local population. In fact, a visit from the White House is *de rigueur* after everything from hurricanes and earthquakes to mass shootings.

But at the beginning of a pandemic, when you have absolutely no idea what the risk factors are, you simply do *not* put the vice president of the United States onto a plane and plunge him into a hot zone where the potential for infection is quite high. There are a lot of reasons why you don't do that, but here's the best one:

You don't do that because, by the very next day, the vice president of the United States, along with all of his staff and Secret Service agents who joined him on the trip, will be back in the West Wing with the potential of infecting some of the highest-ranking officials of the US government—including the president, who saw Pence almost daily.

It was precisely because of that virus denial culture within the vice president's office that the Pence staff *very early on* had proportionately more infections of the virus than any other unit in the White House.

FAILURE REALLY *IS* AN OPTION

As the floor manager for the White House Coronavirus Task Force chaired by VPOTUS, Marc Short wielded tremendous power to steer the course of pandemic history, and as Lord

Acton accurately noted in 1887, "Absolute power corrupts absolutely." In his role, Short suffered from two fatal flaws.

First, because he really did believe that the virus was no worse than the flu, he saw no reason for the Task Force to do much of anything, much less quickly even though the president was demanding action every hour of every day. It was just one more example of bad personnel disobeying the chain of command, resulting in bad policy.

Second, the kind of government actions that might be required to combat the pandemic—including the invocation of the Defense Production Act of 1950 to ensure adequate supplies of personal protective equipment (PPE) and medicines—ran strictly against Marc Short's free-market grain.

It was probably for that last reason alone that Short would get up in my grill every time I, as the Defense Production Act policy coordinator, tried to move an action along.

Truth be told, it was a *huge* unforced error—one of the biggest of the administration—to put Mike Pence in charge of the Task Force. With that decision, the buck was clearly going to stop, if not with the president in the Oval Office, then certainly right down the hall and into the lap of President Trump's 2020 running mate. Talk about an anchor that could drag the Trump-Pence 2020 ticket all the way to the bottom of the Biden sea.

Strategically, it would have been far better to appoint a pandemic czar: someone who was loyal to the president but also tough as nails, smart as the proverbial whip, respected in the scientific community, nimble on his media feet, and welcome on both sides of the political aisle.

If the White House had had such a pandemic czar, we could have better kept the virus at political arm's length. Alas, no such luck.

And here's what bothered me most about Marc Short's central position on the Task Force: he, along with Mick Mulvaney, was always trying to block my efforts to fight the pandemic and use the Defense Production Act to advance a wide range of pandemic-related goals.

I remember well the call I received on March 5 from Mulvaney's administrative assistant telling me to get right over to the Chief's office. *What now?* I wondered.

With Mulvaney at one end of his couch, Short at the other end, and me across from them in the hot seat, Mulvaney ordered me upon threat of firing to stand down from any further work on anything related to either the Task Force or the pandemic. As Marc Short sat there like a cat that had just eaten a six-pack of canaries, I thought to myself, "F– these guys."

What I *said*, which was memorialized in a *Wall Street Journal* article, was something that I will be proud of until the day I die: "Mick, you do what you gotta do. And I'll do what I gotta do."[8]

Then I got up and left without looking back. Mulvaney would be gone from the White House in two days.

There are too many examples to chronicle in this book of the damage Marc Short did while running the White House Coronavirus Task Force. But if I had to reference just one, it would be this.

It is a story that begins on March 22, 2020, with one of my rare appearances at the podium of the James S. Brady Press Briefing Room during what had quickly become the president's daily coronavirus briefing.

By that time, a disturbing wave of profiteering, price gouging, counterfeiting, and hoarding had begun to plague the United States' personal protective equipment markets.

And together with Attorney General William Barr and the full force of the FBI and Justice Department, I was going to put an abrupt end to it.

With POTUS at my right shoulder as I stood at the podium, here is how we promised to lay down the law:

> Brokers are offering millions of items, whether they are goggles, masks, or whatever, and you go through three different brokers, tracing to a warehouse [for example, in Los Angeles] that's allegedly got ten million masks and they want to charge you seven times what they cost. That's price gouging.
>
> A message to the hoarders: If you've got any large quantities of materials that this country needs right now, get them to market or get them to us. We'll pay you a fair price. But if you don't do that, *we're going to come for you and make sure that doesn't happen in this country.*[9]

Unfortunately, my tough sheriff's talk quickly turned into a terminal case of "all talk, no walk." In the weeks ahead, every time Bill Barr and I tried to come down hard on one of those price-gouging predators, Marc Short, along with the vice president's legal counsel, Greg Jacob, blocked the action. In warehouse after warehouse identified by FBI agents as being stuffed with contraband, we just couldn't get anybody busted.

You can see my exasperation in full bloom in my April 29 journal entry:

> *We continue in a stalemate. . . . The Department of Justice has queued up five cases we can bust. . . . Greg Jacob is my new nemesis within the Deep State. . . . Out*

of exasperation—as opposed to desperation—I called Bill Barr once again and asked him to help me work through it.

It was all to no avail. The urgently needed crackdown never occurred.

FOUR

A PEACE CORPS MARTIAN IN THE WHITE HOUSE

Action, Action, Action.
—From the Canon of Bannon

Look, I don't mean to sound arrogant or anything,
but I am the greatest botanist on the planet.
—Astronaut Mark Watney, *The Martian*, 2015[1]

On Saturday, February 8, 2020, Dr. Rick Bright strode grimly into my office. Over the next thirty days, we would draft nearly a dozen guided missives to prod the White House Coronavirus Task Force and Department of Health and Human Services (HHS) into Action, Action, Pandemic Fighting Action.

Not unlike Mark Watney, I turned out to be the "best pandemic fighter in the White House." That was because, at least early on, other than President Trump, I was the *only* pandemic fighter there.

With my doctorate in economics, I was certainly an unlikely candidate to help lead the pandemic fight. I had come to the White House from the Trump campaign with two very clear, and clearly interrelated, missions: help POTUS put an end to China's economic aggression and rebuild America's manufacturing base.

On that note, this might be a good time to clear up a particularly pernicious Fake News myth about my role in the Trump campaign. That particular bad seed was planted by the leftist muckraker *Vanity Unfair*, which miswrote:

> *When Trump wanted to speak more substantively about China, he gave [Jared] Kushner a summary of his views and then asked him to do some research. Kushner simply went on Amazon, where he was struck by the title of one book,* Death by China, *co-authored by Peter Navarro. He cold-called Navarro, a well-known trade-deficit hawk, who agreed to join the team as an economic adviser.*[2]

Now here's the Real News: I had been corresponding with DJT (as I knew him at the time) dating back to 2011. That correspondence began after I read an article in the *Los Angeles Times* in which Mr. Trump had ranked my book *The Coming China Wars* number six among his top twenty favorite tomes on China.[3]

I sent DJT a note at Trump Tower in New York, thanking him, and he quickly responded with one of his trademark handwritten notes in the margin via a letter from his assistant Rhona Graff. The Boss and I began exchanging correspondence thereafter, and when my *Death by China* film was getting ready to debut in 2012 in movie theaters and film festivals across the country, I asked him for a testimonial, which he readily provided. Said Trump about the film, "*Death by*

China is right on. This important documentary depicts our problem with China with facts, figures and insight. I urge you to see it."

So it was that when DJT announced his candidacy, I was not only one of the first to predict that he would sweep the Republican field and likely win the presidency,[4] I also let him know that I would be happy to help in any way.

A TIP OF THE BOSS'S MAGA SPEAR

My office at the White House, the Office of Trade and Manufacturing Policy, was the tip of the spear of numerous policy actions over the first three years of the administration. A short list includes:

- Strengthening and expanding our "Buy American, Hire American" laws.
- Slapping stiff tariffs and other tough sanctions on Communist China.
- Establishing a tariff ring around our beleaguered steel and aluminum industries.
- Increasing arms sales to our allies to strengthen our alliances and create thousands of high-paying manufacturing jobs.
- Reviving our nation's shipyards, strengthening our defense industrial base, and bolstering our merchant marine.
- Protecting our electricity grid from Communist Chinese cyberattacks.
- Freeing Maine lobster fishermen from the tyranny of European tariffs (for which I was dubbed "the Lobster King").[5]

For me it had been a busy three years, and at least up until the point the Chinese Communist Party Virus arrived, the Trump administration's efforts to Make American Manufacturing Great Again had been quite successful.

During the 2020 campaign, I never got tired of saying that the Obama-Biden administration had lost more than three hundred thousand manufacturing jobs,[6] while President Trump had added nearly half a million.[7]

And by the way, Barack Obama himself once said that reshoring American manufacturing couldn't be done. During a PBS town hall on June 1, 2016, Obama, acting as a stalking horse for candidate Hillary Clinton, smugly proclaimed that Donald J. Trump would need a "magic wand" to bring manufacturing back to America.[8] With that kind of "let them eat arugula" attitude, no wonder Obama never got it done.

My point here is that prior to January 2020, I stayed singularly focused at the White House on our two core trade and manufacturing policy missions. Which poses the question: Just how did I wind up as a key field commander in the pandemic fight?

The answer begins with the Peace Corps and ends with the key lesson of *The Martian*.

A GOOSE BUMPS DATE WITH FATE

My Peace Corps adventure began in 1972. Fresh out of Tufts University with a bachelor of arts degree in English and a hankering to get the hell out of a country being torn apart by Vietnam, Watergate, and a depressive Woodstock–Altamont Speedway hangover, I headed out to Berkeley, California.

Berserk-ley, as it has often been called, was not my final destination but simply a pit stop on my way to Japan. My plan was to hang out on the Berkeley campus for a few months, hire a tutor to teach me some Japanese, and then hop on a flight to Tokyo and pick up a job teaching English.

A funny and fortuitous thing happened, however, on my way to the Land of the Rising Sun. The more I read about the country and its culture—its black-suit-and-white-shirt, button-up and button-down salaryman culture—the less I wanted to go to the bland, workaholic Japan and the more I became intrigued with the vibrant colors of Thailand.

As I sat in the South/Southeast Asia Library at Berkeley, freeloading off its marvelous, musty collection, I became intrigued by the Thai culture and its credo of *sanuk*. Popularly translated as "fun" in the West, *sanuk* is much more than that. It is a Buddhist concept that simultaneously reminds you of "the impermanence of everything," "the importance of living in the moment," and the focus on achieving satisfaction in whatever you do.[9]

And speaking of living in the moment, one day coming out of that library on the Berkeley campus in the late afternoon, I had one of the few supernatural experiences of my life. My epiphany as I left the library was that I really wanted to go to Thailand, not Japan.

With that wonderfully pleasant thought swirling through my head, I headed across campus and home to Ward Street and my sweet love, Charlotte, one of only two women—the other was my college sweetheart, Annie—whom I never should've left behind. Youth is indeed wasted on the young and adventurous.

As I was transiting Sproul Plaza, readying to exit the campus, I heard in my right ear somebody ask, "Would you like to go to Thailand?"

The question stopped me in my tracks. Was somebody reading my mind? I got goose bumps.

As I turned to the person who had asked me that question, I saw that he was sitting at a table festooned with big Peace Corps posters and pamphlets. He was on campus to recruit a group of volunteers to teach English in Thailand.

I signed up on the spot. How could I not?

I won't bore you with the details of my next two years as a Peace Corps volunteer at the Sakon Nakhon Teachers' College—but here are a few quick high- and lowlights:

- A white-hot female scorpion sting as I was beating her mate to death with a propane canister in my kitchen (what goes around comes around).
- Nightly serenades *inside* my little house by lizards the size of poodles.
- A fight to the death with a six-foot-long python in my home that liked to eat said lizards.
- Transforming a spider-infested decaying language lab into a bustling virtual classroom that presaged later UC-Irvine innovations in online learning.
- Motorcycling through the Thai countryside with the blazing sun on my face and the humid air blowing through my hair while screaming out the lyrics to "We're an American Band."
- Building a tilapia fish pond the size of a football field in a dirt-poor village with the help of a bulldozer commandeered from a nearby Thai military base.[10]
- Playing rhythm guitar with the stunningly talented Teachers' College band while touring throughout the province.
- A CIA black ops in my little town that went terribly wrong, almost got me shot and put an end to my touring with the band.

- US jets out of the nearby Udon Thani Royal Thai Air Force Base screaming overhead and rattling the windows in my classroom on their way to bomb the bejesus out of Hanoi, a little over three hundred miles away.
- Traveling on holiday breaks to the incredibly crowded Hong Kong and Singapore, the ever-exotic Malaysia, the martial-spirited South Korea, the truly mysterious Burma, the jaw-droppingly beautiful Laos, and the indeed black-and-white Japan that I had imagined exactly right.

When my two-year tour ended, I wasn't quite ready to come home and The Peace Corps mothership down in Bangkok was looking for a volunteer who could both speak the Thai language and repair hospital equipment. As a practical matter, they had two options to fill the position: Either they could find an American biomedical equipment technician who could learn Thai. Or they could find a Thai speaker they could train to repair the medical equipment.

Option two was clearly faster and easier because Thai is an extremely difficult language to learn quickly; a single word can be spoken with five different tones and have five different meanings.

And that was how in 1975 I wound up at a military vocational training school in Aurora, Colorado, for a four-month intensive training gig to get my certificate as a biomedical equipment technician.[11] Yes, I have one of those certificates, along with my Harvard PhD in economics.

Now, here is why this little sentimental journey is important. At that young and tender point in my life, I was strictly a Liberal Arts creative type: touchy, feely, all abstraction. Just not a fix-it, screwdriver kind of dude. But all that changed in the Denver suburb of Aurora.

Working side by side with my military counterparts—I was the only civilian—I had drilled into me the most valuable skill I have ever learned in my life: *how to quickly troubleshoot and fix problems.*

Every Friday, we had a combination test and race to see who could fix the fastest whatever broken machine they would throw at us: an autoclave, a dentist's drill, whatever. They put us on the clock, and God help us if we did not cut to the chase. Sir, yes, sir!

It was one of the greatest experiences of my life, and I can honestly say that what I learned in those four months of vocational training has been just as valuable in my career as what I learned in six years at Harvard.

Without that Rocky Mountain High interlude, I don't think I would have been able to handle the complexity and intensity of the multiple pandemic-related problem sets that would come at the White House like a swarm of Chinese drones.

Of course, the other debt I owe, at least when it comes to preparing me to fight the pandemic, is to Andy Weir's book and movie *The Martian*. Its central lesson, which was invaluable during the early pandemic days, is "work the problem." And in the face of mortal danger, it doesn't matter one whit what your expertise is. When your life depends on it—or in the CCP Virus case, when the lives of millions of Americans depend on it—you damn well better figure it out.

So that was what I tried to do. And starting on Saturday, February 8, 2020, I began to work the problem. I did so with particular urgency, because, as far back as my 2006 book, *The Coming China Wars*, I had foreseen a deadly Chinese virus like this one coming at the United States like a Beijing-to-Shenzhen bullet train flying over the rails.

THE BRIGHT AND THE DARK OF IT

One important strength in problem solving is to have a pretty clear idea about what you don't know. In this particular case, I knew that I knew virtually nothing about confronting a global pandemic. So, the first thing I had to do was to recruit my own team of advisers. And in doing so, I hit a jackpot of sorts in Dr. Rick Bright.

By way of further introducing the good Dr. Bright—who would wind up doing some very bad things to the Trump administration later in our relationship—it may be useful to play a little CCP Virus *Jeopardy*.

So suppose I were to ask you this question: "Which government agency is responsible for quickly mobilizing a coordinated national response to emergencies like a global pandemic?" As a *Jeopardy* contestant, you would correctly answer, "What is ASPR, the Office of the Assistant Secretary for Preparedness and Response."[12]

Suppose I were to ask you next, "Which government agency is responsible for securing our nation from the threats of emerging infectious diseases like the CCP Virus and also moving medical countermeasures like vaccines and therapeutics through research, development, approval by the Food and Drug Administration, and inclusion in the Strategic National Stockpile?"

You might start by saying, "That is way too long for a *Jeopardy* question." And you'd be right. But to win your *Jeopardy* points, you would then have to ask, "What is BARDA, the Biomedical Advanced Research and Development Authority?"

My point here is that if you wanted to quickly find the best experts in the vast Washington bureaucracy to help you fight a global pandemic, the first two places you'd likely start would be ASPR and BARDA. With Rick Bright, the head of BARDA and a deputy assistant secretary at ASPR, I downed the proverbial two birds with one phone call.

I could see immediately upon meeting Rick at the White House on the afternoon of February 8 that he was intense. I also sensed a genuine anguish in him brought about by the glacially slow pandemic response of both the Coronavirus Task Force and the Department of Health and Human Services (HHS).

In truth, Bright and I were kindred spirits. He was a lone voice in the HHS wilderness warning about the urgency of pandemic preparedness. He didn't suffer fools gladly, and he spoke freely—whether given permission to or not.

Though my relationship with Bright began like a beautiful comet blazing through the sky, it would end some months later, after he allowed himself to become a Democrat Party pawn with whom I would not wish to share a foxhole.

I put the blame squarely on HHS secretary Alex Azar for the defection of Rick Bright to the dark Democrat side. On a scale of 1 to 10, Azar committed an unforced error equal to an 11. Here's the quick story behind that story.

In early April, I got a very distraught call from Rick. He had just been told by one of Azar's henchmen that he was being moved over to the National Institutes of Health under the supervision of NIH director Francis Collins to help lead the testing effort.

To be crystal clear, Rick said he had absolutely no problem with that—that he was a good soldier. And I believed him.

What Rick feared, however, was that once his special assignment was over, his old job back at BARDA, which he loved, would not be waiting for him. He asked me to call Azar and ask for his assurance that his job would be waiting for him when his testing mission was accomplished.

Knowing Azar, I thought Rick's concern was well placed. So I promised to get ahold of Azar quickly and firmly make the case on his behalf.

Quite by happenstance, I was able to keep that promise in less than an hour. Shortly after ending my call with Rick, I had thrown on my suit jacket and blue security badge and hoofed it over to the West Wing for a scheduled meeting in the Roosevelt Room. As I entered the lobby, I saw none other than Azar himself sitting on the couch, waiting to see the Boss.

I made a beeline for that couch and took a knee in front of him. It was not in supplication but rather to get close enough to him that I would not be overheard. I looked him straight in the eye and told him in no uncertain terms that he needed to handle the Rick Bright situation *immediately*. Said I, "I get that you and Collins want to move Rick over to NIH for testing, and he's fully on board with that. But—and this is a *big* but—Rick needs to hear from you directly that his job at BARDA will be waiting for him when his mission at NIH is over."

Then I doubled down, saying, "Alex, you really need to do this and you need to do it quickly. Otherwise, this is going to blow up in everybody's face, including the president's. I'm not sure how it will blow up, but I am sure it will."

Regrettably, Azar just blew me off. And blow up it did.

On May 5, Rick's attorney filed a whistleblower complaint that dumped a long litany of mismanagement foibles and follies all over Azar and HHS. Of course, the Democrats, in all their nationally televised public hearing glory, would have a field day using the now-not-so-good Dr. Bright as a star witness to reinforce the partisan messaging that President Trump was mismanaging the pandemic.

THE ITALIAN SWAB JOB AND FEDEX DELIVERS

Now, here's what was really uncomfortably weird for me: Rick Bright's whistleblower complaint would position me as hero to the Trump and Azar villains—not a good position to be in with the Boss.

In particular, the whistleblower complaint laudably noted my "sense of urgency" and that I was "deeply engaged in the issues confronting the United States in responding to the rapidly approaching pandemic." The complaint further noted that "Mr. Navarro was extremely concerned about HHS's laxity in addressing the pandemic."[13]

On the positive side, the whistleblower complaint provided a lengthy reference to one of the coolest capers ever pulled off by my crack White House team of twentysomethings in the persons of Chris Abbott, Joanna Miller, Hannah Robertson, and Garrett Ziegler.

That caper—which I dubbed the "Italian Swab Job"—started on March 14, 2020, as Rick Bright was struggling with a looming testing swab shortage. Here's the problem he brought to me:

Italy had become the epicenter of a particularly deadly outbreak of the virus. With Italian airspace locked down to commercial flights, it was impossible to liberate close to a million testing swabs from a factory in the particularly hard-hit Lombardy region.

Rick had spent the better part of forty-eight hours trying to commandeer an emergency military airlift through the

Pentagon's Defense Threat Reduction Agency. The agency had previously helped Rick move vaccine supplies from Germany to the United States during the Ebola epidemic, but for whatever reason, Rick was hitting a brick wall for his swab job.

In desperation, Rick called me, and here is how his whistleblower complaint described what happened next:

> Mr. Navarro's office worked quickly and secured Secretary [of Defense] Esper's approval in a matter of hours. Approximately two hours later, Maj. Froude confirmed that [the Pentagon] was working to have a flight in the air as soon as tomorrow night.
>
> Later that evening, Dr. Bright emailed Mr. Navarro: You did something miraculous tonight to break through the wall and bureaucratic barrier that was stalling shipment from Italy to US. Four days of bureaucracy that you broke down in 5 minutes.[14]

Yet the Italian Swab Job got even better. I realized early Sunday morning that I had one more problem to solve. The swab crates were coming to the United States in a single military aircraft, but I would have to disperse them to six different American cities. Channeling my inner "work the problem" Martian, I immediately called the Situation Room and had it run down the chief executive officer of Federal Express, Fred Smith.

By the way, one of the things I miss about working at the White House is the ability to call the Sit Room and run to ground just about anyone on the planet within five minutes. It's a beautiful thing, and it never failed to put a smile on my face when my person of interest came on the line.

With Fred Smith on the line, I described my logistics problem and said, "Fred, how about I have the Pentagon plane divert to Memphis. Then six FedEx planes can meet that bird on the tarmac. We'll get the right quantities loaded and shipped off to the right cities. It'll be perfect."

I should say parenthetically that Fred Smith was hardly my best buddy. With his big FedEx exposure in Communist China, Fred, like many multinational corporation CEOs, was strongly opposed to our tariff policies, and we had gone head-to-head in the Oval Office on more than one occasion.

Yet Fred is also a true patriot, and he immediately called his son Richard, who heads up operations at FedEx. Within two In Trump Time hours, we had the whole plan set up.

To make sure it all worked perfectly, I dispatched Garrett Ziegler to manage the boots-on-the-ground operation. Sans suitcase, with just the suit on his back, Garrett scooted over to Joint Base Andrews and hitched a ride on another Pentagon bird headed to the rendezvous point in Memphis; maybe Mark Wahlberg will play the Mighty Ziegler in the Italian Swab Job movie.

So it was that within a mere seventy-two hours of my receiving Rick Bright's SOS, Italian-made swabs were delivered to US soil and to exactly where they were needed. Shortage averted!

If there is a better example of moving in Trump Time, I don't know what it is.

But wait! Upon second thought, I actually do have an even faster example. Why don't I just let reporter Ebony Bowden of the *New York Post* tell it:

> White House officials sprung into action on Monday [March 30] after receiving an "SOS" email from the

> NYPD begging for protective equipment—delivering the frontline gear just 16 hours later. . . .
>
> In a mission dubbed "Operation Blue Bloods," President Donald Trump's equipment czar Peter Navarro, Assistant to the President for Trade and Manufacturing Policy, cobbled together a rapid-response team including company executives who flew thousands of full-body suits on a private plane the next day.

The report in the *Post* continued, describing how police officers were making house calls without necessary protection. It also said that the chief of the NYPD sent an email to the White House requesting help.

The article goes on to describe how I worked in Trump Time get supplies to frontline workers in less than 24 hours. Writes Bowden:

> More than 1,750 crime scene Tyvek suits arrived on [a] private Raytheon plane on Tuesday afternoon, while another 2,125 arrived in the early hours of Wednesday—a total of 4,275.
>
> Some 120,000 pairs of gloves from General Dynamics arrived in New York Wednesday, as did the 111 barrels of hand sanitizer donated by Pernod Ricard.
>
> Detectives responding to house calls will now be provided with a kit including a Tyvek suit, gloves, a face shield, N95 mask, shoe covers and disinfectant wipes.[15]

Yep, I just love that story, and I would be remiss here not to offer my thanks to then Raytheon CEO Tom Kennedy and one of my all-time favorites, Phebe Novakovic, the CEO of General Dynamics. It was a good day during a very bad time.

What was not a good day, however, was the day I had to take on my once brother in pandemic arms Rick Bright. But after Brother Bright filed his whistleblower complaint, duty called. Or, more accurately, the Boss called.

It was just after noon on May 6, and, to shake off some stress, I had hopped onto my trusty Trek road bike to burn twenty-five miles on my favorite loop. It starts at the Potomac River's edge in Georgetown, runs up the Crescent Trail to Bethesda, and then loops back through Rock Creek Park down to Connecticut Avenue and finally to the White House.

As I was pumping up a Rock Creek Park hill, my cell phone rang, and it was none other than the Boss himself. He was appropriately angry at Bright and gave me the green light to counter Bright's hypocrisy. A few days later, when I appeared on ABC's Sunday news show *This Week with George Stephanopoulos*, this is how the discussion went:

> STEPHANOPOULOS: According to all accounts, you were working quite hard during the month of February [with Rick Bright] on all the issues you just mentioned. He said you and he were allies on trying to break through road blocks coming from HHS and other parts of the government.
>
> Yet now you call him a deserter in the war against the virus, why?
>
> NAVARRO: . . . Here's what happened with Rick Bright, and it's an American tragedy, George. This guy is quite talented, but he was asked to be the field commander over at NIH to storm the testing hill with a billion dollars behind him. Instead of accepting that mission, he deserted. He went into a fox hole, wrote up the complaint. And now he's

part of a Capitol Hill partisan circus where he's just become another pawn in the game.

And the tragedy, George, is that this man has talent. He's a smart man. We could have used him on the battlefield. He's not there now. And it was because of the decisions that he made. And it is a shame, George. . . .

STEPHANOPOULOS: [Bright's] expertise is vaccines. He wants to work in vaccine development. They're putting him in diagnostic testing.

Why shouldn't a vaccine expert be working on vaccines?

NAVARRO: So, here's the thing, George. . . . I've been with the President since the campaign, right? I came here to do trade policy, right? What am I now? A conscript in the war on the China Virus. I'm like a quartermaster and a shipping clerk half the time.

Do I complain? No. That's my mission for this President, for this country. We do what we have to do when we have to do it for this country.

And Rick Bright, he made a choice. He could have been making a tremendous contribution over at NIH to testing and you and others have been complaining about testing. He could have been the field general. And now, he's off the battlefield and it was by his own choice, sir.[16]

My only real regret in this whole matter—and it is a *huge* regret—is that Secretary Alex Azar refused to heed my urgent call to help Rick Bright. It was an unforgivable gaffe committed by a charter member of the administration's cadre of bad personnel that would lead to bad politics and yet another wounding of POTUS on the pandemic front.

Here's what too many high-ranking officials in the Trump administration, including Azar, Mnuchin, and Kudlow, never seemed to realize: when bad personnel screwed up, *it was POTUS who suffered the consequences.*

In the Rick Bright case, it was much more of a deep arterial cut than a slight shaving nick, and we would all bleed. But for at least one glorious month, Rick and I did beautiful work together moving the aircraft carrier of the HHS bureaucracy out of the dock and onto the high seas at full throttle.

The fuel that we used to move that carrier was a collection of Action, Action, Action memos I began sending the Task Force on February 9—memos that would dramatically up our pandemic-fighting game and help save hundreds of thousands of American lives.

FIVE

AN UNLOST FEBRUARY AND OFF TO THE VACCINE HORSE RACE

I had an extremely productive session with Rick Bright, my new favorite guy from [the Department of Health and Human Services]. . . . We put together a memo that lays out three immediate asks . . . Buy up all of the doses and raw material for one drug [Remdesivir] that may prove to be efficacious. Ban the export of all N-95 masks and give them a high health priority so we can get domestic production. And jump start vaccine development in a Manhattan Project style approach. . . . It is chilling that Dr. Bright thinks that within two weeks, nervousness and possible panic is going to begin to set in as the virus spreads more through [the] US. We need to get ready.

—Peter Navarro, journal entry, February 9, 2020

On Sunday morning, February 9, as I work at my stand-up desk in the White House, my new right-hand man, Rick Bright, is at my right shoulder. Behind us is Dr. Steven Hatfill, pacing like an expectant father.

At this stage in the emerging crisis, I have already adopted Doc Hatfill as my in-resident medical adviser. Whenever anyone visits my office on a pandemic-related matter, Steven sits in on the meeting, asks questions as needed, and gives me his observations afterward. He always cuts right to the heart of the matter, and for that, I'm grateful.

On this day, Rick Bright, Doc Hatfill, and I are working feverishly on the first of a series of memos to the White House Coronavirus Task Force that will help change the course of pandemic history. These "Navarro memos," as they will become known inside the Task Force (with either fear or derision), will ultimately help frame a Five-Vector Pandemic Attack Strategy focusing on:

1. Jump-starting the "warp speed" development of a suite of vaccines.
2. Advancing a power pack of therapeutics to moderate symptoms and take death off the table.
3. Ensuring sufficient supplies of personal protective equipment such as masks, gowns, and gloves.
4. Filling a dangerous gap in critically needed medical equipment such as ventilators.
5. Deploying broad and rapid testing capabilities.

Taken as a whole, the Navarro memos are clearly exculpatory as regards the oft-repeated criticism that the Trump administration had a "Lost February" when it came to fighting the pandemic.[1] These memos illustrate we were moving in Trump Time in early February and doing so immediately after President Trump issued his travel ban on China at the end of January.

That Action, Action, Action notwithstanding, the facts of a highly productive February will lose out to the Lost February fiction and narrative spun like a whirling dervish by the anti-Trump media. It is a situation not without humor.

Even in a Deep Swamp where nothing is more valuable to a reporter than a leaked memo, as we got closer to election day, I couldn't give the Navarro memos away; they were just too favorable to the president.

Maggie Haberman at the *New York Times* wouldn't touch the memos—Lord knows I tried. Jonathan Swan at Axios wouldn't touch them—the Devil knows I tried. Jennifer Jacobs at Bloomberg News wanted to touch them—but her devilish Never Trump editors wouldn't let her. And forget about the Fake News incarnates, CNN and the *Washington Post*.

In a Washington Swamp full of anti-Trump dogs, it was the ultimate case of the leaked In Trump Time truth that simply would not be barked. At times, it made me want to bay at the moon. At least now I can share these memos with you.

So let's start with the February 9 memo that helped jump-start President Trump's suite of vaccines. This excerpt from that memo presciently predicts the *exact* time frame within which we would be able to mass-produce the Trump vaccines.

> There is currently no vaccine to protect against coronavirus. *If we start this week* to fast track vaccine development with appropriate funding, we can likely have a vaccine to clinical trials within seven months and a workable vaccine by October or November, with a production capacity of 150 million doses by the end of the year. *IF we act NOW.*

The story of how President Trump delivered a suite of vaccines to the American people in a third of the time it had historically taken is a case that should be studied for decades at business and public policy schools. It involves an innovative paradigm shift and a unique application of the Trump organizational culture. Here's that story.

A HORSE RACE AT OPERATION WARP SPEED

When I penned my February 9 memo, there was as yet no slick moniker such as "Operation Warp Speed." Rather, Rick Bright, Doc Hatfill, and I simply viewed the process as a "horse race," while the assistant secretary of Health and Human Services, Bob Kadlec, one of the true unsung heroes of the pandemic, used the hockey analogy of "multiple shots on goal."

As I wrote in homage to both Kadlec's metaphor and my own "Made in America" imperative:

> We don't yet know what type of vaccine would be safe and effective. Therefore, it is critical the [US government] invest in multiple shots on goal to ensure that at least one vaccine is realized. Efforts should be prioritized to focus on US-based vaccine companies.

My urgent recommendation was to "identify [four to five] US-based companies with the experience, infrastructure, skilled labor and resources to most quickly develop a vaccine," equally quickly find the $1 billion to $3 billion we would need for vaccine development, and "place developer contracts within the next one to two weeks."

A follow-up memo on February 19 revealed the "secret sauce" of the Trump vaccine strategy:* We would embrace an innovative paradigm shift for vaccine development that would

* Included in the memo is a document prepared by the Department of Health and Human Services at my request. It laid out "a granular plan to rapidly develop a COVID-19 vaccine in 'Trump Time.'" In doing so, the document perfectly captured both the organizational culture and the strategic thinking of the Trump administration.

make a clean and abrupt break from the traditional *sequential* development approach. Instead, we would focus on a *simultaneous* approach geared toward mass production capabilities at the ready the very moment a vaccine was approved.

In the traditional *sequential* paradigm, vaccine development starts with the initial search for a possible vaccine candidate. A potential vaccine than moves through three distinct phases of clinical trials, starting with a test for safety. This Phase One of the trial is then followed by additional tests for "efficacy"; that is, does the vaccine actually work with a high enough degree of effectiveness to warrant further investment?

In this traditional paradigm, it is only after such clinical trials are successfully completed sequentially that pharmaceutical companies typically make the additional investments needed to mass-produce a vaccine. In economics, we call this slow-paced *underinvestment* during a pandemic a "market failure."

The nature of this market failure should be obvious: the high risk that a vaccine may not work coupled with the large capital requirements associated with mass production virtually ensures that the private sector will move far too slowly.

It was that market failure insight that led the business-oriented Trump administration to turn the traditional sequential paradigm on its head. We did so by moving to a *simultaneous* development process. To wit: even as each of the companies in the vaccine horse race moved through clinical trials, we took all necessary steps to mass-produce every single one of the potentially safe and efficacious vaccines—*without yet knowing which one or ones might work.*

The second key economic principle driving this Trumpian strategy of simultaneity was equally straightforward: It was far cheaper relative to the costs of both the loss of human life and an extended economic lockdown to spend a few billion dollars *up front* to be ready to mass-produce every single vaccine candidate even if some of them didn't pan out.

Clearly, the money we might be accused of "wasting" on vaccines that didn't pan out *would not be wasted at all.* It would be some of the best-spent "insurance policy" money ever expended by the federal government.

ANTHONY FAUCI SHOOTS A GUIDED MAGS MISSILE

It was precisely this kind of business-oriented paradigm shift that traditional medical professionals such as Anthony Fauci simply could not wrap their heads around. Unfortunately, Fauci's lack of economic literacy—and his no small love for the media spotlight—would quickly lead to a sharp clash between him and me.

On the heels of my February 9 memo to the Task Force, I went on television as early as mid-February and tried to reassure the public with my prediction that we would have 150 million doses of a vaccine available as early as October or November. *I was exactly right.*

In sharp contrast, Fauci went on the very same media circuit, saying it would take far longer.[2] *Fauci was exactly wrong.*

What frosted me was not our disagreement; Fauci was certainly entitled to his opinion and could certainly lay claim to more experience in such matters. No, what *really* frosted me was the shadow leak campaign Fauci ran to get me off TV even as he sought to free himself completely from any disciplined White House messaging.

Fauci's attack started on the morning of Friday, February 28, and *New York Times* gossip maven Maggie Haberman would be Fauci's huckleberry. Here is how it all went down in the early a.m. as I was doing my morning exercise routine while watching CNN's ever-bilious *New Day.*

When "Mags" took what my journal would record as a "sharp hit" at me, it was like a gut punch. Here's how her colloquy with *New Day*'s John Berman went:

> HABERMAN: Appearances by Peter Navarro, one of the president's economic advisers . . . were mentioned to me by a number of administration officials as something that they saw as unproductive. . . .
>
> We saw Dr. Fauci speak yesterday but only alongside Mike Pence. We did not see him on television. . . .
>
> BERMAN: Part of that reason, Maggie, is because what we had heard from some of the medical experts and public health experts was different from what we're hearing from the political leaders.
>
> Anthony Fauci saying it will take a year to a year and a half to get a vaccine, side by side with the president telling us it's coming very soon.[3]

The clear message Mags was sending was "less Navarro and take the muzzle off Fauci." In this case, it was easy enough to read between the leak lines to see what game was afoot. And I eventually tracked the Haberman hit right back to the Fauci Fountainhead.

By the way, if you wonder why I have zero respect for Fauci, this is at the bottom of my list. At the top is Fauci's likely role in helping spawn the pandemic by funding dangerous gain-of-function experiments at the Wuhan Institute of Virology.

New Day's bile notwithstanding, here is my all-time favorite CNN quote about Fauci's fallibility from Fareed Zakaria's show *Fareed Zakaria GPS*:

> ZAKARIA: It was Dr. Anthony Fauci who initially downplayed the dangers of the coronavirus. On January 26th he said it's a very, very low risk to the United States. . . .
>
> At the same time, Trump adviser Peter Navarro, a non-scientist looking at the same data coming out of China, warned in a January 29th memo of the risk of the coronavirus evolving into a full-blown pandemic imperiling the lives of millions of Americans and [Navarro] urged aggressive action.
>
> It looks like the layman was right and the scientists were wrong.[4]

And here's the rub: When President Trump needed the best advice of the "scientists," and more important, needed a preparedness plan to immediately implement when the pandemic hit, scientists and bureaucrats with names such as Fauci and Collins and Hahn and Redfield and Brett Giroir and Azar had nothing. Nothing, that is, but excuses.

Even worse—and Fauci was always the worst—those Deep Administrative State bureaucrats would, over the course of the pandemic, constantly and quickly cover their rear ends even as they sought to shift the blame to the president for a situation that *they, with their own signal failure, had failed to properly anticipate or prepare for.*

JOE BIDEN WEAPONIZES THE TRUMP VACCINES

Now, the last thing to say about Operation Warp Speed is this: never in my wildest dreams did I imagine that a Biden regime would turn the Trump vaccines into a weapon of cultural, economic, and social control.

Here the idea that a vaccination "passport" might be used to deny us jet travel, restrict our entry into restaurants or sports arenas, turn our children into pariah "others" in their own schools, and even take our jobs away is not just morally repugnant; it is bad science and poor risk management.

That individual choice should be our guiding principle when it comes to the vaccine is evident in the following four observations.

First, as Doc Hatfill warned me at the outset of our quest to develop a vaccine, a vaccine will *always* have side effects. In this case, they range from tolerable chills, fever, fatigue, muscle pain, and headache to far more dangerous blood clots, heart muscle inflammation (myocarditis), heart lining inflammation (pericarditis), Bell's palsy, Guillain-Barré syndrome, anaphylaxis, and even death.

Second, the vaccines are administered under an Emergency Use Authorization (EUA) rather than full Food and Drug Administration approval, and the FDA itself has acknowledged the possibility of "serious and unexpected side effects" as it continues clinical trials.[5]

Third, several of the vaccines, including Moderna and Pfizer-BioNTech, have been produced with experimental messenger RNA gene therapy technologies. What can go wrong? Who knows? And that poses additional risks.

Fourth, and perhaps most important, risk varies markedly across different segments of our population. On the one hand, seniors and individuals with significant comorbidities such as lung and heart disease have a much greater incentive to be vaccinated. This is because their own individual risks and complications due to an infection may be significantly higher than the not-inconsequential risks of the vaccine itself.

On the other hand, young, healthy individuals are likely to suffer only moderate or no symptoms from the virus while facing little risk of death. It follows that:

- Forcing or pressuring our young children to be vaccinated is tantamount to forcing a large unnecessary risk and cost upon them in exchange for a small and speculative benefit to adults.
- This kind of government mandate gives a whole new meaning to the phrase "women and children first."

It's not just age and comorbidities that factor into each individual's risk calculus. People infected by the virus can build up powerful natural antibodies and immune cells known as *memory T-cells.* The immunity they derive from them is likely to be every bit as effective as that generated by the vaccines. It likewise follows that:

- Forcing individuals to be vaccinated who have these antibodies is to force them to take on the risks and costs of vaccination with little or no incremental immunization benefit.
- This is as scientifically foolish as the forced jabbing of our children.

Let us note the irony of a Democrat Biden regime that is anything but "pro-choice" when it comes to the vaccination decision. A second-term Trump administration would *never* have tolerated the tyranny and bad science we are now witnessing.

SIX

TAKING DEATH AND FEAR OFF THE THERAPEUTICS TABLE

Buy all existing U.S. doses of Remdesivir and bulk materials.

—Peter Navarro, memorandum to Coronavirus Task Force, February 9, 2020

OMG. What a difference a day makes. The Boss and the First Lady test positive for the China virus at midnight . . . . It's all messed up at the West Wing. Everybody is unreachable as the virus hits the President.

—Peter Navarro, journal entry, October 2, 2020

The Boss is suffering from symptoms big time and went to Remdesivir. That's a bad sign.

—Peter Navarro, journal entry, October 3, 2020

Little did I know on February 9 that the first two therapeutic drugs I would be pushing to develop rapidly—Remdesivir and Regeneron's monoclonal antibodies—would be administered to help save the life of the president of the United States. And Dr. Steven Hatfill gets a *huge* assist for enlightening me on both of those therapeutics.

That morning, as the doc and I were awaiting the arrival of Rick Bright for our first marathon memo-writing session together, I was kicking back in a chair at my sit-down desk. In my hand was a big, beautiful mug given to me as a gift for being the Commencement speaker for the Class of 2019 at the United States Merchant Marine Academy—truly an epic day.

In my mug was ice-cold water laced with Airborne, my own sugarless version of what we used to call "soda pop." As I sipped from the mug, I began a rapid scan of the pile of newspapers that had been plopped onto my desk that morning.

The good news was that the guy we thought we could beat, Bernie Sanders, was up in the polls in New Hampshire. The very bad Endless War news was that four more American soldiers had been killed in Afghanistan.[1]

On the Marie Antoinette "don't let them use carbon" front, the king of crappy software, Bill Gates, was reported to have just bought a half-billion-dollar hydrogen-powered megayacht. The Globalist megabillionaire had sat not ten feet from me at my conference table the previous year to lobby my good offices about one of his endless Globalist initiatives.

Of course, conspicuous in its absence across many of the front pages was any real news about a possible looming pandemic. The dancing bourgeoisie in the ballroom of the *Titanic* had more situational awareness than most of the mainstream media did.

A WAR OF ATTRITION WITH A VIRUS

When Doc Hatfill walked into my office with a cup of whatever concoction was in his cup, I asked, "What's up, Doc?" I never got tired of using that old line.

Ever the Grim Reaper, Steven replied in his raspy voice, "We've got to take death off the table."

"Do tell," I said. And he did.

As he explained it, we definitely needed to push the Task Force hard for a vaccine. But we should not look at the vaccine as a panacea for two reasons.

First, even if we hit our target of developing a vaccine by October or November, there might be many dire months before that. In the short and medium term, our only hope to take death off the table would be a powerful suite of therapeutics.

Therapeutics are medicines that can both moderate symptoms and reduce the mortality rate, that is, take death off the table. Effectively, what a really good suite of therapeutics might be able to do is to transform covid-19 from Xi Jinping's demon of death into nothing more than a bad case of the common cold.

As a practical matter, there are three main types of therapeutics we could search for: those that might be administered intravenously, such as Remdesivir; pills or tablets that you can pop, such as hydroxychloroquine and ivermectin; and injectable serums, such as the aforementioned monoclonal antibodies, which strengthen a patient's immune system and therefore the ability to fight the virus. Said Doc Hatfill, "If we can take death off the table, we take fear and panic off the table. That way, we can keep people at work and have far less impact on the economy. And the best way to take death off the table other than with a vaccine is to go full bore on therapeutics."

The second reason Steven emphasized a heavy focus on therapeutics was sobering. Even if we developed one or more viable vaccines, he believed that the virus would continually mutate. As he put it, "Viruses are clever little beasts. And a really clever virus builds up its own defenses almost as fast as humans can develop antibodies or vaccines. Viruses fight back by mutating, and make no mistake here, we are going to see thousands of mutations over decades upon decades of this damn China virus, and this will be a war of attrition."

"Well, aren't you a bundle of joy this morning," said I. All Steven could say was, "I wish it weren't so. So let's get our butts to work. I'm antsy."

So, get to work that day we did. If Doc Hatfill, Rick Bright, and I had not pushed *hard* for the development of both Remdesivir and Regeneron's monoclonal antibodies in February, it is unlikely either would have been ready in October when the president's pulse oximeter reading plummeted, he had extreme difficulty breathing, and really needed some powerful therapeutics to take his own death off the Walter Reed hospital table.

CORNERING THE MARKETS UPSTREAM AND DOWN

Here's how the Remdesivir part of the story went down. With Rick by my side and Doc Hatfill doing his pacing thing, I started out in my February 9 memo by noting that "Remdesivir was originally developed to treat Ebola cases." Among possible therapeutics, Remdesivir "has the highest probability of an existing drug for being efficacious for treating coronavirus."

Now here's the important part: In seeking to develop this speculative therapeutic, we had to hit the proverbial two birds with one stone. More specifically, we needed to corner not one but two markets—the market for the current supply of Remdesivir *and* the upstream market for the raw materials and supplies needed to produce the drug at mass scale.

Purchasing the current supply—which was relatively small at the time—was absolutely critical if we were going to be able to rush the drug into the kind of randomized clinical trials we would need for rapid FDA approval. Any delay in the start of such clinical trials would delay the medicine's use and therefore lead to needless deaths if the medicine turned out to work.

Purchasing the existing raw materials *and supplies* was equally critical because we would no doubt be competing with countries such as China in the marketplace. If we did not lock up those materials and supplies early, we would not have enough ingredients to produce Remdesivir in the quantities that Americans would need.

Said I in the February 9 memo—and note the "Buy American" component here:

> *Gilead [Sciences] has 4,500 doses on hand at a cost of $2,200 per dose. It also has sufficient bulk material to produce an additional 100,000 doses.*

Based on these observations, here is what we recommended to the Task Force:

- Immediately purchase the existing 4,500 doses.
- Secure the right of first refusal for all doses coming out of the factory.
- Enter into a contract to buy all 100,000 additional doses as they are produced.
- Immediately work with Gilead to on-shore *all steps* of the Remdesivir supply chain, including chemical-based intermediate production steps that are currently being performed in Canada.

Yes, as history had painfully taught us, our brothers and sisters to the north in Canada posed potential problems for the security of our Remdesivir supply chains. Here's the warning I sent to the Task Force on February 14:

> *Failure to onshore this upstream production capacity will put the US at a significant disadvantage to access additional drug supply after the initial 100,000 doses are exhausted.*
>
> *REMEMBER: In 2009, during H1N1, Canada withheld vaccines from the U.S. until their national need was satisfied.*

ANTHONY FAUCI MOVES THE GOALPOST

Because of the early action we took on Remdesivir, we were indeed able to expedite clinical trials, gain control of at least some of the supply chain, get to market with the medicine, and get it to President Trump, along with tens of thousands of other Americans, in their darkest hour of need. That was the good news.

The bad news is that Remdesivir, a drug costing thousands of dollars per treatment and offering whopping profit margins to Big Pharma, has turned out to be hardly a magic bullet. Particularly in the early stage of a CCP Virus Infection, Remdesivir is likely to be no more, and probably less, effective than hydroxychloroquine, a $12 generic with an extremely low profit margin. Plus, you can just pop hydroxy pills, whereas Remdesivir has to be administered as an IV.

The stark price and profit differences between the cheap, abundant, and low-margin hydroxychloroquine and the expensive and scarce Remdesivir with whopping profit margins for Big Pharma lay the basis for an interesting sidebar to this story. Of course, it is one involving yet another piece of sleaze from Anthony Fauci: even as he was bashing hydroxy-chloroquine, he was greasing the skids for the approval of Big Pharma's Big Profits Remdesivir. It would be a classic bait and switch.

To wit: rather than judge the efficacy of Remdesivir on the basis of *a reduction in the mortality rate*—the original "death off the table" endpoint of the study—Fauci surprised the scientific community by abruptly moving this goalpost to the much less consequential *time to recovery.*[2]

When I heard about that, I found it just plain weird. At least I found it weird until Doc Hatfill told me to follow the money. And as it always is with Fauci, the money trail leads directly back to Fauci's patron saint, Big Pharma, an industry that has helped make Fauci the highest-paid bureaucrat in the entire US government.[3]

In any kind of normal times, Fauci would have been intensely criticized by both the media and the scientific community for his moving of the Remdesivir goalpost. However, during the Trump administration, Saint Fauci—the anti-Trump media's favorite POTUS foil—was always off limits.

A BATTLE ROYAL WITH OMB PENNY PINCHERS

Now, what about the story behind the Regeneron story? Our efforts to help jump-start Regeneron's monoclonal antibodies treatment has a nice little humorous twist.

The jump start began in earnest in my February 19 memo to the Task Force, which noted:

> *Regeneron has a proprietary . . . platform that can rapidly identify and produce monoclonal antibodies with*

*extended half-life. . . . The company's expertise and capabilities are suitable for accelerated development.**

To catalyze this "accelerated development," and more broadly press forward with key elements of our Five-Vector Pandemic Attack Strategy, I pressed the Task Force in a follow-up memo on February 23 to support a supplemental congressional appropriation of $3 billion for vaccines, PPE, testing, and therapeutics. Fully $198 million of that appropriation would be earmarked for Remdesivir and another $169 billion for Regeneron's monoclonal antibodies.

To help close the deal, in a follow-up memo of March 1 I noted the need to fill the gap between any eventual vaccine and the carnage that might ensue absent a suite of viable therapeutics. Wrote I, channeling Doc Hatfill:

In the absence of a vaccine . . . Regeneron's antibodies should be expedited for development and evaluation for use as a prophylactic treatment. This approach would provide protection against . . . infection for healthcare workers and prioritized emergency and critical infrastructure personnel.

Now, here is the humorous twist: I would get into a huge fight over the proposed supplemental appropriation with Acting Chief of Staff Mick Mulvaney and his replacement as Office of Management and Budget (OMB) director, Russ Vought. Neither of them wanted to pony up a dime for a problem they didn't believe existed. Ergo, they were lowballing at

* This observation is contained in an attachment to my memo from the Department of Health and Human Services, prepared at my request.

a mere $300 million. Of course, at $3 billion, I was asking for ten times that.

So what's the humorous twist? Congress would eventually approve almost three times the amount of money that even I was pushing for.[4]

The moral of this story is the same one I learned when winning the China travel ban: in government, paper the hell out of opponents.

I want to share with you one of our finest "paper the crap out of them" hours. Here is the memo of February 23, subject line "Request for Supplemental Appropriation." The first paragraph is designed to scare readers with the prospect of accountability for all of the American lives that might be lost because of failure to act. Here goes:

> *There is an increasing probability of a full-blown COVID-19 pandemic that could infect as many as 100 million Americans, with a loss of life of as many as 1–2 million souls. To minimize economic and social disruption and loss of life, there is an urgent need for an immediate supplemental appropriation of at least $3.0 billion dollars to support efforts at prevention, treatment, inoculation, and diagnostics.*

In the second paragraph, I invoked the God of In Trump Time:

> *This is NOT a time for penny-pinching or horse trading on the Hill. Uncertainties associated with developing a vaccine and viable treatment options should NOT slow down investments in these high risk, high reward ventures. In this Administration, we take appropriate risks*

> *to protect the public. We move in Trump Time to solve problems. We always skate to where the puck might be—in this case a full-blown pandemic.*

Now for the Grand "Wrong Administration" Finale, here's the coup de grâce:

> *We CAN develop a vaccine and treatment therapeutics in half the usual time. We MUST get appropriate protective gear and point of care diagnostics. Any member of the Task Force who wants to be cautious about appropriating funds for a crisis that could inflict trillions of dollars in economic damage and take millions of lives has come to the wrong administration.*

SEVEN

THE SCURRILOUS CASE OF HYDROXY HYSTERIA

My big mission of the day is to make sure hydroxychloroquine gets sent to [the hot zones of] Detroit, Chicago, New Orleans, and New York. . . . We agree on a distribution of three million tablets per distributor—McKesson, Cardinal, and AmerisourceBergen. They will provide me with granular addresses so that we can ship directly to the hot zones and cut out all the middlemen distribution centers.

It's a good plan. Let's see if we can execute. I have promises from FEMA [the Federal Emergency Management Agency] that they will move the stuff out tonight or early tomorrow morning, and I am awaiting the addresses.

—Peter Navarro, journal entry, April 6, 2020

On March 19, as the US economy was beginning to be shut down in what would be a futile effort to stop the spread of the CCP Virus, President Donald Trump declared that hydroxychloroquine might be a "game changer." POTUS further promised that the FDA would swiftly provide emergency approval of the potentially lifesaving medicine for treatment of the virus.

The very next day, Dr. Anthony Fauci would stomp all over the president's message of hope by countering that hydroxychloroquine was *not* an effective treatment. Ignoring reams of hard scientific evidence in support of the drug's safety and efficacy, Fauci falsely claimed that any alleged effectiveness of the drug in fighting the virus was "anecdotal."[1] And he completely ignored an email he had received two days earlier from a prominent scientist who had described hydroxychloroquine as an "effective and safe treatment."[2]

With Fauci's throwdown, thus began the biggest and bloodiest battle of wills between a US president and a US government employee since President Harry Truman went toe-to-toe with General Douglas MacArthur. Thus also began round two of my fight with a wildly overpaid bureaucrat who would soon emerge as the guiltiest party—along with Jeff Zucker's CNN—in the Scurrilous Case of Hydroxy Hysteria.

NOTHING TO FEAR BUT HYDROXY HYSTERIA ITSELF

Hydroxy Hysteria is the irrational and unjustifiable fear of taking a medicine that almost certainly won't hurt you and almost certainly can help save your life if you are ever attacked by the CCP Virus. Here are the nonhysterical facts:

For more than sixty years, hydroxychloroquine has safely treated malaria as well as autoimmune conditions such as rheumatoid arthritis and lupus. It's on the World Health Organization's Model List of Essential Medicines, and the CDC even labels hydroxychloroquine safe—drumroll, please—for nursing mothers and pregnant women.[3]

And then there is this: lupus and rheumatoid arthritis patients take about the same amount of hydroxychloroquine *every day of their lives* that a CCP Virus patient is advised to take daily for *just a single week*.* On this basis alone, you can

* The recommended daily hydroxychloroquine dosage for lupus is up to 400 milligrams (mg) per day, while for rheumatoid arthritis, it is up to 600 mg per day. By comparison, covid-19 patients are treated with 600 mg the first day followed by 400 mg per day for up to seven days.

see how ridiculous it was for the anti-Trump media to fraudulently warn about the dangers of hydroxychloroquine, especially as a deadly pandemic began to grip Americans by the throat and lungs.

Now, here's the underlying science: hydroxychloroquine can be an effective therapeutic *when used within the first five to seven days* of a CCP Virus infection. This is true irrespective of any particular variant strain or mutation of the virus.

In such so-called early-treatment use, two 200 mg tablets of hydroxychloroquine per day can reduce the viral load along with the need for hospitalization, supplemental oxygen, and mechanical ventilation. These benefits in and of themselves help alleviate physician congestion and hospital overcrowding.

Most important, by significantly reducing the mortality rate, hydroxychloroquine also helps take death off the table.[4]

Just how does hydroxychloroquine work its magic? In layperson's terms, it does so through two primary biological pathways: an *alkalinity effect* and a *blocking effect*.

When you become infected with the CCP Virus, the virus first attacks the cells of your airway and then spreads into the rest of your body. By taking hydroxychloroquine, you raise your cellular pH level into a more alkaline state—this is the alkalinity effect. It is the antiviral alkalinity effect inside your own cells that serves to slow down the replication of the virus or kill the virus outright.[5]

In fact, the antiviral properties of hydroxychloroquine—the drug chloroquine is a close analogue—were first observed in a landmark *in vitro* study that appeared in 2005 in the *Journal of Virology*. Wrote the authors of this landmark article:

> Chloroquine has strong antiviral effects on SARS-CoV infection of primate cells. These inhibitory effects are observed when the cells are treated with the drug *either before or after exposure to the virus, suggesting both prophylactic and therapeutic advantage.*[6] [Emphasis added.]

Note here the reference to a possible prophylactic advantage. This is where the *blocking effect* of hydroxychloroquine comes into play.

To understand this blocking effect, it is first critical to understand the architecture and weaponized nature of the CCP Virus. Here, when you look closely at a magnified picture of the virus, you will immediately notice the *spiked* or *club-shaped crowns* that protrude from the virus's core. It is precisely these crowns from which the virus gets its name as a coronavirus—*corona* is the Latin word for "crown."

It is these crowns—called *spiked proteins*—that are the true weapons of the virus. They serve as the tips of the spears that attack the so-called ACE-2 receptor proteins on your airway cells. When the spiked protein spears are able to attach to and penetrate your cells through your ACE-2 receptors, the virus streams into your cells, and you are now infected.

Now here's the prophylaxis punch line: *Hydroxychloroquine helps* ***block the spiked protein attacks****. It does so by removing sugar molecules from your ACE-2 receptors.*[7] *With this change in "terminal glycosylation," as it was referred to in the landmark 2005 study, it becomes more difficult for the virus to attach to your own airway cells through spike proteins.*[8]

It's not for nothing that thousands of doctors, nurses, and first responders around the world from the very beginning of the CCP virus pandemic, began using hydroxychloroquine to prevent their own infections as they found themselves cast into hot viral infection zones. Numerous studies have since strongly validated this prophylactic effect.[9]

By the way, a useful analogy here may be found in the use of hydroxychloroquine to prevent malaria. Travelers heading to a malaria zone take hydroxy for a week or two prior to going there to build up a similar kind of prophylactic effect.

EARLY- VERSUS LATE-TREATMENT USE

Now here's a key plot point in the Scurrilous Case of Hydroxy Hysteria, one tied directly to hydroxychloroquine's *alkalinity effect*: *though numerous scientific studies have found hydroxychloroquine to be highly effective in* ***early treatment of outpatients*** *within the first five to seven days of infection,*[10] *hydroxychloroquine is likely to be* ***less effective*** *in the* ***late treatment of hospitalized patients****.*

Here's the obvious problem: once patients have been infected for more than seven days and they are in the late-treatment stage, the virus has replicated millions of times and likely surged into the heart, kidneys, and other organs. At such an advanced stage of the disease, hydroxychloroquine is simply not powerful enough to work well.

Therefore, *using hydroxychloroquine in the late-treatment stage is like trying to treat the pain of a gunshot wound with aspirin*. To mix metaphors, when your kitchen stove is on fire, you don't wait until the entire house is in flames to call the fire department; you get your fire extinguisher and put the fire out immediately. For the CCP Virus, hydroxychloroquine is the early-treatment fire extinguisher.

At the time of this writing, there have been more than three hundred hydroxychloroquine studies involving more than four thousand scientists around the world and nearly four hundred thousand infected patients.[11] A meta-analysis of those studies indicated a *66 percent overall improvement* with the use of hydroxychloroquine compared to matched control groups not receiving the drug.[12]

In addition, early-treatment mortality studies estimated an average *75 percent reduction in deaths* with the use of hydroxychloroquine, while later-treatment studies showed a *22 percent reduction* in the mortality rate.* Talk about taking death off the table!

A ROGUE FDA WITH BLOOD ON ITS HANDS

Now, you might think that the top doctors and scientists at the US FDA might be smart enough to distinguish between early- and late-treatment use of hydroxychloroquine and shape their policies accordingly. Yet you would be wrong.

Indeed, the FDA committed one of the worst blunders of the entire pandemic by taking what amounted to a rogue and foolish action in defiance of both President Trump and the secretary of the Department of Health and Human Services, Alex Azar. Here's the story behind this important part of the story.

On March 23, four days after President Trump had promised that the FDA would expedite the use of hydroxychloroquine, Azar and his deputy at HHS, Bob Kadlec, gave several FDA bureaucrats very clear and explicit instructions to make hydroxychloroquine widely available to the American public *as an early CCP Virus treatment on an outpatient basis.* (As shown by the use of hydroxychloroquine in other countries, early-use outpatient treatment would be an important key to

* These statistics are based on 11 early-treatment studies and 174 late-treatment studies.

interrupting the exponential spread of the virus and minimizing deaths in the United States.)*

Nonetheless, five days later, those very same FDA bureaucrats—including FDA commissioner Stephen Hahn and his eventual replacement, Janet Woodcock—completely countermanded the POTUS-Azar-Kadlec order. Instead, on March 28, the FDA issued a rogue directive *restricting the use of hydroxychloroquine to the late treatment of hospitalized patients.*[13]

With its rogue directive, the FDA effectively ensured that hydroxychloroquine would be diverted ***from its best possible use*** *as an early treatment for outpatients* ***to its worst possible use*** *as a late-treatment medicine for hospitalized patients. At least in the court of public opinion, that single decision was tantamount if not to murder, then certainly to negligent homicide.*

Now I would like to tell you that I uncovered a very good reason in my subsequent investigation as to why Hahn and Woodcock, with the apparent help of Dr. Rick Bright, would make such an egregious decision. Yet in the absence of a smoking gun, all I can do is surmise that the decision was either gross incompetence or an intentional attempt by the Deep Administrative State to sabotage President Trump's hydroxychloroquine policy. Both are nearly unimaginable.

Either way, there is considerable blood on the hands of the FDA for that decision alone. Yet there would be even more blood on Anthony Fauci's hands.

FEAR IN HIS EYES, LOATHING IN MINE

On April 4, I had my second major facedown with Saint Fauci in the Situation Room. Recall that in my first go-round with

* A key benefit of hydroxychloroquine that is seldom discussed is this: as their viral load and severity of infection are reduced, patients have to spend less time in the hospital, freeing up space for other patients and putting the brakes on an exponentially increasing number of cases.

him on January 28, Fauci had strenuously opposed President Trump's travel ban on China. If we had not prevailed in that fight, hundreds of thousands and perhaps millions of Americans would have needlessly died due to Fauci's bad advice.

This time, the facedown with Fauci was over hydroxychloroquine. In preparation, I had Doc Hatfill and my team prepare a large dossier with the hundreds of pages of scientific studies I had reviewed on the safety and efficacy of hydroxychloroquine. I knew that Fauci would play the "there's only anecdotal evidence" card and wanted to be ready to prove that that assertion was false.

The meeting started off civilly enough. Vice President Mike Pence was at the head of the table, chairing the meeting, along with his chief of staff, Marc Short; Jared Kushner had come to make a cameo appearance; and the big guests of honor were Fauci along with Surgeon General Jerome Adams and the FDA's Hahn.

To my pleasant surprise, at the outset of the meeting, the surgeon general offered strong words in support of hydroxychloroquine along the lines of "The medicine certainly can't hurt you, and there seems to be some evidence that it may help." I greatly appreciated those words because I knew he was taking a risk. His peers—Fauci in particular—might well try to come down hard on him.

Adams was followed by Hahn, and to my surprise, even Hahn had some encouraging words for hydroxychloroquine—perhaps because of all the heat the FDA had been taking for its moronic March 28 directive.

That support from Adams and Hahn notwithstanding, when it was Fauci's turn, right on cue, he immediately played his "there's only anecdotal evidence" card. Just as immediately, I stood up from my backbench chair just behind Vice President Pence and walked straight toward Fauci.

As I approached him, I saw fear in his eyes. I'm sure it crossed his mind that I might physically assault him. Instead, I dumped my large dossier of studies onto the table in front of him and said to Fauci as much as to everyone else in the room—especially VPOTUS—"Tony, these are not anecdotes. That's more than fifty scientific studies in support of hydroxy. Fifty! So stop spouting your crap about there only being anecdotal evidence because not only is it counterfactual. You are going to kill people just like you did during the AIDS crisis when you refused to approve medicines that everybody but you knew worked."

Now, keep in mind that discussions conducted in the Situation Room are generally considered confidential. Yet—and there was only a very small handful of very senior officials attending this meeting—my confrontation with Fauci was immediately leaked to Jonathan Swan at the DC gossip website Axios.

Swanny, as I liked to call him whenever he called to confirm a fact or try to coax a leak from me, gave a detailed account of what he described as an "epic Situation Room showdown" featuring a "heated exchange" between Fauci and me.[14]

His reporting was not wrong. But that kind of leak was *just not right*—and I told him so.

At least my confrontation with Fauci would shut him up for a couple of days. Then a tragic hat trick of Hydroxy Hysteria would hit Doc Hatfill, POTUS, and me harder than an Alex Ovechkin body check.

THE FRENCH MISCONNECTION

This tragedy of scientific errors began on April 14, 2020, with a French study posted on the online bulletin board medRxiv. Its Yale sponsorship notwithstanding, the website is an embarrassment that does far more harm than good. It does so by providing a thin patina of respectability to any kind of so-called research that hacks around the world might want to post without adequate peer review.

The French hacks in question took a small sample of a mere 181 patients stuck in a French hospital in the late-treatment stage of their infection and divided them into one group that received hydroxychloroquine and a "control group" that did not. Not surprisingly, the researchers found no difference in mortality rates between the two groups; remember, hydroxychloroquine does *not* work well in late-treatment use.[15]

Of course, the Hydroxy Hysteria media immediately pounced on the French Misconnection. CNN, in particular, tried to hang the meaningless finding like a millstone from the Boss's neck, crowing, "A drug that's been touted by President Trump as a 'game changer' didn't help hospitalized patients with coronavirus."[16]

MURDER IN BRAZIL

The next Hydroxy Hysteria puck was fired at our heads two days later, on April 16. The "Murder in Brazil Study," as I would dub it, was literally designed to kill.

After a very small sample of eighty-one subjects was divided into "low-dosage" and "high-dosage" groups, patients in the "high-dosage group" were given enough medicine to bring an elephant to its knees.

Oh, did I mention this? The Brazilian researchers also put the patients most likely to die—those over the age of seventy-five—into the high-dosage group.

It wasn't therapy; it was euthanasia. And enough of these senior citizens died quickly for the study to be quickly canceled.

Like the cherry blossom trees in Washington that month, Hydroxy Hysteria sprang into full April bloom following the publication of the Murder in Brazil Study. Fearmongering headlines included phrases such as "Fatal Heart Complications" (*New York Times*),[17] "Lethal for Some Patients" (*The Guardian*),[18] and "Study Ends Early Due to Deaths" (CNN).

A FAKE DEPARTMENT OF VETERANS AFFAIRS STUDY

As Doc Hatfill and I sat in my office on April 23 bitching and moaning about the media's ginning up of Hydroxy Hysteria, we got hit right in our foreheads with the third puck in the hat trick. It was a study[19] believed to be sponsored by the Department of Veterans Affairs—only it wasn't.

After Doc Hatfill read that fake Veterans Affairs study,* he was particularly incensed: here we had yet another poorly designed late-treatment-use study in which hydroxychloroquine had been administered to the most vulnerable of patients with the lowest chance of survival.

Most egregious—and this was truly unbelievable sloppiness—the hydroxychloroquine group contained a statistically higher percentage of smokers than the control group did. That alone would account for the alleged negative results the researchers reported.

---

* The study had used data obtained from the VA but had not been sponsored by the VA.

BLOOD ON THE FDA'S HANDS

As if all that weren't bad enough, on April 23, FDA commissioner Stephen Hahn took yet another rogue and inexplicable action that would blow even more fetid air into Hydroxy Hysteria's billowing sails. Under Hahn's signature, the FDA issued a "Drug Safety Communication" that warned of "abnormal heart rhythms and possible death" associated with hydroxychloroquine. The FDA also warned practicing physicians that the drug should be used only in hospital settings and not with outpatients.

The ludicrous new "Fauci-Hahn-Woodcock National Pandemic Strategy" would keep early-stage infected patients quarantined at home and ***without hydroxychloroquine treatment*** *until they became so ill that they had to be admitted to a hospital. Once in hospital, they would finally be given hydroxychloroquine, which, in that late-treatment use, would not work very well.*

More than six hundred thousand dead Americans later, we still have no accepted early outpatient treatment for the CCP Virus—even though hydroxychloroquine is just such a treatment.

It can't be said too forcefully: what the FDA did was flat-out Grim Reaper ridiculous. There was *no, absolutely* ***no****, legitimate evidence* whatsoever to support the FDA's new policy—only deeply flawed studies such as the French Misconnection and Murder in Brazil. Remember, hydroxychloroquine has been used safely for more than sixty years, and it is safe even for pregnant women and nursing mothers.

That exceptional safety record notwithstanding, the FDA announcement had a noticeably chilling effect on my ability as the Defense Production Act policy coordinator to distribute the *more than 60 million tablets* of hydroxychloroquine sitting in the FEMA stockpiles. This May 5 entry from my journal describes the deadly coffin the FDA and anti-Trump media had put me and thousands of other Americans into:

> *We are in a situation where the demand for hydroxy[chloroquine] has dried up significantly after a couple of bad newspaper stories and hysteria on TV, and the FDA announcement which . . . was widely interpreted as telling people NOT to use it. Demand for hydroxy through my office channels and the distributors has slowed to a trickle.*

To fully understand the "blood on their hands" implications of the FDA's announcement, it may be time to stop and do a little Hydroxy Hysteria Grim Reaper math. Consider, then, those 63 million tablets of hydroxychloroquine gathering dust in FEMA warehouses. They were enough to treat about 5 million Americans infected with the virus.

If we conservatively assume a case fatality rate of 1 to 2 percent,[20] anywhere from fifty thousand to one hundred thousand of the 5 million Americans diagnosed with the disease would die absent an effective therapeutic. *If, as studies now clearly indicate, hydroxychloroquine can reduce that fatality rate by up to 75 percent,[21] it means that the amount of hydroxychloroquine that was ready to dispense from the FEMA stockpiles could have saved up to seventy-five thousand American lives.*

It is also worth pointing out here that case fatality rates increase exponentially with age, which is to say that the older you are, the far more likely you are to die of a CCP Virus infection.[22] If we had been able to target those more than 60 million tablets of hydroxychloroquine to seniors over the age of fifty-nine, we could have saved even more lives.

It may also be useful to point out here that the war waged on hydroxychloroquine by CNN, the FDA, and a lot of anti-Trump journalists in between was about as pure a case of racial discrimination as you can get. Here was a medicine we could have quickly dispensed in the hot-zone days of March and April to the low-income, primarily Black and Brown communities being hammered in our largest cities.

This medicine would not only have reduced the death rates in those communities, it would have prevented hospital overloading, reduced the need for ventilators, and reduced the need for extra health care workers.

THE BIG FDA CHILL ON CLINICAL TRIALS

The FDA's rogue announcement did not just hamper our ability to distribute hydroxychloroquine to physicians and patients; it had an equally chilling effect on the ability of researchers such as Dr. William O'Neill at Detroit's Henry Ford Health System to recruit subjects for the randomized clinical trials many of the critics of hydroxychloroquine were clamoring for.

Ford is one of the largest hospital systems in the country and disproportionately serves lower-income African Americans. With the grace of God—and no shortage of FEMA and UPS trucks—my White House office helped keep Bill O'Neill's troops sufficiently stocked with enough gowns, gloves, and N95 respirators—and, yes, hydroxychloroquine—to keep at least most of his doctors, nurses, and first responders safe. But it was touch-and-go there for a long while, and many of the times I talked with Bill, I could hear anguish in his voice.

It was easy to understand Bill's anguish. He was operating in a very special kind of Motor City hell, as the vast majority of his patients were Black. By that time, it had become all too apparent that Blacks were disproportionately vulnerable to the CCP Virus, with both higher infection rates and higher mortality rates.[23]

A big part of the problem was the wide range of comorbidities that African Americans are subject to because of growing up in poverty and often subsisting at the lower rungs of our economy and society. Obesity, high blood pressure, heart disease, and diabetes are all prevalent in the brownstones and mean streets of Detroit, making Black Americans easy prey for the Chinese Communist Party Virus.

May 5 was a particularly emotional day for Bill O'Neill, as indicated by this entry from my journal:

> *[Dr.] William O'Neill at the Detroit Hospital is absolutely livid at how fear has disrupted his clinical trials and he, along with eight other fairly famous doctors, have drafted a letter to [the Journal of the American Medical Association] condemning the witch hunt atmosphere that has been created by the media.*

Bill was in the middle of one of the worst viral hot zones in the country, trying to deal with a flood of highly vulnerable patients. At the same time, this truly good doctor was desperately trying to conduct his randomized clinical trials that would show once and for all that hydroxychloroquine is highly effective in early-treatment use. Yet day after day, both the FDA and the anti-Trump media, along with Tony Fauci, threw dagger after dagger after dagger at the heart of his operations.

As a case in point, on August 1, Bill O'Neill finally struck back against the Hydroxy Hysteria empire. His research team at Ford would publish a landmark article in the debate over hydroxychloroquine. The study's key finding is worth reporting here in all its scientific-lingo glory: "According to a protocol-based treatment algorithm, among hospitalized patients, use of hydroxychloroquine alone and in combination with azithromycin was associated with a significant reduction [in] in-hospital mortality compared to not receiving hydroxychloroquine."[24]

The study clearly proved that tens of thousands of American lives could have been saved if only hydroxychloroquine had been used early on in the pandemic as President Trump had wished and the FDA had been commanded to make happen. As soon as the Ford article came out, however, Saint Fauci himself would go out of his way to condemn the Ford study as "flawed" in congressional testimony.[25] As reported on The Hill website, "When Rep. Blaine Luetkemeyer (R-Mo.) interjected to say the [Ford] study was peer-reviewed, Fauci replied with this dagger: 'It doesn't matter. You can peer review something that's a bad study.'"[26]

"You've got to be kidding," said I to Doc Hatfill when I watched Fauci's testimony. "Where was his 'bad study' smack-talking jive when the French Misconnection or Murder in Brazil reared their ugly and truly flawed heads?"

Clearly, Fauci had his own agenda in stoking Hydroxy Hysteria, and the only possible reason could be his desire to take down the president. *That* was becoming clearer and clearer to me.

But Fauci was hardly alone in the upper echelons of science in pushing an anti-Trump, Hydroxy Hysteria narrative. He would soon be joined from "across the pond" by one of the most scurrilous actors in this Scurrilous Case: Richard Horton, the editor in chief of the British journal *The Lancet*.

THE LANCET'S MORAL DECAY

On May 16, Richard Horton took the unprecedented step of using his journal to editorialize against the reelection of Donald Trump.[27] In doing so, he crossed the unspoken red line between science and politics. As if that weren't bad enough, he would soon bring even more shame to a journal that once ranked as one of the most prestigious in the world.

Indeed, just days later, on May 22, Horton published an anti-hydroxychloroquine journal article that, in a thinly veiled attack on President Trump, was the equivalent of a neutron bomb.

Unlike the French Misconnection and Murder in Brazil, the *Lancet* article was not a too-small sample study published on some garbage bulletin board. Rather, it was a peer-reviewed article based on what appeared to be a massive database of almost one hundred thousand hospital patients spread across six continents. Based on the results, the study's lead author, Dr. Mandeep Mehra, warned of "immutable" and "grave harm" from the use of hydroxychloroquine,[28] and with that warning, the anti-Trump Hydroxy Hysterics in the media were off to the races.

That morning, in my White House office, my heart raced as I raced through the *Lancet* article for the first time. On that first pass-through, my thoughts were *Mayday! Mayday!*—and *Where the heck is Doc Hatfill?* Yet after I calmed down a bit, my Harvard training kicked in.

The second time I went through the article and its statistical tables, in a moment of crystal clarity, I had an epiphany: *This database is too good to be true. The summary statistics across the six continents are just not differentiated enough to be other than massaged or cooked.*

When Doc Hatfill rolled into the office an hour later, he told me he had *exactly* the same impression.

Sure enough, within days, the anti-Trump Richard Horton was forced to retract the study of Mandeep Mehra and his colleagues and acknowledge that the database was flawed.[29] *Yet before Horton's retraction,* The Lancet *weapon of mass hydroxychloroquine destruction would do incalculable harm.*

The World Health Organization would soon announce a temporary halt to its global clinical trial of hydroxychloroquine. The French government would ban the prescription of hydroxychloroquine to treat the CCP Virus, and France's infection and death rates would soon be out of control. One of the major manufacturers of the drug, the French company Sanofi, would even suspend the recruitment of new patients for its clinical trial. And thousands of preventable global deaths would follow.

A SIGNAL FAILURE OF SCIENCE AND JOURNALISM

The Mayday! Mayday! *Lancet* attack, coupled with April's Hydroxy Hysteria hat trick of poorly designed, late-treatment-use studies and the FDA's multiple rogue actions would represent a catastrophic and signal failure of both the scientific and journalistic communities. The result would be the needless sacrifice of tens of thousands of Americans and hundreds of thousands of victims worldwide on the altar of Hydroxy Hysteria.

Maybe one of those who died needlessly was your husband. Or your wife. Or perhaps one of your grandparents. It was all so unnecessary, and there were many nights I had trouble sleeping when I allowed myself to think about it. It was all so terribly wrong.

All of my anger and disgust about so many needless deaths would spill over during an acid-tinged CNN interview on July 29 with John "Holier than Thou" Berman. Said I:

> Americans are dying. [Yet FDA Commissioner Steve Hahn] has acknowledged fully [that hydroxychloroquine] will not hurt you. . . . The only question is whether there's any upside, and I would maintain having read over 60 studies on this that the evidence for early treatment use is overwhelming. . . .
>
> *If I'm wrong [about hydroxychloroquine working], nobody gets hurt.*
>
> . . . If I'm right, thousands of Americans are dying because the media and the FDA have made hydroxychloroquine something that appears to be dangerous when it's a 65-year-old drug that can't hurt you under doctor supervision.[30] [Emphasis added.]

And here is what I wanted to say to Jeff Zucker right after that interview with the callow Berman:

It's one thing to use your Cable News Network like Roger Ailes once used Fox to influence the political process and help determine the outcome of a presidential election. I get it, and I might even be able to say that's all fair and good in a free and open democratic system.

But, Jeff: what you are doing with CNN in promoting Hydroxy Hysteria is as wrong as it ever gets. If hydroxychloroquine works in early-treatment use—and the preponderance of scientific evidence certainly says it does—there is the blood on your hands of tens of thousands of Americans.

After that CNN interview, I called up Saint Fauci and suggested a powwow with his panel of scientists to figure out why he was so adamantly opposed to hydroxychloroquine. The result was a Zoom call on August 5 with me and my team at the White House and Fauci's team dialing in from various portals or at the National Institutes of Health.

Early in the meeting, I asked one of Fauci's top lieutenants which studies he believed proved that hydroxychloroquine was ineffective. After hemming and hawing—it was clear that he was not an expert in the literature—he finally cited a University of Minnesota study of prophylaxis in the *New England Journal of Medicine* of June 3.[31]

I found that to be a very curious choice because the subjects in the study who took hydroxychloroquine actually had *a noticeably lower rate of infection* than the control group did.

The only problem with the study was that the result was not, as we say in the trade, "statistically significant." Yet it took neither an NIH scientist or a social scientist like me to understand that its lack of statistical significance was due to *too few participants*, which is to say, again in my trade, that the study was "statistically underpowered."

Of course, rather than seeing that promising news of a lower rate of infection staring them straight in the eyes, Fauci's Merry Band of Morons simply didn't get it—or, more likely, simply didn't want to get it. And when I say morons, what comes to mind is Barack Obama's observation about how many times in his eight years as president, he had met "highly credentialed, high IQ morons."[32]

Of course, nothing I was going to say that day was going to change anybody's minds at the Hydroxy Hysteria factory otherwise known as the National Institutes of Health. By agreeing to meet, Fauci was just humoring me so he could tell the media he had an open mind.

The real humor came, however, at the end of the conference, after we had ostensibly signed off. What Fauci didn't know was that his microphone and camera were still hot; my assistant Joanna Miller had not yet dropped the Zoom call.

As soon as Saint Fauci thought he was off camera, he dropped that sweet awe-shucks Manhattan TV persona and went full Brooklyn in front of his team, just ripped me up and down, saying with a smirk, "See what I have to put up with?"

I literally had to restrain the enraged Doc Hatfill from trying to jump through the jumbo TV monitor so he could grab Fauci by the throat and shake him like a rag doll.

All I can say is: God bless hot mikes—they are so revealing. If I'd had any doubts about the two faces of Anthony Fauci before that incident, that moment of candor shattered all of them.

Over the next three months leading into the November 3 election, there would be many more twists and turns in the Scurrilous Case of Hydroxy Hysteria. But for all practical purposes, the Fauci-Zucker-CNN Fat Lady had already sung her funeral dirge for the lifesaving medicine.

In light of what has been a totally unnecessary American carnage, I will let Doc Hatfill have the *next-to-last* word. Here's what he told me with that signature exasperated shake of his head on March 21, 2020: "India's population is five times larger than that of the United States, but India's death toll has been only about thirty percent of America's. The difference is India's widespread use of hydroxychloroquine both as a prophylactic and in early-treatment use."

Now, Victor Davis Hanson gets the *last* word. That's because his December 9, 2020, take on the political dynamics of Hydroxy Hysteria—late in coming though it was—is nonetheless so very spot on:

Only hydroxychloroquine has prompted furious partisan debate over its possible usefulness. Why?

Probably because Donald Trump endorsed its usage months ago. Almost immediately, the media, the university and government medical community, and the progressive political opposition declared hydroxychloroquine useless and dangerous.[33]

A REQUIEM FOR RATIONAL ACTION

And finally, in the "Just Thought You Should Know" bin, in Switzerland, France, and Panama, when hydroxychloroquine was banned at the height of Hydroxy Hysteria, the number of daily covid-19 deaths increased significantly. When alarmed authorities brought the drug back, the daily number quickly returned to the baseline.

- No other therapeutic has repeatedly and consistently demonstrated the benefits, safety profile for early use, low cost, ease of manufacture, rapid dispensing, and ease of outpatient use than hydroxychloroquine when used under a doctor's supervision. It is even sold without prescription in some countries.
- No other drug, when properly utilized by private physicians and public health authorities, has such a dramatic ability to minimize patient hospital admissions and reduce the number of deaths in high-risk populations.

Here's the sad truth: not only did the FDA and Anthony Fauci fail to keep a proper check and balance on the pharmaceutical industry and select the best drug for the operational management of the pandemic. Those denizens of the Deep

Administrative State actually assisted pharmaceutical company interests by snuffing out the use of hydroxychloroquine in favor of Remdesivir.

With the benefit of hindsight, we now know that the Fauci-Hahn-Woodcock-Bright Doctrine of not treating high-risk patients early, upon clinical suspicion, led the United States down a path that destroyed any chance for a successful pandemic response—and Jeff Zucker at CNN played the role of an anti-Trump Pied Piper.

EIGHT

KILL THE GM CHICKEN, SCARE THE VENTILATOR MONKEY

I spend all day moving product to New York City. Ventilators, Tyvek suits, and PPE. In addition to the 400 [ventilators] I got sent, FEMA sends another 4,000 after [New York governor Andrew] Cuomo bitches and moans. I try to make sure that the White House gets some credit and let [Mayor] Bill de Blasio know that they're coming because Cuomo will play "hide the ventilator" from de Blasio as they hate each other. Cuomo takes a really hard hit at me at his press conference and claims the Defense Production Act should be used more. I rip back hard at him on Tucker Carlson after spending 40 minutes with the Guv on the phone.

—Peter Navarro, journal entry, March 24, 2020

Just for the record, Andrew Cuomo is one of the biggest jerks I have ever had the displeasure of meeting and trying to work with. At least New York mayor Bill de Blasio was pleasant, albeit wrong about just about everything—and Bill and I would get some great stuff done for the people of New York, including an incredible "Easter Miracle." But first Cuomo.

In the difficult months of March and April, with the CCP Virus hammering New York, Detroit, and New Orleans particularly hard we at the White House were facing the very real prospect of a massive ventilator shortage. It was literally a deadly situation.

For many people severely infected with the virus, a ventilator is literally their last hope in delaying that inevitable meeting with their maker. As to why a ventilator can be a lifesaver: the CCP Virus inflames the small air sacs in the lungs.

This inflammation thereby cuts off oxygen to other vital organs, and pretty soon, you are too weak to breathe fully and create the *negative* pressure necessary to draw air and oxygen into your lungs.[1] A ventilator can solve this problem by creating a compensating *positive* pressure.

Throughout March and April, in their zeal to get the federal government to send them ventilators from the Strategic National Stockpile, many big-city mayors and big-state governors began making over-the-top demands on our ventilator inventory. Those demands not only raised Americans' fears; they also threatened to exacerbate the looming shortage.

This is because these panicked demands would put needless pressure on the Trump administration to dispense ventilators based not on need but rather on raw political power. Of US politicians, no one was more guilty of sowing such fear and panic and attempting to flex his political muscles than the Big Bad Apple of New York, Governor Andrew Cuomo. (Good riddance, by the way.)

THE FREDDY KRUEGER OF GOVERNORS

In his now-infamous "hair on fire" March 24 press conference, Cuomo hysterically claimed that the state of New York needed thirty thousand ventilators or thousands of New Yorkers would die![2] It was a wildly absurd overestimate of any conceivable need, and with his famous forked tongue, Cuomo not only chastised President Trump and the White House for denying his state ventilators from the federal stockpile. He called me out personally as the Defense Production Act policy coordinator for turning a blind eye to the plight of the Empire State, whining, "What am I going to do with four hundred ventilators when I need thirty thousand?"[3]

Let's do some forked tongue Cuomo math: when I had my staff track down all of the ventilators we had already sent New York, we discovered thousands upon thousands of them piled high in an Albany depot rather than having been pony expressed by Cuomo to the city of New York, where they were most needed.

Cuomo was indeed trying to play hide the ventilators from his archnemesis, Mayor Bill de Blasio. Yet a good part of his "ventilators gathering dust in Albany" problem was due to bureaucratic incompetence and inertia. *It was unforgiveable ineptitude by a loudmouthed politician in the middle of a pandemic.*

The very next day, and after a talk with the Boss, I lit Cuomo up like the Empire State Building at Christmastime. That same day, he would be forced to issue this lame version of a New Yorker's nonapology: "Yes, they're in a stockpile because that's where they are supposed to be, because we don't need them yet. We need [the ventilators] for the apex, the apex isn't here, so we're gathering them in a stockpile."[4]

Apex, smaypex. Andrew Mark Cuomo will never take responsibility for anything. Not for hiding ventilators from Bill de Blasio when New Yorkers were dying. Not for killing thousands of senior citizens in New York nursing homes by forcing those homes to admit infected patients.[5] Not for sexually harassing a raft of women in his own tyrannical workplace.[6]

Memo to Andrew Cuomo and the rest of the world: The miracle that President Donald J. Trump pulled off in dramatically boosting the US ventilator supply in Trump Time is second only to that of his vaccine miracle.

The abiding truth of the ventilator matter is this—and I'm proud to have been the tip of the president's spear—*no American who needed a ventilator was denied a ventilator on President Trump's watch.*

LORDSTOWN OF THE FLIES

Though part of POTUS's ventilator miracle involved several of the recommendations I made in my February memos, the bigger and better part of the ventilator story actually starts with a call I received in early 2019 from Molly Michael, the president's executive assistant. Molly wanted me to quickly sprint over to the Oval Office, and sprint I did.

POTUS then waved me in from the Outer Oval Office and introduced me to Mary Barra, the CEO of General Motors, and Craig Glidden, GM's general counsel. The two of them were there to beg the president's forgiveness for one of the dumbest economic and political moves any major corporation would make during our four years in office.

To wit: in her finite wisdom, Mary Barra had decided to save a few shekels by closing a major auto production facility in Lordstown, Ohio, that was employing more than 1,600 workers.[7]

The announcement of the plant closure on November 26, 2018, hit the White House like shrapnel from an IED,[8] and the

Boss was hotter than a GM engine with a bad oil leak.[9] And why shouldn't he be angry?

After all, *Candidate* Trump had run on a platform of saving both manufacturing jobs and our auto industry, and Ohio was the mother of all critical battleground states. If we lost the Buckeye State because of plant closures like that one, we would almost certainly lose the election.

Despite the political significance of her decision, Mary Barra had never bothered to give the White House a heads-up. That was no doubt because she thought POTUS would try to browbeat her out of the decision. No doubt she was right about that.

At any rate, Barra and Craig Glidden were there to make amends, as POTUS had been relentlessly cutting up GM in the press. So enter the Oval Office, stage right, Navarro, chased by autoworkers. Said the Boss to me immediately upon my entry, "Peter. I need you to work here with Mary and Craig to get Lordstown up and running again. I'm sure the three of you can get it done. It'll be amazing. An amazing story for the whole Mahoning Valley. Let's go!"

Did I mention that both Mary and Craig were squirming uncomfortably in their chairs by that point? Thought I, watching this squirm and scrum and looking into Barra's downcast eyes, *The last thing Mary wants to do is throw any GM bucks Lordstown's way. But really, the last thing she should want is having the president of the United States up in her grill. And he won't be going away until this problem goes away.*

My read of the situation was that although Mary Barra was tone deaf, Craig Glidden seemed to get it. With that read, I saw Craig as my path to reimagining the Lordstown footprint and raising this manufacturing Lazarus up from the dead before the 2020 election.

SETTLING A GM-UAW AUTO STRIKE IN TRUMP TIME

Over the course of working with GM to restore Lordstown to its former manufacturing glory, I was able to build considerable goodwill with Craig Glidden. To borrow a word from Governor Cuomo, the goodwill reached its "apex" when, beginning on October 17, 2019, I quietly intervened in what was a fractious GM-UAW labor strike.

By working with both sides behind-the-scenes—and having the trust of the United Auto Workers leadership because of my street cred boosting American manufacturing—I was able to help resolve a strike that had dragged on for weeks at great cost to both sides, and it was settled in *less than four days.* Trump Time, baby!

Reported Fox News under the headline "GM-UAW 'Catalyst' Peter Navarro Helped Seal Deal," "Turns out top White House trade advisor Peter Navarro can add General Motors and the United Auto Workers to his resume of deals negotiated."[10]

Not bad for a guy who had a reputation in the Fake News of not being able to get along with people.

FORD V FERRARI REDUX

Fast-forward to March 2020 as I was working with a wide variety of US companies as the Defense Production Act policy coordinator. My mission, in many cases, was to convince them to repurpose some of their factory capacity toward the manufacture of personal protective equipment and medical equipment such as ventilators.

The strategy took a page right out of the World War II history book. In that era, our forebears in the "Greatest Generation" transformed auto factories into Arsenal of Democracy weapons that churned out airplanes and tanks in great numbers.

Two of the companies that I was trying to enlist in the "fight the pandemic" repurposing were GM and Ford, both of which needed to start producing ventilators rapidly. In our negotiations, the contrast between the two companies could not have been starker.

Even as Ford forged rapidly ahead at a repurposed factory in Ypsilanti, Michigan, GM dragged its heels on building a similar facility in Kokomo, Indiana. The company did not want to move forward without a signed contract from the federal government.

For me, it was another MBA lesson in organizational culture. Ford, by its culture, is far more nimble and less risk averse than its bigger competitor, GM. I had learned that sad fact of corporate life up close and personal while working with GM executives on the Lordstown venture and GM strike.

So one of the things I did to try to jump-start the process, in a rather overt homage to one of the great movies of 2019, *Ford v Ferrari*, was to issue a Ford v GM challenge: Which company would be the first to start rolling ventilators off the assembly line?

The second thing I did was far more important: at the president's direction, I brought the hammer of the Defense Production Act squarely down on GM's risk-averse, unpatriotic skull.

POTUS' BIG DPA STICK

At this point, it may be useful to explain that neither the president nor I saw the DPA as some big "command-and-control" policy fix-all in the great Soviet Union Leontiev matrix in the sky—Andrew Cuomo's Stalinesque tendencies notwithstanding. Instead, we saw the DPA as a tool to be used sparingly in the spirit of Teddy Roosevelt's famous dictum "Walk softly and carry a big DPA stick."

Our thought—and our strategy—was to appeal first to the patriotism of America's corporations. If that failed, we would then play on the corporate fear that might come from the threat the Big Stick DPA might be used. Only if that failed would we invoke the DPA.

With GM, the president indeed had to use Teddy's big stick. POTUS signed an executive order on March 27, effectively directing GM to belly up to the ventilator manufacturing bar. We then tag-teamed the company in the media. Said POTUS at a same-day press conference, "We thought we had a deal for 40,000 ventilators, and all of a sudden, it became six [thousand] and price became a big object. . . . But Peter Navarro is going to handle that. . . . Maybe they'll change their tune. But we didn't want to play games with them."[11]

It turned out to be the perfect moment to "kill the chicken to scare the monkey"—that's an old Chinese proverb. This is because two things happened after the president used the DPA on the chicken General Motors.

First, many of the monkeys of Corporate America shuddered as our DPA stick suddenly looked a whole lot bigger than they might've imagined. That got us a lot more cooperation than we might otherwise would have gotten on many other fronts. Second, we got to bear witness to one of the greatest miracles in US industrial history.

In just seventeen days, GM, in partnership with a small company from Seattle named Ventec, stood up a ventilator factory in Kokomo. Just three days later, with the stellar help of UPS, we were able to deliver desperately needed ventilators to hospitals in Gary, Indiana, and Chicago, Illinois.

I daresay that this seventeen-day In Trump Time GM miracle will never be duplicated, and it's important to end the story by saying that those were damn good ventilators. They embodied state-of-the-art Ventec technology, and I couldn't have been prouder of the GM workers who'd built them.

This, too, is worth repeating: *every American who needed a ventilator got a ventilator.*

A GARMENT LAZARUS RISES FROM THE DEAD

As for Bill de Blasio and that Easter Miracle I alluded to earlier, it was a thing of pure In Trump Time beauty. That miracle did indeed start on Easter Sunday—April 12, 2020, to be exact. Even though it was Easter, I had a pandemic to contend with, so I was at my White House office when I got a panicked call from de Blasio for yet another shipment of surgical gowns.

Parenthetically, panicked calls were the only kind I ever got from Brother Bill. Here's my candidate for best understatement of this book: Bill de Blasio was *not* one of President Trump's favorites. That was particularly true after de Blasio allowed Black Lives Matter to deface the streets around Trump Tower in New York City.

Now, here's the backstory to this Trump–de Blasio Easter Miracle. My mom spent much of her adult life working in retail for Saks Fifth Avenue, and one of her duties was to travel twice a year to New York's Garment District to select the latest styles for the ladies' dress shop that she managed. She took me on those adventures a number of times, which was when I got my first big look at the Big Apple—along with the storied Garment District.

So as I was talking to Bill about his situation, I asked him why we couldn't raise that Garment District Lazarus back up and running to its former glory by transitioning into the production of personal protective equipment such as gowns and masks. A light bulb went off above de Blasio's head to go with the one shining brightly in mine.

I will let Ebony Bowden of the *New York Post* finish the Easter Miracle story of how de Blasio and I worked together to get the garment district sewing and provided jobs for up to 500 New Yorkers. As Bowden and her coauthor, Julia Marsh, wrote in a nice little bit of free press for the White House:

> Working with private enterprise and the National Council of Textile Organizations, the White House was able to secure a million yards of waterproof fabric from healthcare company Owens & Minor and within days have it on a UPS truck bound for the Big Apple.
>
> In another act of goodwill, UPS volunteered a truck and driver which drove the fabric from North Carolina to the Big Apple in just two days. . . .[12]

Not bad for government work.

NINE

SWEET ON HONEYWELL, HIGH ON PERNOD, AND A PPE MISSION

China produces about half of the world's N-95 masks . . . is prohibiting N-95 mask exports [and seeking to buy] a U.S. factory and export it to China. . . .

Currently, U.S. companies are ramping up, but they are exporting much of their production. The U.S. therefore faces the real prospect of a severe mask shortage!

—Peter Navarro, memorandum to White House Coronavirus Task Force, February 9, 2020

On Thursday, March 12, I got a call from Romina Khananisho, a vice president at Honeywell. She would turn out to be one of the most helpful guardian angels in our quest to address a looming and severe shortage of the gold standard of masks for our frontline health care workers and first responders: N95 respirators.

After Romina got over the shock that she actually had me on the line so quickly—accessibility was the culture of my office—she told me that Honeywell was ready, willing, and able to stand up two additional N95 factories: one in Smithfield, Rhode Island, the other in Phoenix, Arizona. All she needed was a quick turn of a contract proposal so Honeywell could start moving the two projects in what Romina called "Trump Time."

After I stopped chuckling—Romina certainly knew how to push my buttons to close her deal—I told her to immediately jump-start both projects. When she expressed reservations about moving before the contracts were signed, I told her—going out on a long limb—"Don't worry. You have my word on this."

On the basis of my word, Honeywell did indeed get the projects moving in Trump Time. In fact, within twenty-four hours, Romina had trucks moving N95 production machinery from Massachusetts to Rhode Island, and Americans' mask future was already a little brighter.

It took a few days and nervous nights and more than one phone call to the bureaucratic maze of the Department of Health and Human Services to clear the contract decks for Honeywell. But I was eventually able to get all the paperwork moving even as Honeywell hit the manufacturing ground running.

Today, Honeywell's two new factories are producing more than 30 million "Made in the USA" N95 masks a month.[1] They are employing more than a thousand Americans and saving American lives.[2]

"Buy American, Hire American" doesn't get much better than that! Yet even today, we as a country remain dangerously overdependent on foreign suppliers, particularly China, for much of our PPE.

CAUGHT WITH OUR MASKS DOWN

When the CCP Virus came to US shores, our PPE situation was particularly dire. Because we as a nation were caught with our masks and gowns down, health care workers and first responders needlessly died in beleaguered cities such as New York, New Orleans, and Chicago.[3]

The Obama-Biden administration had left the United States with a bare-bones Strategic National Stockpile. However, more than three years into the Trump administration, we could rightly be criticized for not having filled that stockpile more quickly.

Rightly criticized, yes, but perhaps not altogether fairly. Like the administrations of Clinton-Gore, Bush-Cheney, and Obama-Biden before us, Trump-Pence viewed the possibility of a pandemic as a highly unlikely "black swan" event. Through that long-odds prism, building up our stocks of pandemic-fighting PPE was barely on our radar, much less a battle worth fighting during the annual budget wars on Capitol Hill.

As the Bush administration's HHS secretary, Mike Leavitt, noted about his own failure to aggressively push for adequate pandemic relief funds, "Over time, when the snake is not at your ankle, you're worried about other things that are dangerous. And this is not just a function of our generation. This has been the case in virtually every pandemic in human history."[4]

Well, now the snake *is* at our ankle, and if that experience has taught us anything, it is that the United States is dangerously dependent on foreign countries for the production of its essential medicines, medical supplies such as PPE, and medical devices such as ventilators.

To be clear, our foreign dependencies are not just on Communist China—although our greatest and most dangerous vulnerabilities are with that authoritarian beast. During the pandemic, eighty countries[5] circled their wagons and imposed some form of export restrictions on everything from PPE, test kits, and therapeutics to the raw materials needed to produce them.[6]

Based on such realpolitik observations, my February 9 memo called for the "halt of the export of all N-95 masks," a prohibition "on the sale of U.S. N-95 factory equipment to China," "immediate purchase guarantees for all U.S. supplies at maximum production capacity," and "over the longer run," the enforcement of "Buy American provisions for N-95 masks." Call me an Economic Nationalist, and I will wear that like a badge of honor on my sleeve.

VOLTAIRE AND I TOSSED OUT OF A PLANE

Honeywell's Romina Khananisho wasn't the only PPE angel who came to America's rescue. Three others who became an important part of the story were Tara Engel, a vice president at the liquor distiller Pernod Ricard; Kim Glas, the chief executive officer of the National Council of Textile Organizations; and Laura Lane, the chief corporate affairs, communications, and sustainability officer of United Parcel Service (UPS).

By the way, anytime I hear the word "Pernod" or see one of the labels on its bottles in a restaurant or bar, I think of the time when I was a junior in high school and my older brother came home from college for a visit. Brother Brad was a wild one at that age, still finding his way. When he arrived at our Bethesda, Maryland, apartment, up from Emory University for what was supposed to be his first night home, he was drunk as a freshman frat boy on, yes, Pernod.

Now, my mom was not exactly puritanical. But she was damn frugal. So she absolutely ripped Brad up and down for getting high on Pernod—one of the most expensive drinks a teenager can buy. So, too, with little ceremony, Mama Bear threw her oldest spawn out of the house, and I wouldn't see Brother B again for more than two years. When I did, he was at the University of Michigan in Ann Arbor, to which he had transferred on an ROTC scholarship and where he had gotten sobering religion as a fledgling navy pilot.

During my visit, my brother would literally push me out of an airplane. Skydiving, I think he called it. At least I had a parachute on. It was an exhilarating ride down—the quietest few minutes I've ever spent—but I haven't tried it since. As Voltaire once remarked, "Once is philosophy; twice is perversion."

At any rate, Tara Engel sent me an SOS email on March 16, offering to repurpose part of Pernod's production lines to make hand sanitizer. However, like Romina, she needed the White House to cut through some red tape quickly.

Apparently, the FDA has a higher safety bar for the alcohol you put on your hands than the alcohol you put into your mouth. Go figure.

On top of that bureaucratic absurdity, the Treasury Department wanted to slap an excise tax on the alcohol-based sanitizer comparable to that of alcoholic beverages. Go figure again.

As soon as I hung up, I made some quick calls and did indeed work the problem Martian-style and slash through the red tape. It took less than two hours; In Trump Time strikes again!

Over the ensuing months, Pernod would *at no cost* send hundreds of thousands of gallons of its sanitizer primarily to law enforcement agencies around the country. And all of the sanitizer would be made in good old US of A factories in Arkansas, Kentucky, Texas, and West Virginia.[7]

In that venture, Tara's "Partner In Trump Time" crime was Laura Lane at UPS.[8] Laura arranged for whatever transportation was needed with no questions asked—just a stiff, crisp UPS salute to the American flag. True patriots, they!

A JARED KUSHNER AIR BRIDGE TO NOWHERE

Though working with Romina and Tara was a dream, trying to help Kim Glas was a Made by Jared Kushner Nightmare. Kim is the chief executive officer of the National Council of Textile Organizations, and my relationship with her started in exactly the same way as it had with Romina and Tara—with a frantic phone call asking for my help.

Glas was working with top executives such as Andy Warlick, the CEO of Parkdale Mills, and Mike Faircloth, the group president, global operations, of Hanes, and she had assembled a broad consortium of US manufacturers willing to produce as many as 5 million masks a week. They could start within a matter of days, but *only if* the White House could break through some regulatory barriers at the FDA related to sterile production protocols.

One of the side benefits of Kim's proposed venture was that much of the employment gains that we would reap would be in blue-collar manufacturing in lower-income states across the South, where the dying embers of much of our once vibrant textile industry are located. That jobs boost would come at a time when millions of Americans were being kicked to the unemployment curb by the CCP Virus. So I was double in on *that* project.

Little did I know, however, that even as I was trying to help Kim Glas rejuvenate and rebuild US manufacturing capabilities in PPE, Jared Kushner was getting ready to cut the legs out from under the effort with his Project Airbridge to Nowhere. In his typical back-channeling fashion, Kushner was secretly negotiating with his high-level contacts in the Chinese Communist Party to purchase huge quantities of overpriced, low-quality masks, gowns, gloves, N95 respirators, and other PPE.

Make no mistake: Kushner's Project Airbridge was a zero-sum game. To be exact it was a pure "Made in China" versus "Made in the USA" game.

Under Kushner's backdoor, back-channeling gambit, the United States imported nearly 1 billion gloves, 50 million gowns, 2.5 million face shields, and 1.5 million N95 respirators.[9] In the process, Kushner squandered much of the money Congress had made available for the purchase of *domestically* produced PPE from companies such as Parkdale Mills and Hanes.

Oh, did I mention? This kind of Kushner panda hugging—a common occurrence around the West Wing for four insufferable years—also helped drive up the trade deficit even as it careened this country further into its foreign import dependency ditch.

Lest you think Kim Glas and I were the only ones totally ticked off about the whole situation, take a gander at this high and tight "Buy American" fastball whipped at Kushner's head by the office of the Democrat governor of Washington, Jay Inslee:

> From the start, Project Airbridge has done nothing to increase American manufacturing of [personal protective equipment] or even global production of PPE. It has only continued our reliance on foreign supply chains. It is both a public health and national security concern that we cannot manufacture the protective equipment necessary to keep Americans safe.[10]

When I saw that little bit of news break, all I could say from across the country and across the aisle was, "Amen, brother."

As to why Kushner gave me no heads-up about his secret operation, he knew full well that I would oppose it. Just before the news broke on March 29, he said to me, "Please don't be mad at me." "For what?" I said. "You'll see," said he. See I did, and I was absolutely livid.

By the way, Kushner's chop block of "Buy American" was not just behind my back but behind the president's back as well. The first four words of this March 20, 2020, CBS News coverage of a Kushner press statement is a total lie:

> "*At President Trump's direction* we formed an unprecedented historic public-private partnership to ensure that massive amounts of masks, gear and other PPE will be brought to the United States immediately to better equip our health care workers on the front lines and to better serve the American people," Kushner said in a statement.
>
> The search for much-needed health care equipment from abroad comes as top administration official Peter Navarro, who the president has tasked with coordinating the Defense Production Act, has been crafting an executive order to cut U.S. dependence on medicine and medical supplies manufactured abroad. Navarro wants to bring that manufacturing back to the U.S., a need he sees as exemplified by the ongoing pandemic.[11] [Emphasis added.]

When I saw that coverage, I didn't know whether to laugh, cry, or simply fly the "Buy American" flag atop the White House at half-staff.

What I do know is this: this pandemic should be a teachable moment for our country. Regardless of political party, future administrations should take note of the bureaucratic tendency *not* to prepare for black swan pandemics or, more broadly, for the possible use of bioweapons by enemies of the American state. If we are not to be chronically foolish on these matters, let us not let past once again be prologue.

TEN

ROCKING WITH THE GODFATHER OF POLITICAL SOUL IN TEST SWAB LAND

At the [test swab] plant it's a beautiful sight. One of the busiest beehives I've ever seen. Brightly lit, nice looking factory with mostly women in masks working in Trump Time. As the President walks in, one of them like Clark Kent turning into Superman rips off her uniform to show her big red Trump-Pence 2020 T-shirt. She brings the house down and gets a picture with the Boss.

After a great speech that sounds the closest to a rally that we've had in months, we take the [Night Hawk] choppers back to Air Force One and fly into Washington in the middle of a thunderstorm. There's virtually no news coverage of the[great] jobs numbers that day or the event.

—Peter Navarro, journal entry, June 5, 2020

Whenever I wanted to get a natural buzz on at the White House—neither drugs nor alcohol has ever been my bag—I'd sign up for an Air Force One trip involving a side sojourn on the Nighthawk helicopter fleet.

Whether flying toward the demilitarized zone between North and South Korea or landing on the parking lot of a high school football field in Guilford, Maine, a Nighthawk flight was, as the psychologist Abraham Maslow might call it, a "peak experience." Strapped into a jump seat with soldiers armed to the teeth on either side of me and gazing at the spinning landscape through the big open bay located at the back of the chopper, I always found it the best view of any town.

The trip to Guilford, Maine, proved to be one of the few unequivocal victory laps Team Trump would be able to take on the testing front. From the very beginning of the pandemic, starting with a massive screwup by the Centers for Disease Control and Prevention, testing was the Achilles' heel of our Five-Vector Pandemic Attack Strategy.

In any pandemic, testing will always be critical. Yet with the CCP Virus, testing turned out to be particularly important because of the high degree of so-called asymptomatic spread.

Asymptomatic spread means that a person without any symptoms may still be infected and capable of seeding and spreading the virus. Yet in a world where test kits were in short supply—as they were in the early months of the pandemic—people without any symptoms would not initially be considered as "front of the queue" candidates for testing. So an asymptomatic "super spreader" who goes undetected because he or she is not tested could do tremendous damage as a modern-day Typhoid Mary.

To be clear, significant asymptomatic spread is *not* a normal characteristic of viral diseases. However, with the CCP Virus, the asymptomatic spread was off the charts from the very beginning of the pandemic.[1] That sobering fact alone provided one of the best pieces of evidence that the CCP Virus may well have been weaponized (either accidentally or intentionally) through so-called gain-of-function experiments in a Chinese laboratory—experiments, by the way, sanctioned by none other than Saint Fauci here in the good old US of A.

In fact, what we have witnessed since January 2020 could well be the plotline of a new season of the old Kiefer Sutherland melodrama *24.* In this example of life imitating art, infected Chinese nationals from Wuhan enter the United States without any symptoms and mingle with the American population. By the time these human bioweapons manifest symptoms, the seeding and spreading of the virus in cities like New York and New Orleans and Chicago is a *fait accompli.* As to how Jack Bauer might have stopped the attack, he probably would've had no more luck than President Trump did—which was perhaps why the script was tossed into the trash.

And by the way, the high degree of asymptomatic spread was not the only reason I thought the CCP Virus might be weaponized. As another piece of circumstantial evidence, there is the equally suspicious imperviousness of the CCP Virus to summer heat and humidity.

As we headed into the summer of 2020 after a deadly winter and spring, many experts in the medical community[2]—along with no shortage of celebrity TV doctors—predicted that the rate of infection would slow, or perhaps the virus might even disappear, until the following winter. Instead, we had a summer of hellish rates of infection and an upward-spiraling death count.

This lethal combination of asymptomatic spread and the resilience of the virus to seasonal change made it all the more essential for us to quickly develop a broad range of testing capabilities. However, it was with testing that POTUS—with no small thanks to Robert Redfield's incompetent CDC—had to endure some of the earliest and most punishing political body blows.

THE CDC FLUNKS ITS MOST IMPORTANT TEST

In its "haste did indeed make waste" effort to develop a testing kit, the CDC had spent just seven days on its formulation. On February 8, the CDC began to mail out limited quantities of the tests to hospitals. However, it quickly became evident that the results were fatally flawed by a high degree of false positives.

Making a bad test was not, however, the CDC's worst mistake—not by a long shot. Under the rules set by the CDC, and zealously enforced by Redfield for petty turf reasons, *no* private commercial laboratories, public health laboratories, or university labs were allowed to develop and distribute tests—only the CDC. So even if the CDC tests had worked flawlessly, this bungling bureaucracy *still* did not have anywhere near the production capacity to move quickly to large-scale manufacturing.

In sharp contrast, the South Korean government put us to shame precisely by using the private-sector commercial lab model. By mid-March, South Korea was conducting 3,600 tests for every 1 million South Korean citizens, compared to only five—that's right, five tests—for every 1 million Americans.[3]

Redfield was not the only one to blame for the fiasco. Health and Human Services secretary Alex Azar and FDA commissioner Stephen Hahn together made one big rookie mistake. On January 31, Azar took the seemingly responsible step of declaring the situation a "health emergency."

What neither Azar nor Hahn appeared to understand—Hahn had been on the FDA job barely seven weeks—was that such a declaration created a far more stringent rule regarding testing. To wit: in such a declared health emergency, would-be testers would have to file for, and receive, an Emergency Use Authorization (EUA) from the FDA.

Obtaining an EUA is a difficult-to-navigate, mazelike process at the best of times. Under the stress of the looming pandemic, that process completely and utterly broke down.

The Mayo Clinic's director of clinical virology, Matt Binnicker, ripped the Band-Aid off the festering CDC wound with this lament: "The public health infrastructure is really not set up to handle a pandemic."[4]

As to how we wound up in Guilford, Maine, on June 5 to take one of our rare testing victory laps, that's an ode to the famous Ben Franklin quote that begins with "For want of a nail" and ends with "the kingdom was lost." In business school parlance, whenever you are seeking to manufacture and distribute something, the most important thing supply chain analysts look for is the "long pole in the tent"—any bottleneck that might constrain the ability to produce or use the end product.

Fresh off my adventure with the Italian Swab Job, I was deeply concerned as early as March that we might mightily manufacture all the tests in the world. But if we didn't have enough swabs to go into the test kits, it would all be for naught.

Fortuitously, the way we would solve that particular supply chain problem would not be without its political advantages. As it turned out, the United States' largest test swab producer, Puritan, happens to be located smack in the middle of Maine's 2nd Congressional District.

THE AMERICAN SWAB JOB AND LOBSTER KING

Unlike forty-eight other states in the union, Maine does *not* use "winner take all" rules for the distribution of its Electoral College votes. Instead, if a presidential candidate wins the vote in a Maine congressional district—the Pine Tree State has two such districts—that candidate is entitled to that district's Electoral College vote.

In the 2016 election, from my perch in the War Room in Trump Tower, I had taken it upon myself to make sure that we at least won Maine's 2nd Congressional District. I knew that Maine 1 was a hopeless cause because most of its voters lived in Portland, a bedroom community of Boston and not coincidentally a liberal bastion.

To help win Maine 2, I had done numerous media interviews leading up to the 2016 election. I had also penned a number of op-eds appealing to the working men and women of that hardscrabble state. Perhaps not coincidentally, President Trump had trounced Hillary Clinton in Maine 2 by 51 percent to 41 percent[5]—and it was the first time in Maine's history that it had divided its electoral votes.[6]

My read of the chessboard was that the 2020 election would be much closer than 2016 and the entire election might come down to that single Maine 2 vote with a 270–268 Electoral College margin for either the Boss or Biden.

Given the high political stakes, I had, over the entire four years of the administration, worked the Maine 2 angle hard, pushing a variety of "Buy American" and tariff actions that would benefit industries ranging from lumber and blueberries to lobsters. But my American version of a Swab Job with Puritan took all of it to a new level. It was like hitting the Electoral College lottery: as Guilford and its surrounding communities went, so, too, would likely go Maine 2.

So it was that beginning in April 2020, the Trump administration—with no fingers on the scale, mind you—awarded three different contracts totaling more than $130 million for Puritan to dramatically expand its "Made in the USA" facilities.[7] It was to celebrate the Boss's victories that I hopped onto Air Force One on June 5 for the trip to Puritan.

On the way to Guilford, we first made a pit stop in Bangor, where POTUS held a roundtable meeting with a group of commercial fishermen. At that televised event, the president dubbed me the "Lobster King" and tasked me with getting rid of the punitive tariffs that Europe had imposed upon US lobster fishermen—to the sorry-ass benefit, I might add, of the ever-rapacious Canadians.

After my Lobster King coronation, we jumped onto a gaggle of Knighthawk helicopters and choppered our way up to Guilford. On the motorcade ride through the township, with POTUS waving from his signature Beast limo, the reception was so warm it was cool.

For more than a mile, the streets were lined with a quintessentially Deplorables crowd smiling, waving, and exhorting the president on—hail to the Government Contracts Chief. And there was nary a protester in sight. Truly, peace in the Trump Deplorables Kingdom.

Whenever I went to events such as these and got outside the Washington Swamp and anti-Trump media bubble, my spirits soared. It once again became clear to me that at least out in Deplorables Land and Flyover Country, President Trump had captured the hearts of working-class Americans.

As good as the motorcade ride was, things got even better at the Puritan facility. The place was electric. When POTUS strode in, the workers, decked out in starched white lab coats and hairnets, started dancing and waving wildly at their Blue-Collar King. And, yes, the superwoman I noted at the beginning of this chapter stole the show.

The closest thing I have ever seen to the raucous rapture I witnessed in that Guilford factory was at a James Brown concert at the old Howard Theatre in DC when I was a high school teenager in the 1960s. On that long-ago night, beautiful women danced and swayed in the aisles, screaming for the Godfather of Soul.

Things weren't quite as bawdy that day at the Puritan facility. But it was damned close.

With that Heartland love, you could see the entire weight of the Washington Swamp fall off of POTUS as he put on the biggest smile I had seen in months.

The only downside was that in their rambunctiousness, some of the Puritan workers breached a sterile swab protocol. And all of the swabs produced that afternoon had to be deep-sixed.

I guess you can't win 'em all. But we did wind up winning Maine 2 again.

ELEVEN

A MORNING CNN PRAYER, A NIGHTLY MSNBC WAKE

This morning American citizens won't go to church because of the Chinese Communist Party. This afternoon there's no baseball games. Tomorrow, American adults won't go to work. American children won't go to school. Cruise ships around the world are sitting out in the sea like flying Dutchmen. And we have these great, big, beautiful flying machines sitting on the ground gathering dust. That's all because China hid this virus from the world. It could have been contained. And instead it turned into a pandemic. And I think it's important that the question be asked, should China be held accountable?

—PETER NAVARRO ON *FAREED ZAKARIA GPS*, MAY 3, 2020[1]

I certainly can't get more eloquent than that. At least off the TV cuff. All to no avail.

By the spring of 2020, POTUS was getting steamrolled over and over again in the mainstream media by his perceived mishandling of the pandemic. From virtually every direction, he was getting eviscerated, splayed, flayed, sliced, diced, pickled, and cubed.

Every time I went to the Oval Office for a meeting, the Boss didn't quite seem himself. His usual swagger, good humor, and relentless charm had been replaced by the seething anger of a stuck bull being tormented by a gang of picadors.

In the print media, it was hit piece after hit piece by the likes of the Amazon Post and the Big Apple Times. On cable news, it was a morning CNN prayer for the dead and a nightly MSNBC wake. And on Main Street, it was antifa arsonists, BLM looters, and history-killing statue topplers running wild and chanting defund the police.

Amidst this propaganda and chaos, fear and loathing blossomed. A growing Cancel Culture bloomed. And a locked-in, locked-down, restive American population was increasingly ready to explode.

Of course, all that pent-up anger was being directed by the likes of "Morning Joe" Scarborough, Al Sharpton, and Rachel Maddow at a great tower of a man who had achieved more than they ever would yet whom they relentlessly portrayed as a hapless president. It didn't matter that their attacks were lies; they still stuck like a pit bull's jaws to a postman's leg.

For me, long enough in the tooth to remember the 1960s, it was déjà vu all over again. Every time I watched CNN or MSNBC in living color in 2020, it reminded me of my teenage years in the 1960s watching Walter Cronkite on a black-and-white TV chronicling the Vietnam War dead.

Cronkite's "And that's the way it is" closing dirge was the devastating nightly body count from the rice paddies of Asia, the corpses of young men barely old enough to shave piled up so high that the carnage crushed the reelection hopes of Lyndon Johnson.

That history certainly was not lost on the likes of Never Trump corporate media kingpins such as Jeff Zucker and his cadres of on-demand propagandists. They no doubt thought that CNN's prominently displayed daily body count would do to DJT what Cronkite had done to LBJ.

But it wasn't just incoming missiles from flacks in the anti-Trump media. Inside the Trump administration, the White House communications team had to cope on almost a daily basis with the passive-aggressive "TV Tony" throwing his Fauci-isms at the Boss.

President Trump's descent into CCP Virus hell was evident in two simple statistics. In March 2020, his approval rating for his handling of the pandemic was at 60 percent.[2] By July, that rating had plummeted to 42 percent.[3] Moreover, the administration's perceived incompetence on the pandemic front was bleeding Biden Blue into the Boss's *overall* approval and job performance ratings, which were at the lowest of his administration.[4]

As we descended further and further into that public perception hell, I increasingly saw only one way out of the pandemic box: correctly shift the blame for the pandemic off the back of the Boss and put it squarely onto the shoulders of Xi Jinping and the Chinese Communist Party.

To be crystal clear here, I did not seek to blame China for something it did *not* do. Rather, I sought to assign it its *rightful* blame for a catastrophic pandemic that was killing hundreds of thousands of Americans and millions worldwide while draining trillions of dollars from the US and world economies.

From the outset, I knew that the mission would be a difficult one. This is because the anti-Trump media had a huge vested interest in *not* blaming China in any way, shape, or form for the pandemic. *From Jeff Zucker on down, these Twisted anti-Trump Sisters of the Fourth Estate knew exactly what I knew: to blame China for the pandemic was to* ***not*** *blame Donald Trump.*

TWELVE

A FAUCIAN GAIN-OF-FUNCTION BARGAIN WITH A WUHAN DEVIL

What we know is that ground zero for this virus was within a few miles of that [Wuhan] lab. If you simply do an Occam's razor approach that the simplest explanation is probably the most likely, I think it's incumbent on China to prove that it wasn't that lab.

—Peter Navarro on *Sunday Morning Futures*, April 19, 2020

"Oh, my God, there's been an outbreak of chocolaty goodness near Hershey, Pennsylvania. What do you think happened?" Like, "Oh, I don't know, maybe a steam shovel mated with a cocoa bean? Or it's the [expletive] chocolate factory! Maybe that's it?"

—Jon Stewart on *The Late Show with Stephen Colbert*, June 15, 2021

Yes, to me, it was Occam's razor obvious from the get-go that the CCP Virus had come from the Wuhan Institute of Virology, just as Jon Stewart's parody noted. Of course, what wasn't obvious at the time was Dr. Anthony Fauci's likely role in the paternity of that deadly virus.

I daresay you will find nothing more ironic in US history than Saint Fauci turning out to be the likely arsonist who started the world's Wuhan virus fire.

Oh, if I had only known then what I know now. I would've blown Saint Tony right out of the water at the very start of the pandemic. I would have done it right up on the stage of the James S. Brady Press Briefing Room in the West Wing in a way whereby Anthony Fauci would never, *ever* darken the door of the White House or light up a TV set again, and everyone in the United States—especially Donald J. Trump—would have been all the better for it.

But blowing up Tony Fauci as the likely Godfather of the Pandemic would come only later—and long after election day. In the meantime, in that dark summer of 2020, if we were going to win a second term, we had a pandemic to move from the shoulders of President Trump to those of the dictator Xi Jinping and the Chinese Communist Party.

THE AIKIDO MAN IMPERATIVE

In politics and in life, I have always been a karate kind of guy: kick, punch, repeat. Maybe that's why the Boss appreciates me. His martial arts motto is "If someone hits me, I have to hit them back harder."[1]

That said, in the case of trying to shift the responsibility for the pandemic from POTUS to China, I would learn the hard way that the direct karate approach—blaming China simply for cooking up the virus in a Wuhan lab kitchen—wasn't going to cut it. Not with the anti-Trump, lab-denying media taking China's side.

Instead, I had to try a more nuanced aikido approach. I sought to accurately blame China for everything that had happened *after* the virus had popped up in Wuhan, including the failure to contain the pandemic itself.

It was the White House's chairman of the Council of Economic Advisers, Kevin Hassett, who first introduced me to the finer art of political aikido as I confronted numerous Globalists within the administration. In fact, Kevin initially was one of those—an avowed Globalist cut from the free-trade-at-any-cost cloth of the American Enterprise Institute.

Yet over time, he would come to see up close and personal—including with the benefit of thousands of pages of classified documents—the sheer evilness that is the Beijing regime, and the Hassett Man would leave the White House every bit as much of a tariff-slapping China Hawk as I was.

About Kevin, I can say two things with certainty: First, he is one of the gentlest guys I have ever met. Second, as an umpteenth-degree black belt in aikido, he was the only White House official with the skills to use the force and energy of an attacker to subdue that attacker within ten seconds or less.

That's the essence of aikido—use your opponent's energy to defeat that opponent—but it would take me a few bloody karate noses from the anti-Trump media before I would fully understand it.

OCCAM'S RAZOR TAKES A SUNDAY BOW

My karate phase of the China Pandemic Blame Game began with an appearance on April 19, 2020, on Maria Bartiromo's show *Sunday Morning Futures*. You can see from the quote opening this chapter that I raised the question on that show of whether the CCP Virus had originated from a bioweapons lab in Wuhan, China.

I might just as well have screamed "God is dead!" from the pulpit of Washington's National Cathedral. The reaction to my heresy in the anti-Trump media was fast and furious. Incanted the Greek Chorus of anti-Trumpers intent on insulating China from any possible blame: "What proof do you have, Sir?"

Today—and I feel far more disgust than vindication—what I first claimed about the laboratory origins of the virus has become the conventional wisdom. Even Jon Stewart eventually jumped on the chocolate lab theory bandwagon—to the utter dismay of Stephen Colbert.

What surprised me was not Stewart's epiphany; it was that the former CDC director, Dr. Robert Redfield, was the first to break from the pack of Wuhan lab deniers—albeit just about a year after I broke "Wuhan lab bad" on Maria Bartiromo's show.

My take on Redfield, dating back to my Fauci showdown on January 28, 2020, in the Situation Room, was that Dr. Bob was a meek sheep. Yet here is what Redfield boldly said on March 26, 2021, in an interview with CNN's Sanjay Gupta:

> I still think the most likely etiology of this pathogen in Wuhan was from a laboratory, you know, escaped. . . .
>
> I am a virologist. I have spent my life in virology. I do not believe this somehow came from a bat to a human. . . . Normally, when a pathogen goes from a zoonotic to human, it takes a while for it to figure out how to become more and more efficient in human to human transmission. I just don't think [what has happened with the virus} makes biological sense.[2]

Shortly thereafter, CNN's Gupta broke ranks with Jeff Zucker's head office and sided with Redfield. After that, the floodgates broke, and yesterday's heresy has become today's conventional wisdom.

What troubled me most at the time about all this propaganda in a petri dish was how key institutions in our country—not just the media but academia and the scientific community as well—rallied round the Communist Chinese flag in denial of what, at least to me and my trusty Occam's razor, was the painfully obvious laboratory origin of the virus. I would wonder many times, *Have we reached a point in this country where the anti-Trump media and the academic and scientific elites hate Donald Trump so much that they are willing to sacrifice any and all claims to both their own integrity as well as common sense?*

Of course, the answer to that question is a resounding and highly disturbing "yes." That's why I think it's important now to offer the *quod erat demonstrandum*, or QED, proof that led me to the prescient view not only that this was a "Made in China" weaponized virus but also that Anthony Fauci and his enablers were the likely Godfathers of the Pandemic.

A BATTLE OF TWO COMPETING THEORIES

When the CCP Virus first popped up its deadly little spiked proteins in the fall of 2019, it did so within yards of both a Wuhan wet market and the Wuhan Institute of Virology. Applying Occam's razor that the simplest explanation is also the most likely, there were immediately two "most likely" theories of the origin of the virus.

The "wet market," or "zoonotic," theory postulated that a naturally occurring virus had jumped from an animal to a human as the infected animal was being butchered, cooked, and consumed in a Wuhan wet market. Alternatively, the "Wuhan lab" theory postulated that a virus—likely a genetically engineered one—had either accidentally escaped or been intentionally released from the Wuhan lab.[3]

Initially, the wet market theory seemed plausible, even highly probable. That was because of a clear, close, and recent historical precedent. To wit: in 2003, China's first SARS virus, SARS-CoV-1, had been quickly tracked to an almost identical virus found in raccoon dogs and Himalayan palm civet cats. In scientific parlance, SARS-CoV-1 therefore had a very clear *direct progenitor.* That is to say, it had the direct progenitor dogs and cats from which China's first SARS virus had jumped to humans. Virus from nature. Origin determined. QED. Zoonotic case closed.

"So surely the same must be true of China's second SARS virus, SARS-CoV-2" was the logical thinking in the early days of the pandemic. That was particularly true given the closeness of the Wuhan wet market to ground zero of the outbreak.

Yet there was an obvious problem, one that quickly threw freezing water on the wet market theory. Try as they might, scientists could find *no* direct progenitor of SARS-CoV-2 (i.e., the CCP Virus). No cats. No dogs. No raccoons. No pangolins. *Not even a bat-shit crazy bat.*

This remains true to this day. After testing thousands of animals, scientists have still not found a direct progenitor.[4] Accordingly, we must firmly rule out the Wuhan wet market. That observation leads us right back to another and deeper cut of Occam's razor: *If a deadly and possibly weaponized virus pops up within a few kilometers of a wet market and a virology lab engaged in bioweapons research, and that deadly virus did* ***not*** *come from the wet market, the most likely explanation is that it came from, yes, the Wuhan Institute of Virology.*

"So where's the evidence?" once again screams the Greek chorus of anti-Trumpers. Well, there's plenty to see—if only you are willing to look.

Let's start with the lab itself. China's Wuhan Institute of Virology is home to some of the most dangerous pathogens on Earth, including the deadly Ebola virus.[5] Though the lab has the highest possible biosafety rating of P4, you should take that information with a hefty grain of salt. Even the best P4 high-security labs in the world, including those in the United States, are vulnerable to accidents and leaks that can release dangerous pathogens into the world. In 2018, the US State Department warned of just such a possibility. That Citadel of Diplomacy noted quite undiplomatically that, despite its P4 rating, the Wuhan lab was awash with sloppy safety protocols that raised the specter of a "new SARS-like pandemic."[6] You can't say we weren't warned.

By the way, we now know that a massive shutdown of the Wuhan lab in October 2019 points squarely to a catastrophic leak.[7] So, too, does the disturbing fact that at least three workers from the lab came down with CCP Virus–like symptoms the very next month.[8] And a Congressional investigation by the House Foreign Affairs Committee has unequivocally concluded that "the preponderance of evidence proves the virus did leak" from the Wuhan lab.[9]

As for the demon spiked protein virus itself, it most closely resembles viruses found in horseshoe bats in caves nearly a thousand miles from the Wuhan lab in China's Yunnan province. So how did a huge collection of these viruses wind up at the Wuhan lab as templates for the genetic engineering of designer demons? Enter stage right the Bat Lady of China.

Shi Zhengli, the director of the Center for Emerging Infectious Diseases at the Wuhan Institute of Virology, is a temptress of fate and nature right out of a James Bond novel. It was this Bat-Shit Crazy Bat Lady who would lead a crusade to conduct so-called gain-of-function experiments that would turn already dangerous bat viruses into human-attacking bioweapons of mass destruction. It may be worth quoting one other little epiphany from Jon Stewart on the obvious dangers of gain-of-function experiments. Quipped Stewart to his foil, Colbert, "Science has, in many ways, helped ease the suffering of this pandemic, which was more than likely caused by science."[10]

As to what "science" we are actually talking about, "gain-of-function" is macabrely defined as that which "improves the ability of a pathogen to cause disease,"[11] and here the "Colonel Mustard did it in the Wuhan lab with gain-of-function" plot doesn't just thicken; it comes with a very twisted Faucian twist.

For it was Anthony Fauci's National Institute of Allergy and Infectious Diseases (NIAID) that spent millions of US taxpayer dollars to help finance the Bat Lady and fund the very gain-of-function experiments at the Wuhan lab that likely led to the pandemic. In fact, Fauci *directly* funded the Bat Lady's experiments through NIAID grants; and Shi Zhengli even acknowledged Fauci for his support of gain-of-function research in her own research papers.[12]

And by the way, before she was muzzled by her Communist censors, China's Bat Lady publicly expressed the fear that the virus might have leaked from her lab.[13] Bat-shit crazy or evil though she might be, she knew damn well the viral Chernobyl with which she was playing God.

PETER DASZAK'S TERMINAL CASE OF HUBRIS

The Bat Lady Shi Zhengli wasn't the only one spending Fauci dollars. Fauci also *indirectly* funneled money to the Wuhan experiments through third-party US grantees such as Eco-Health Alliance president Peter Daszak and Professor Ralph Baric at the University of North Carolina at Chapel Hill.[14]

Baric, nicknamed "Dr. Coronavirus Hunter," would himself become the hunted soon after the pandemic hit. He went into hiding and assiduously dodged many media inquiries.

As for Daszak, that extrovert dark clown had bragged before the pandemic during several TV appearances about how easy it is to inject material into the backbone of bat viruses to weaponize them. Here is just one bitter taste from a February 23, 2016, C-SPAN recording that also reveals China's culpability. Boasted Daszak, "So we sequence the spike protein . . . then we—well, I didn't do this work, but my colleagues in China did . . . you insert the spiked proteins [into the backbone of the horseshoe bat virus] . . . [and] you end up with a small number of viruses that really look like killers."[15]

Now, that is one devilish dumb arrogant oaf playing God if there ever were one. Daszak, with his terminal case of hubris, belongs either in jail or in an insane asylum—certainly not in a collaboration with a Bat-Shit Crazy Bat Lady operating in a People's Liberation Army bioweapons lab using wads of US taxpayer money.

A REVERSE GOLDILOCKS BIOWEAPON

Here, too, it should be noted that if China's Bat Lady and the People's Liberation Army were going to weaponize a coronavirus in a P4 lab like the one in Wuhan, that bioweapon would likely have many of the same characteristics that we observe today in SARS-CoV-2, aka the coronavirus, aka the CCP Virus.

I have already told you about so-called asymptomatic spread, the ability of infected people without symptoms to rapidly seed and spread the virus. I have also told you about how China's demon virus appears impervious to both heat and humidity, which was why we did not observe any noticeable downturn in the rates of infection during the summer season of 2020 that most virologists had predicted. But here are two additional observations in support of a weaponized virus.

First, as my good friend Doc Hatfill once told me, curdling my blood, "A truly successful virus, at least from the virus's point of view, is one that kills as many people as possible, and to do that, it can't be as lethal as a virus like Ebola because that kills people too quickly and doesn't allow efficient spread."

And that is exactly what we've got here: a perverse, reverse Goldilocks virus from China that is just lethal enough to allow an optimal rate of spread—not too mild and not too deadly but just efficient enough to have already killed more than six hundred thousand Americans.

Second, to go a little highbrow wonk on you, the CCP Virus has what are called "nucleotide triplets." These triplets appear to be *specifically engineered to attack human cells.* Moreover, they are ***not** present in any other known coronaviruses.* Any gain-of-function alarm bells going off here?

FAUCI BACKDOORS THE TRUMP WHITE HOUSE

Here's an even more twisted Faucian twist to this gain-of-function plot: in 2017, Fauci and NIH director Francis Collins engineered an end run around the Trump White House to quietly reauthorize the use of gain-of-function experiments.

With that end run, Fauci and Collins subversively overturned a 2014 decision by the Obama White House to restrict gain-of-function experiments—precisely because they were judged to be very dangerous. In fact, the Obama White House's decision had been made after what had been reported as an alarming "series of laboratory biosafety incidents at U.S. Government research facilities."[16]

Having been a White House official in 2017, I can tell you unequivocally that Fauci and Collins pulled a fast one on President Trump. Rather than going through the front door of the West Wing and Oval Office, Fauci went through the back door of a low-level office staffer in the Eisenhower Executive Office Building to lift the gain-of-function ban.[17]

Here's how the normally business-friendly Business Insider website dolloped up the gain-of-function story with a heaping spoonful of justifiable alarm:

> The NIH's policy shift will allow researchers to take already dangerous viruses and genetically engineer them to be more contagious or deadly. That could mean taking a flu strain or a virus like MERS or SARS and modifying them so they spread more easily or become more fatal.
>
> These types of experiments are known as "gain of function" experiments, since they add new—and riskier—functions to diseases. . . .
>
> Such research is controversial because of concerns that a modified deadly disease could escape into the wild and infect the public. That could happen if a terrible accident were to occur, or if the know-how for creating a deadly superbug were to fall into the wrong hands.[18]

So which was it in the case of the CCP Virus and the ensuing pandemic? Just a terrible accident in which the virus happened to escape from the Wuhan lab? Or did the very "wrong hands" of the Bat Lady and the Chinese military use Fauci's gain-of-function tools to design a "deadly superbug"?

Either way, if the virus escaped from the Wuhan lab, the blood of millions of people is on Anthony Fauci's hands. Here's how I framed this issue in an article in the *Washington Times* on June 10, 2021, as I helped lead the campaign to fire Fauci: "If the virus came from the Wuhan lab—which it almost certainly did—if the virus has been weaponized using so-called gain-of-function tools—which it almost surely has—and if those experiments were paid for by Fauci's NIH—which they certainly were—then Dr. Fauci is the American godfather of the pandemic."[19]

Now think about the implications of this for one last minute:

A virus that has done untold damage to the world economy and killed nearly half a million Americans may well have been developed and perhaps weaponized with the help of millions of US taxpayer dollars ***and*** *the approval of gain-of-function research experiments by the very same pious, wildly overpaid bureaucrat who sabotaged an American president even as he lied to us about masks, kept our kids out of school, killed hydroxychloroquine, and lectured us on everything from closing churches to hookup sex on Tinder.*

Yes, ***that*** *Dr. Fauci.*

Instead of coming clean with President Trump and the American people at the outset of the pandemic, "that Dr. Fauci" engaged in arguably the worst cover-up since Watergate. It began on January 31, 2020, with an email from Scripps Research Institute scientist Kristian Andersen. He advised

Fauci that although the murderous pathogen resembled a horseshoe bat virus, its "unusual features" indicated that it had been "potentially engineered."[20]

If Fauci had simply admitted at the time that the virus might have been designed in a lab to attack humans instead of covering his ass, *we could have had a much quicker and more accurate read of the enemy we were up against and thereby saved hundreds of thousands of lives with a more targeted response.*

On the basis of that knowledge, we would also have demanded immediate cooperation from Communist China on sharing the genome of the virus and any other information about its weaponization for what was arguably an act of war. Of course, we would also have held China both financially and morally accountable for the carnage it had unleashed on the world.

Instead of coming clean, Fauci appears to have persuaded Andersen to publish an article in *Nature Medicine* on March 17 that completely dismissed the lab origin theory.[21] A month later, in a White House press briefing with President Trump by his side, Fauci used that very same study—without mentioning his contact with Andersen—to argue that the virus "is totally consistent with a jump of a species from an animal to a human."[22] Just another stone-cold Fauci lie.

That was not just a cover-up; it was *the* most cynical cover-up by a US public health official ever witnessed.

My broader point in this chapter's interlude with Occam's razor is simply that I felt perfectly justified going on television at the dawn of the pandemic and blaming China for a deadly and weaponized virus that almost certainly came from a lab in Wuhan. Yet after that TV appearance on Maria Bartiromo's show—and the ensuing anti-Trump media firestorm—I learned that my karate approach to shifting the blame for the pandemic from President Trump to China by holding China responsible for creating the virus was not going to work.

The Greek "Where's the proof?" chorus of anti-Trump naysayers would simply beat me into submission every time I tried to make that argument on TV. Ergo, I would have to figure out another way.

And with no small irony, Fareed Zakaria would show me the aikido way.

THIRTEEN

A CHINESE COMMUNIST PARTY TRAGEDY IN FIVE HEINOUS ACTS

You said in an interview with FOX [that China] spawned the virus. And you said it was likely from a bioweapons lab. Now the scientists I've talked to all say that it's highly, highly unlikely that this came out of a lab . . . the scientific consensus is that this came from a wet market in Wuhan. Do you have evidence that suggests that the Chinese . . . spawned the virus?

—Question to Peter Navarro on *Fareed Zakaria GPS*, May 3, 2020[1]

As TV interviewers go, Fareed Zakaria is one of my favorites. Though we rarely agree on anything, he has always been a gentleman during our jousts and respectful of our differing points of view.

I would put George Stephanopoulos into the same category, along with Michael Smerconish, Judy Woodruff, and Gerard Baker. Among America's left-leaning Sunday news show hosts, Chuck Todd and Margaret Brennan are also usually quite civil.

As for CNN's Jake Tapper, he was always a bit of a hard pill to swallow during my White House years. Yet I actually liked him. So I was saddened when, a few months out from election day, he decided to cancel me from his show after a particularly contentious interview that went something like this:

> TAPPER: You're not answering my question.
> NAVARRO: I am answering it. You just don't like the answer.[2]

Toward election day, CNN had only one rule: if it was going to let a Trump surrogate onto the air, it would have to be a relatively pliant surrogate, and I had a reputation of giving at least as good as I ever got. So canceled I was by CNN after that Tapper interview, and that cancellation has held to this day.

FAREED POPS THE EVIDENCE QUESTION

At any rate, two weeks after I floated the idea on Maria Bartiromo's Sunday show that the CCP Virus had come from the Wuhan lab, I went on Fareed Zakaria's *GPS* weekend show, and sure enough, he tried to hit me right in the chops with the "Do you have evidence?" question, as featured in the opening quote of this chapter. By then, however, I was more than aikido ready.

After Bartiromo's show, I quickly began to work the Pandemic Blame Game problem Martian style, and what I came up with as a media strategy was to make a clear and critical distinction between "Speculative Blame" versus "Indisputable Blame."

Speculative Blame is the blame associated with a virus that might have been spawned in a Chinese lab. Going forward, it would be Speculative Blame that I would pivot away from as I quickly moved to Indisputable Blame.

Indisputable Blame is associated with the Five Heinous Acts the Chinese Communist Party committed in the early days of the pandemic. These Five Heinous Acts virtually ensured that an otherwise containable virus slipped the bounds of Wuhan and metastasized into a global biological Chernobyl.

A CCP TRAGEDY IN FIVE HEINOUS ACTS

China's first heinous act was to hide the possibility of a deadly pandemic from the world for more than sixty days. As early as October 2019, Xi Jinping and the Chinese Communist Party knew that China had a deadly virus on its hands.[3] As the Year of the Pig drew to a close, Wuhanians were dying in the streets. Local doctors were warning of asymptomatic spread, and there was no question that this was an unusually deadly SARS-like infection.[4]

Yet China not only hid those dangers, it did so behind the shield of the puppet World Health Organization (WHO). For even as Chinese government officials were dropping a bamboo curtain around Wuhan, WHO's puppet director, Tedros Adhanom, was repeatedly lavishing praise on Chinese officials for their handling of what the WHO refused to brand as a pandemic until March 11, 2020.

In sharp contrast, I had called the pandemic forty-three days earlier in the January 29 travel ban memo. I, a lowly "doctor" of economics, got it right long before the doctors at the World Health Organization. And Steve Bannon beat me by four days when he launched a new show called *War Room: Pandemic* on January 25. Steve, a lowly Harvard MBA in finance. Just saying.

And, yes, due to China's first heinous act of hiding the virus, the world lost more than precious months not just of preparation to fight the pandemic but of the opportunity to contain the virus.

As its second heinous act, the CCP refused to release the genome of the virus to origin trackers and vaccine researchers.[5] That utter lack of transparency significantly delayed any attempts to understand the latest pathogen from China, much less develop a viable vaccine or safe and effective therapeutics.

Moreover, even as China was hiding the genome from the world, it refused to allow international inspectors to investigate either the wet market *or* the Wuhan lab. Scientists from the US Centers for Disease Control and Prevention seeking to assess the dangers were even barred from Wuhan.[6]

As still a third heinous act, CCP officials orchestrated a thorough cover-up by destroying evidence at the Wuhan wet market. They just scrubbed down—and away—every possible piece of evidence that no doubt would have proven early on that the Wuhan wet market was clearly *not* the source of the virus.[7]

Even worse, even as some Chinese workers were lathering up the Wuhan wet market with soap and bleach, others were wiping computer hard drives and shredding evidence at the Wuhan lab.[8] It wasn't just critical data that disappeared; many of the laboratory workers and whistleblowers also disappeared—many never to be seen again.[9]

Together, the shredded information and the firsthand witnesses would almost certainly have proved that the Wuhan lab *was* the source of the virus.

Heinous Act 4 is the worst: while the Chinese Communist party was hiding the genome and full dangers of the virus from the world and destroying evidence, the Chinese government was locking down the whole country to domestic travel tighter than the zip ties on the wrists of a Uighur prisoner.

Yet those same government officials freely allowed hundreds of thousands of Chinese nationals to board gleaming Airbus and Boeing jetliners bound for cities from Milan and New York to Tehran.

Those airships—really weaponized disease vectors—thereby heavily seeded the virus in cities around the world and turned them from bustling metropolises into pandemic hot zones. By committing Heinous Act 4 alone, China lost the opportunity to contain the virus in Wuhan and thereby *guaranteed* a global pandemic. Just think about that for a minute:

As Communist China was hiding the dangers of the virus from the world, the CCP was locking down ***all*** *of its own citizens to* ***any*** *kind of domestic travel whatsoever with the* ***greatest*** *of urgency. That urgency was driven by the knowledge that CCP officials had with the new Viral Hell otherwise known as Wuhan.*

It is well worth repeating here that this heinous act alone guaranteed that what otherwise could and should have been a *fully contained* outbreak in Wuhan would become a global pandemic. The virus would kill millions of people and cost trillions of dollars, euros, yen, rubles, and bitcoin.

For Heinous Act 4 alone, China should bear the entire blame for the pandemic. SARS-CoV-2 was a virus that could have been contained in Wuhan. It should never have caused a pandemic of covid-19. And it is rightly and righteously called the CCP Virus.

Yet there is one more heinous act to consider in our compilation of Indisputable Blame for the pandemic. Here is the quick backstory.

Before the pandemic, the world's "factory floor," China, was a huge net exporter of PPE. Yet once China knew it had a global pandemic on its hands—and even as it hid that information from the world—Chinese state-owned and state-directed enterprises sallied forth and vacuumed up all the world's personal protective equipment. I am not just talking about masks, gloves, goggles, gowns, and N95 respirators; China would even corner the PPE markets for critical peripherals such as thermometers and pulse oximeters.

The resultant PPE scarcity condemned tens of thousands of defenseless health care professionals and first responders to an early grave in the early stages of the outbreak. And every time an American, Italian, or Iranian doctor, nurse, or first responder perished because of a lack of adequate PPE, that Death by China's PPE Hoarding would kill numerous other victims down the chain.

Why? Because when a health care professional or first responder was taken off the duty roster, scores of patients went without timely and adequate treatment, and many of those poorly attended patients wound up dying.

PPE AND HEARSES PASSING IN THE VIRAL NIGHT

As if this market-cornering behavior weren't bad enough, the ever-opportunistic and Machiavellian China would compound Heinous Act 5 by putting some of its hoarded PPE *back* onto the world market at exorbitant prices.[10] At the same time, to advance its geopolitical interests by acting as a "good Samaritan"—really, that was too darkly funny, given the circumstances—China would donate PPE to the very same countries it had infected with the virus and deprived of PPE in the first place.

And so it was that in northern Italy, delivery trucks festooned with Chinese flags streamed in from airports loaded to the gills with donated Chinese PPE even as they passed hearses filled with the Italian dead who had lost their lives as the result of Chinese hoarding. Irony is as irony does.

The indisputable point to draw from these Five Heinous Acts and China's Indisputable Blame for the pandemic is this: *Even if the virus did not originate in the Wuhan lab, China's behavior once it was unleashed not only guaranteed a global pandemic; it led to the needless deaths of heroic doctors, nurses, and first responders in countries around the world.*

So how did I use that information to answer Fareed Zakaria's opening "Where's the proof?" question? Here goes:

> [I think] we should let the question of whether it came from the lab or whether it came from the wet market ride for a little bit, and simply stay with the fact that China hid the virus from the world. That's number one.
>
> Number two, while they were hiding the virus from the world, they went from a net exporter of personal protective equipment to a huge net importer, basically vacuuming up all the world. That killed people because public health officials at the front lines from Milan to New York didn't have that. And even as we speak, they are now profiteering from that . . .
>
> *It could have been contained. And instead it turned into a pandemic.* And I think it's important that the question be asked, should China be held accountable and there should be a lot of other people asking that question, including yourself, to search for a good answer to that.[11]

My answer to Fareed illustrates that at least every once in a while you can teach an old karate dog like me a new aikido trick. You can see in that answer how I quickly tacked away from the origins of the virus question and Speculative Blame to the dead center of Indisputable Blame. Yet it would still be several more months before I finally figured out how to play the China Pandemic Blame Game.

FOURTEEN

A CCP VIRUS COMMISSION AND THE ULTIMATE INTERNATIONAL TORT

I meet Jason Miller at the campaign headquarters and we go over some [internal] polling data. The data shows very clearly that about two-thirds of the respondents blame China for the pandemic, want reparations, and see Joe Biden as weak. They like the idea of a Presidential Commission . . . and it appears to move voters off the fence [toward Trump]. This is a hot buttered croissant ready to eat.

—Peter Navarro, journal entry, September 6, 2020

On a hot August 2020 evening, I was sweltering in my Washington, DC, apartment, thinking about the best way to use a presidential executive order to seamlessly shift both the Speculative and Indisputable Blames for the pandemic to Communist China, and this idea hit me right between the eyes: *Form a national presidential commission to investigate the origins, costs, and geopolitical implications of the Chinese Communist Party Virus.*

I couldn't wait to get into the office the next morning and start drafting an executive order that would lead to the formation of just such a CCP Virus Commission. To jump-start the process, the first thing I did was to have our team pull up all previous examples of presidential commissions.

I specifically wanted to determine under what legal or statutory authorities such previous commissions had been formed. I also wanted to know details such as: How many people were usually on them? How were they financed? Who appointed the members? How long did the commissions usually last? And what were their typical work products?

By 10:30 a.m., while at my stand-up desk, I hit the jackpot. Actually, my staff member Garrett Ziegler hit the jackpot for me. He came rushing in with a piece of pure digital gold.

By the way, from my stand-up desk, I had an absolutely gorgeous view overlooking the "Pebble Beach" media complex on the North Lawn in the foreground and both the East and West Wings of the White House in the background. Truth be told, my office and that view—along with being able to hunt down anyone in the world within five minutes from the Situation Room and popping in to see the Boss—are really the only things I really miss from my days at the sweatshop. The only thing, that is, other than the exercise of raw power in defense of American workers. Just saying.

So just what was the digital gold Garrett had for me? It was an absolutely perfect YouTube link to a video address recorded in the Oval Office in May 2010 by none other than President Barack Obama.[1] He was announcing by executive order the formation of a presidential commission to investigate the origins and costs of BP's *Deepwater Horizon* oil spill in the Gulf of Mexico—although to describe that humongous gusher as a "spill" would be to describe the Gulf of Mexico as a bathtub.

That was indeed a fortuitous grab by Ziegler. We now had both recent precedent for a commission and at least one legal template to follow.

Here's a simple rule that may come in handy if you ever wind up in the White House and are tasked with drafting executive orders and presidential memoranda.

Imitation is not just the sincerest form of flattery; it is the best way to make sure that whatever executive order you are drafting will pass legal muster. Just use the boilerplate language from whatever has been used before and been shown to be bulletproof to any legal challenge, and you will have the best template for whatever action you are contemplating.

So throughout the day, using the Obama oil spill order as my lodestar and using several other previous commissions such as those on Pearl Harbor and the John F. Kennedy assassination as models, I worked up a solid draft of the proposed executive order. Here's the relevant mission and purpose statement from that first draft:

> The National Commission shall investigate the origins of the COVID-19 pandemic; the economic, political, social, human, and other costs of the pandemic borne by the United States; and whether the People's Republic of China or the Chinese Communist Party have used the pandemic to advance their own economic, geopolitical, military, or territorial agendas.[2]

DON'T FORGET THE KIDNEY DIALYSIS

As an expression of pure aikido, the mission to "investigate the origins" of the pandemic would *not* be explored in any finger-pointing, accusatory way but rather carried out by an independent team of prestigious experts simply seeking the truth.

Such an approach, with the imprimatur of an objective scientific panel, would thereby raise the politically sensitive

Speculative Blame issue of the possible Wuhan lab origin of the virus in a way that would be sufficiently passive-aggressive that it could not be credibly criticized by the anti-Trump media. At least I had learned one tactical ploy from the Patron Saint of Passive Aggression, Anthony Fauci.

As the second key of the draft order, it wouldn't just be the economic costs the CCP Virus Commission would calculate; the commission would also be directed to "estimate the human costs."

Importantly, the estimate would include not just the "loss of life directly from the virus." It would also account for any costs incurred "*indirectly* from factors such as pandemic-related delays in delivering health screenings or medical treatments."

The beauty of *this* provision from a political messaging point of view was that it would remind people that the CCP Virus not only kills people it *directly* infects; it also kills people *indirectly* through the postponement of procedures such as breast cancer screenings, kidney dialysis, and chemotherapy.

Finally, as its third major focus, the commission would be asked to hold China to account for its use of the pandemic to advance its geopolitical and military objectives. By that time, the CCP had already crushed democracy in Hong Kong by using the pandemic as a means of keeping protesters inside their homes.[3] And there would likely be more Communist Chinese aggression soon in the Taiwan Strait. The commission would shine a bright, blaring spotlight on all such aggression.

All in all, the commission idea was a beautiful aikido fusion of great policy with great politics, and I couldn't wait to get started on moving that potential savior of the Trump Campaign first through White House process and then to a possible finish line.

Of course, at a point in time where I was more than three and a half years into a job whose primary description was banging my head against an East meets West Wing, China Appeaser wall, you might ask: Navarro, how can you be so naive as to think this might actually work?

You do have a point. And as I think about that point, the quotation that pops into my mind now is Samuel Johnson's famous reference to the "triumph of hope over experience."

But it was hope that I indeed had. My previous experiences notwithstanding, it was an absolutely beautiful idea and the magnitude of its beauty was topped at that point in time only by the magnitude of the political hole this administration had dug our president into. So surely, thought I, common sense would prevail.

But wait! I left out the best part of the national commission executive order. To wit: the China Commission would be tasked by the president to figure out a way to stick Communist China with a multitrillion-dollar bill for compensatory damages and costs. Yowza! It would be the *ultimate international tort.*

In fact, the preliminary estimate of such damages and costs quickly approached the value of an entire lost year of the US gross domestic product. That's more than $20 trillion!

Lest you think that is an extravagant *overestimate* of the costs of the pandemic to America, think again as we do some simple CCP virus math.

Consider first, then, the aforementioned value of the loss of American lives *directly* due to the virus. And let's stipulate for the record, so you don't think that I am some goblin or ghoul, that at a purely humanistic level, a human life is impossible to put a price tag on.

Still, when confronted with that task, the US government has decided that the average value of an American life is $10 million.[4] So given that we've already lost over six hundred thousand American souls to the CCP virus, they alone add up to damages well north of $6 trillion.

Of course, this estimate of loss of human life doesn't even count the aforementioned costs associated with the indirect loss of life due to virus-related alcoholism, depression, increased drug use, and the inability to get proper and timely medical diagnostics and care for other diseases and conditions. So add a few trillion dollars more.

Now what about straight economic damages? Consider here that the United States government has already spent more than $10 trillion in fiscal and monetary policy relief measures. These costs range from increased expenditures on unemployment benefits and small-business loans to the more targeted relief aimed at highly impacted sectors of our economy such as cruise ship lines, hotels, and restaurants.

Based on these considerations alone, you can see how the costs and damages associated with China's Wuhan virus quickly add up to at least—yes, at least—the annual value of the United States' gross domestic product.

And did I mention that the presidential executive order also had a provision in it to collect reparations from China, which currently holds more than a trillion dollars' worth of US debt?

By sticking China with a bill for the havoc it has wreaked on the US economy and American people, we could effectively cancel our debt to China and still lay claim to trillions of dollars more in damages for the havoc inflicted by the CCP.

THE AMERICAN JURY IS IN, AND CHINA'S GUILTY

In fact, this kind of damage recovery and reparations from Communist China is strongly supported by the American people. A July 28, 2020, Rasmussen Reports poll found that over half of the respondents thought that "China should help pay at least some of the financial costs that have resulted from the global transmission of the coronavirus."[5]

After that poll came out, I asked Jason Miller at the Trump Campaign to quietly conduct a poll on the issue and our proposed executive order. As my journal entry leading off this chapter documents, Miller reported to me over Labor Day weekend that the issue was a political gold mine.

That "hot buttered croissant," as I framed it in my journal, had the power to do the most important thing that any political issue can do: move undecided voters off the fence and into the Trump camp. Those persuadables would ultimately determine the outcome of the election, so the formation of my proposed presidential commission was clearly, as they say, "salient" to the outcome of the election.

And note here: neither the idea for the CCP Virus Commission itself nor the "Make China Pay" provision was the truly genius part of the executive order—at least from a political perspective. Rather, the really important part was to *require an interim report* from the commission just a few weeks *before* election day!

That interim report would be issued by a gaggle of respected economists, scientists, and geopolitical strategists, and it would provide an eye-opening blockbuster of an Archimedes lever that would enable us to move a whole lot of Speculative and Indisputable Blame and hurt from President Trump to Communist China—and thereby move a whole lot of swing voters. It had the added benefit of being precisely and factually true.

Writ large, I saw the interim report not just as essential information for the American people but as the immutable object that would blow past the Great American Firewalls of CNN, MSNBC, the *New York Times*, and the Amazon Post.

None of the Never Trump media wanted to make any connection whatsoever between the pandemic and from whence that pandemic had come for fear of shifting blame from Orange Man Bad to China. But the report would have to be, dare I say it, ***fully reported***.

I was utterly convinced that if we executed the executive order crisply, smartly, and unequivocally, we would create a perfect campaign message that would carry us straight to victory.

In truth, and as a meta-element of the China Commission gambit, I also thought there was a very good chance that it would finally push Xi Jinping and the CCP over their own hawkish edge. As Steve Bannon once said to me right after a Jared Kushner–triggered blowup with state councilor Yang Jiechi and several other top Chinese officials at a meeting in New York City during the transition in 2016, "The Chinese Communists are the most rational people in the world—until they aren't."

The risk was that if we pushed too far and too hard, Beijing's own "America Hawk" hard-liners in the Politburo and the People's Liberation Army would surely both beat the drums to threaten the United States publicly and take actions designed to punish the president and the American people. Think stiff Chinese tariffs here on American products such as autos, oil, and whiskey; cancellation of the purchases of American soybeans, beef, and pork; renunciation of the Phase One trade deal; and maybe, just maybe, Chinese jets screaming over the Taiwan Strait.

BEIJING'S "AMERICANS IN A POT" STRATEGY

In assessing that risk, I thought, *So be it.* I knew that if the CCP tried to flex its economic and/or military muscles at that critical juncture, when Americans were already close to the tipping point with a steal-our-jobs-and-stick-us-with-a-pandemic China, that kind of hawkish overreaction by the CCP would only backfire on it.

Of course, Xi Jinping and his top strategists clearly knew, as I did, that if China went after the American people hard, we as a voting nation would almost certainly rally around both the president and the American flag rather than kowtow to China's pressure. Because that was true, Xi Jinping and the CCP, despite repeated humiliations, had shown what some might call remarkable restraint over the first three and a half years of the administration.

In the Oval Office, the president frequently remarked on that restraint. And whenever he spoke about the CCP's willingness to endure our humiliation, it would always be in the same breath as a comment such as "They are smarter than us and more cunning."

In fact, what Xi Jinping and the CCP were showing was not remarkable restraint but much more *strategic* restraint. As scholars such as Michael Pillsbury, the director of the Center on Chinese Strategy at the Hudson Institute, and journalists such as Bill Gertz of the *Washington Times* have noted, the last thing the CCP wants to do is to reveal its true Evil Empire self to the American people and thereby further stoke the passions—and accompanying policy actions—of a widely perceived "China threat."

Stripped of rhetoric, Beijing's strategic restraint was just the CCP's own version of a "Trump and the Americans in a pot" strategy: don't boil the Americans too quickly, and we clever Communists will eventually boil them surely.

So throughout much of the Trump administration—aside from the occasional "all for show" grenades thrown by CCP propaganda organs such as the *Global Times* and *People's*

Daily—Xi Jinping and the CCP leadership had remained stoic as POTUS had heaped tariff indignity after tariff indignity upon them.

Still, as a bonus of the gambit we were planning, I thought the announcement of the commission might finally break through that Chinese restraint and we would be off to the "wag the Chinese running dogs" races.

A CAST OF PRESTIGIOUS CHARACTERS

Once I finished drafting the executive order, I had one more task before taking the document over to the West Wing to socialize and proselytize it within the building. I had to line up a gaggle of respected experts whom the president could appoint to the commission. In my mind, those members would have to have both the professional chops to be taken seriously and also be trustworthy enough not to go over to the dark side of either China or the Democrats.

On those criteria alone, my first thought was the appointment of Senator Tom Cotton of Arkansas as chair of the commission. Smart as the proverbial whip, true blue on the China issue, and a trustworthy Trump Loyalist, Cotton was also one of the first to point a finger at the Wuhan lab as the possible origin of the virus. So he would not shy from that topic.

The commission would also need several virologists and bioweapons experts capable of untangling the CCP's web of deceit about Wuhan. The obvious move was to tap the local talent at the US Army Medical Research Institute of Infectious Diseases at Fort Detrick in Frederick, Maryland—Detrick is the premier biological weapons research lab in the world.

Next I would need a gaggle of Mensa-level economists to parse what is, hands down, *the* most complex "general equilibrium" problem the United States has ever faced. General equilibrium analysis focuses on how changes in one or more individual or "partial equilibrium" markets of an economy might ripple through the broader macroeconomy and financial markets—and often trigger permanent structural adjustments in the process.

To anticipate and parse these Rubik's Cube–like structural adjustments—and thereby provide a full accounting of the costs of the CCP virus—the commission's macroeconomists would have to sort through and estimate the changes in key variables such as GDP growth, productivity, inflation, and real wages. They would also need to carefully track the massive but largely hidden covid-caused damage to our small businesses that drive nearly half of employment and job growth in America.[6]

To conduct the analysis, I was hoping to enlist the help of two of my favorites inside the West Wing perimeter—the former and the current chairmen of the Council of Economic Advisers, Kevin Hassett and Tyler Goodspeed. Neither needed any nudging on this mission—they were gung ho.

Finally, the commission's band of experts would have to include China scholars and geopolitical experts to sift through mounting evidence that Xi Jinping and the CCP were indeed using the shield and chaos of the pandemic to advance their geopolitical and territorial ambitions. The aforementioned Mike Pillsbury, a POTUS favorite, immediately jumped to my mind, as did General Robert Spalding, who had done a brief stint at the National Security Council. As a bonus, having Pillsbury on the marquee would make it easier to sell the venture to the Boss.

With at least a tentative cast of experts assembled, my next task was to socialize and sell the package not just over in the West Wing but also to Secretary of State Mike Pompeo, who would have a key role in the gambit. That sales job would turn out to be more fun than a barrel of monkeys—particularly with National Security Advisor Robert O'Brien—but it would be a barrel that also contained no shortage of bad personnel apples.

FIFTEEN

THE LAST DAYS OF POMPEO AND THE THREE FEARS

Pompeo at 9 a.m. at State is a big disappointment. We went to get [name redacted] appointed as the temporary Principal Deputy Assistant Secretary to move POTUS' arms sales and . . . Mike reveals he used to be in the arms sales biz and views the defense contractors as perpetual whiners and us as their errand boys.

I push right back saying that I'm working for a very pissed off POTUS [not the defense contractors] and that PM [the Bureau of Political-Military Affairs] is a rat's nest of folks whose org culture is not conducive to the Trump mission. It's a polite standoff but a missed opportunity.

—Peter Navarro, journal entry, May 24, 2018

Yep, the newly minted secretary of state got right up in my grill the very first time I asked for his help.

In a typical rogue move, Pompeo's predecessor, Rex Tillerson, had decided to use President Trump's signature megabillion-dollar arms sales deal to Saudi Arabia and the United Arab Emirates as a bargaining chip to pressure them into resolving their bitter dispute with Qatar.[1] As a result, the PDAS or principal deputy assistant secretary at the Bureau of

Political-Military Affairs at the State Department had been sitting on the approvals.

When the Boss found out about Rex's scorpion in the arms sales ointment, he told me to fix it and fast—of course, in Trump Time. As to why me?

Arms transfers to our allies were part of my trade and manufacturing policy remit, because every time we sold a new F-16 fighter plane or Terminal High Altitude Area Defense missile defense system to the Saudis or Bulgarians or Japanese, we not only strengthened US alliances but helped create thousands of high-paying manufacturing jobs on American soil.

To fix the Rogue Rex problem, I immediately invited State's PDAS and her team over to the White House Situation Room. Once a week, they would march in grim-faced with their spreadsheets, and my then deputy, Alex Gray, and I would go over which transfers would be needed both within the State Department and up on Capitol Hill. I'd then direct the PDAS to prioritize them appropriately and move them along.

By the time Mike Pompeo replaced Tillerson, things were moving along reasonably well. But the PDAS was a very well seasoned Deep Administrative State bureaucrat who was ideologically opposed to many of the arms transfers we were trying to move forward, so she periodically dragged her heels and played little Deep State bureaucratic tricks to stall them.

Parse that for a minute: the person in charge of arms transfers at the State Department was ideologically opposed to most of such transfers!

Welcome to Washington. Now you know why nothing in the Swamp ever seems to work.

At any rate, with Tillerson tweet-beat out the door, Alex Gray and I wanted to put a friendly Trumper into the PDAS position, and we had a great candidate. But as you can see from my journal entry, Pompeo wanted no part of it.

What surprised me most about the encounter wasn't that Mike had told me to go pound sand; it was worth a try. What surprised me was that he had ever worked as a lobbyist in the defense industry to begin with, and I was especially annoyed at his suggestion that somehow I was an errand boy for the military-industrial complex.

At any rate, things got way better with Mike over time as we made common cause on the China issue. He was as hawkish as I was, and two of his top aides—Mary Kissel and Miles Yu—became my go-to contacts at the State Department. So whenever a China issue came up at the White House where I was going to need Mike's help in yet another Situation Room showdown with Steve Mnuchin and Larry Kudlow, I would give Mary or Miles a holler. They would then give Mike both a heads-up and a thorough briefing.

As to why I'm telling you all this, it was Pompeo, Mary Kissel, and Miles Yu whose help I would need to ultimately seal the deal for the proposed CCP Virus Presidential Commission. That's because we would need one cabinet-level agency to both house the commission and pony up the funding. And State was by far the most logical choice, as I could completely trust Pompeo and his crew to deliver a fine and fine-edged product.

In the meantime, I had to get POTUS on board with the idea, and to do that, I did not want to hit him cold. He would simply say to me, "Peter. What's the team think about it?"

First things being first, the next part of my own process was to work with and woo that team—or, as Abe Lincoln might have more accurately put it, that "team of rivals." So it was that the day after I drafted the China Commission executive order, I made my way over to the West Wing to make my usual daily rounds.

Typically, on these daily trips to the West Wing, I would pop in and see what was shaking with all the key players: Meadows; Kushner; Deputy Chief of Staff Chris Liddell; Robert O'Brien; Stephen Miller; the two "Pats" in the Office of the White House Legal Counsel, Cipollone and Philbin; the crew down in the Office of the Staff Secretary; Hope Hicks; maybe Director of Strategic Communications Alyssa Farah; and certainly Dan Scavino for both laughs and moral support. Always Scavino.

I should say here as an aside—and you may find this curious—that the easiest person for me to see in the entire West Wing was the president himself. All I had to do was call Molly in the Outer Oval for a quick appointment or just drop by and stick my head in the door, and POTUS was always happy to see me.

In contrast, when I needed to see Chief of Staff Mark Meadows on an urgent matter, I would go over to his office and ask his assistant to put me onto his calendar. She would dutifully scribble my request down on an oversized notepad that was usually filled with other scribblings. And then I would never hear from her again.

After about the third time that happened, when the urgent matter I really needed to see the Chief about was indeed urgent and wound up harming POTUS, I gave up and went directly to the Boss. It just wasn't worth my time trying to play courtier to Meadows's court jesters—except perhaps today.

In this case, as I made my rounds, my hope was that Meadows would finally like one of my ideas, and it was my good luck to bump into the chief in the Outer Oval Office as

I was filling in Dan Scavino about my idea for the commission. Dan loved the idea and urged me to call the Boss that very night at the residence to pitch it. Copy that, Brother Dan!

As I was leaving Dan's office—really a little cubbyhole tucked away inside the Outer Oval—I saw Meadows moving past me from the Oval Office on his way back to his office. It was a *carpe diem* moment, so I fell in by his side and quickly briefed him on the China Commission idea as we walked down the narrow hall to the chief of staff's suite.

To my surprise, Meadows loved the idea. So far, so good.

My next stop was down the next hall past the vice president's suite to see National Security Advisor Robert O'Brien. My luck was holding here as well, as O'Brien was holding court with Alex Gray, who had left my office to take the job as Robert's chief of staff—a "lateral movement," as I liked to joke with them.

With my brother in arms O'Brien, it would be a case of "fourth time is a charm," as he followed the crucifixion of Michael Flynn, the Globalism of H. R. McMaster, and the Dr. Strangelovian reign of error and terror of John Bolton to become Donald Trump's fourth national security advisor.

I had gotten along swimmingly with Flynn dating back to our days at Trump Tower during the transition after the 2016 election win. He admired my work, and we were locked and loaded to advance an uber-tough-on-China agenda.

That Flynn was taken out by a group of rogue FBI agents and Democrat operatives who remain free and unindicted to this day was one of the worst abuses of government power in US history. The abrupt and early loss of Flynn was a great blow to POTUS and the administration because it took a Trump loyalist off the board even as it led to the far too hasty appointment of the Globalist H. R. McMaster.

I liked H.R. well enough. For a former tank commander who was built like a brick outhouse and trained to kill people with big guns and brutal efficiency, H.R. was surprisingly amiable and likable. And unlike most of the treacherous connivers in the West Wing, he always played it straight when it came to process.

The problem with H.R. was that he simply was not one of Us, meaning a Populist Economic Nationalist. Instead, he was one of those Globalist Thems who always thought it was more important to maintain our foreign alliances than to take care of our blue-collar workers. As a result, whenever there was a conflict between a trade issue and a national security issue, I found myself on the other side of H.R. with our guns drawn. Here was the essential problem: *McMaster simply didn't understand a favorite mantra of the Boss: economic security* ***is*** *National Security. And if you try to sacrifice economic security on the altar of national security, as Globalists are wont to do, you wind up losing both.*[2]

A classic case in point was my clash with McMaster over the president's resolute campaign promise to renegotiate what was an awful, auto industry–killing South Korean trade deal. McMaster wanted absolutely no part of such a trade dispute because he didn't want to disrupt the military alliance we had with the South Koreans.

From my perspective, that was just damn foolish from a negotiating position. The Koreans needed our military bases and nuclear umbrella far more than we needed to station massive amounts of troops on the Korean Peninsula, so we were holding all the cards. And there were tens of thousands of American jobs in the auto industry at stake in such a negotiation. And how can you even have a strong national defense without a strong auto industry? Economic security *is* national security.

At least on this particular issue, I ran right over McMaster as though I were in one of his tanks. As a result, the Boss got his renegotiated South Korean deal, and we saved America's pickup truck industry in the process.

It was one of my few trade victories with H.R. on watch at the National Security Council—although Secretary of Commerce Wilbur Ross and I would use one of McMaster's tanks to roll over National Economic Council director Gary Cohn on steel and aluminum tariffs and, in the process, help drive him right out of the building. Now, that was a very good day.

TOO MANY ROOMS WHERE BOLTON HAPPENED

When John Bolton came along, I figured it would be heaven on West Wing earth, as his rhetoric on China was as tough as anyone's. He turned out, however, to be the consummate turf-conscious bureaucrat who was far more concerned with blowing up Iran or Syria and invading Venezuela than taking on Beijing.

In far too many of the rooms where Bolton happened, John's libertarian mean streak would collide with the Trump "Buy American" and trade agendas, and the mustachioed Dr. Strangelove would repeatedly use his NSC bureaucracy to bury all manner of Make America Great Again actions that the White House otherwise should have carried out.

So when Dr. Strangelove bolted, it was more than good Bolton riddance. It was also more than a big sigh of relief. *It was time for me to take Action, Action, Action.*

So as soon as Bolton left, I vowed that I would not be stuck with yet another non-Deplorable for a national security advisor. Of course, the person who immediately came to mind as the perfect replacement was none other than Robert O'Brien.

In 2017, I had helped Robert get his job over at the State Department as the administration's chief hostage negotiator, but he was clearly underemployed. With the kind of legal, political, and policy chops he had, he could just as easily have been secretary of state—and he probably would have been if Trump had been reelected to a second term and Pompeo had moved on.

So when I heard about Bolton's exit, I immediately called O'Brien and told him to start working all the contacts he had to get his wonk hat into the big ring. After I hung up, I wrote his name down on a White House card in big red letters with an exclamation point and walked over to the Oval Office. It was the afternoon of September 10, 2019, and I remember it like it was yesterday.

It was again a time when I wasn't really interested in going through the protocol of asking Molly to get me in, so I just popped my head in front of the open door to the Oval, where the Boss could see me. When I gave him a small salute, he quickly waved me in.

With that, I walked over and put the card down in front of him on the Resolute Desk. As he looked at the name I had written down, I simply said, "Boss. That's your guy for NSC." After he gave me a quick smile and "message received" nod of his head, I turned and walked out the door.

That's not the end of the story, however. It's not even the best part of the story. The best part is this.

After I saw the Boss, I went back and called Robert and told him what I had done. Of course, he thanked me; Robert is nothing if not always gracious. But he also wanted my advice on what his next move should be. Said I, "Look, the Boss is heading out to LA for a fundraiser that's going to feature your buddy [former California governor] Pete Wilson. You need to get your butt on a plane out to the Left Coast and make sure you show up at that fundraiser in your best suit with a Trump red tie around your neck and with Pete the Guv Wilson on your arm. Art of the deal, baby!"

The gambit worked like a charm. Wilson put in a good word to the Boss for Robert right on the spot. The Boss offered Robert the job on that very same spot. By the time Robert was heading back to Washington, he was the de facto national security advisor, and both he and I could not have been happier.

Of all the operations I ran during my four years at the White House, that one was both the most successful and the most fun. And 99.9 percent of the time, Robert was a dream to work with—and it would thus be so with the China Commission executive order.

In fact, when I pitched him on the idea, he paid me the ultimate compliment. Ever the jokester, Robert said to me with his best deadpan delivery, "Peter, this is so good I'm going to tell everybody that it was my idea."

Yes, Robert O'Brien absolutely loved the China Commission. He immediately saw what a powerful aikido tool it could be to shift the blame for the pandemic from the Boss to China.

A POKER-FACED PAISAN CHINA HAWK

From O'Brien's office, I next headed down the hall and up the stairs to visit my only other true-blue tough-on-China ally in the West Wing, White House legal counsel Pat Cipollone.

In terms of value added, Pat was critical to moving any executive order as swiftly as possible through the staff secretary process within the White House. At the staff secretary level, Derek Lyons would, as his bad personnel predecessor, Rob Porter, invariably had done, give me endless grief and create endless bad process delays simply because he could.

That said, Lyons would never dare try any of that obstructionist crap with Pat Cipollone. So when I needed to goose the staff secretary process, my golden gooser was Pat.

One of the most pleasant surprises of my tenure at the White House was when I learned that Pat Cipollone was cut from the same tough-on-China cloth as I was. When the poker-faced Pat had first come to the White House in October 2018 after the soap opera–style exodus of Don McGahn, I'd had no idea what Pat was thinking.

After Pat came on board, he just started showing up every Monday for the 9:00 a.m. senior staff meeting in the Roosevelt Room. He always entered the room early. And he always sat there in his bland lawyer's suit and skinny red tie in a chair right next to the chief of staff, who at the time was John Kelly.

Like a sphinx at a poker table at the Luxor in Vegas, Pat spoke only if he was spoken to. Whatever question he might be asked by Kelly or anyone else in the room, he would answer in a clipped fashion. Throughout those first few months of his tenure, he was just a poker faced enigma.

That all changed one day after Pat invited me up to his office to ask for some assistance on a trade-related mission that POTUS had given him. "Do you have a way to accomplish this mission by executive order?" he asked me.

Since that was a classified matter, I'm not going to say anything more specific. But when I did have a really good solution for him, he not only was thankful; he went off on a long thoughtful soliloquy about the need to crack down harder on China for both policy and political reasons. "At last," I thought, "I have an ally in the Office of the White House Counsel."

NOTHING TO FEAR BUT THREE FEARS THEMSELVES

At this point, I could pepper you with all manner of anecdotes and details as to why America never got its National Commission on the Origins and Costs of Covid-19. But in the end, it all boiled down to bad personnel—think mostly Mnuchin and Kudlow—interacting with what I would come to call the Three Fears.

The First Fear was that any tough action on China might cause the Chinese side to cancel the Phase One trade deal and all of the agricultural purchases that were allegedly going with it to critical farm states such as Iowa, Iowa, and Iowa. I say "allegedly" because the clever Chinese Commies were always ordering far more product than our farmers were putting onto cargo ships for export and delivery.

I say "clever" because the essence of the Phase One trade deal trap was for the Chinese side to always dangle the promise of large purchases but never quite consummate the deals. Said the China scholar Professor Aaron Friedberg of Princeton in another context that is nonetheless applicable here, "The Chinese are always very good at setting the table, but they rarely deliver the meal."*

The Second Fear fit tongue and groove into the First Fear because the mother of all market crashes might come if the Phase One deal got dumped into the tough-on-China toilet. Or so the Neville Chamberlain–Lord Halifax, Mnuchin-Kudlow stoking of the Second Fear with the Boss went.

* I interviewed Friedberg for my *Crouching Tiger* book and film. That was one of his gems.

Of course, I didn't believe for a minute that a canceled Phase One deal would crush the stock market. The big hedge fund managers and other Smart Money on the Street who set the longer-term market trends with their massive money moves knew full well that Phase One was of no practical consequence for the real economy. Ergo, any cancellation would lead at worst to a few down days in the market, and, after some day traders got a little richer off the volatility, the market would shrug it off.

Regrettably, I never got to test that hypothesis, as the Mnuchin-Kudlow "Don't rock the China boat" Second Fear view would prevail.

The Third Fear was to me the most perplexing. It was that any further antagonism of Beijing might start a hot war.

The very first time this came up in the Oval Office, I found it curious as it was my own belief that we were already in a hot war with China, both economically and in cyberspace.

The abiding fact of the matter here is that modern Chinese warfare, particularly if you read landmark People's Liberation Army documents such as *Unrestricted Warfare: China's Master Plan to Destroy America*,[3] favors *nonkinetic* forms of warfare such as economic, cyber, information, and legal warfare.

To me, and to other China scholars such as Michael Pillsbury, the idea that China would dare attack us militarily simply did not parse. Perhaps in five or ten years. But certainly not in the next few years.

The People's Liberation Army simply was not yet at military parity with us, and Beijing knew it. And anyway, the CCP was already having its way with us through its Seven Deadly Unfair Trade Sins, its information warfare, and all manner of other nonkinetic means. So why bother to attack with conventional arms?

Still, as the Third Fear kept creeping more and more into Trade Team discussions with POTUS, it began to give me pause. As much as he and I thought alike, and we surely did to the point where sometimes it was just plain eerie—the Boss actually said to me one time, "It's like you're in my head"—Donald J. Trump was playing a much higher dimension of chess. So if he thought kinetic war might be on the table, I needed to pay attention.

KUDLOW, MNUCHIN, WAR, DISHONOR

So it was that over the last few fateful months before election day, whenever I pitched the CCP Virus Commission—or other tough on China actions in the Oval Office—Mnuchin and Kudlow shamelessly tag teamed the Boss with the Three Fears to short-circuit any possible action.

Since I was hardly a shrinking violet, sparks flew. Insults were hurled. And the Boss would sit there and shake his head in exasperation.

Toward the bitter without any hint of sweet end in the few short weeks before election day, the president grew to dislike Mnuchin's weakness and double dealing almost as much as I did. But before he got to that epiphany, when we were speaking privately, he often asked me, "You really don't like Steve, do you?"

I would tell him that emotion had nothing to do with it. In the cold light of a Rust Belt day, I simply believed, and very strongly, that of all the bad personnel in the White House, Mnuchin and Kudlow were doing the most to both destroy the working men and women of this country and his presidency.

"At the end of this," I told him, "if you are a one-term president, Mnuchin is going to laugh all the way to the bank in Beijing as Chinese money funds his new movie productions.

And Kudlow is going to wind up back on TV as a high-priced Fox pimp for Wall Street Globalism disavowing your trade policies."

When I told him that, the Boss never pushed back—and eventually he understood that I was exactly right in the hardest of ways. But by then, it was too late; the Mnuchin-Kudlow damage was irrevocably and irreversibly done both economically and politically.

Here, there is absolutely ***no*** *question in my mind that Donald J. Trump* ***won the 2020 election by a significant margin of LAWFUL votes****. Yet here there is equally no question in my mind that bad personnel such as Mnuchin and Kudlow pushing bad soft-on-China policies* ***made the 2020 election close enough to steal****. And steal it the Democrats did.*

When I think about all that and my many days in hand-to-hand combat with the likes of Mnuchin, Kudlow, and others, and when I think about how it all ended, I'm reminded of Winston Churchill's words to Neville Chamberlain upon the occasion of the Munich Agreement, which handed Czechoslovakia over to the Nazis and triggered World War II. Said Churchill, "You were given the choice between war and dishonor. You chose dishonor, and you will have war."

And war we will continue to have with Communist China, nonkinetically for the foreseeable future and perhaps kinetically at some point, because of the weakness that those White House advisers exhibited—and most of all, because we no longer have Donald Trump in the White House.

As a coda, it is worth noting that Mnuchin and Kudlow would show their true Wall Street colors quite soon after election day. Mnuchin would be implicated in the possible application of the Twenty-fifth Amendment to remove the president from office soon after the January 6 Capitol Hill meltdown.

When confronted with his treachery by the press, Mnuchin didn't even push back; he simply declined to comment.[4]

Kudlow—no doubt to smooth any turbulence on his glide path back to Wall Street and a cushy gig on Fox Business—would join the chorus of RINO Republicans criticizing the president for "falsely" insisting he had won the election and blaming the Boss for inciting the Capitol Hill riot. It was just heartbreaking to watch Larry act in such an untruthful way to a great larger-than-life president who had rescued Larry from the ash heap of history and his life of oblivion.

In the end, Mnuchin and Kudlow got it wrong on just about everything. And nowhere were they more wrong than on the issue of Communist China.

SIXTEEN

THE CURIOUS CASE OF THE DELAYED VACCINE

I do a Fox and Friends *hit in the A.M. with the primary mission to advance the message that Trump is the only president who can get a vaccine done in half the normal time. He has turned the traditional paradigm on its head by moving from a sequenced multistage process to a simultaneous one. Instead of waiting to discover the vaccine and then going through clinical trials before manufacturing, we are doing it all at once.*

—Peter Navarro, journal entry, July 27, 2020

If they pull a vaccine out of their a--, it will be the October surprise of October surprises. I think you'll see some of the angst lifting off of the American electorate.

Democrat pollster Cornell Belcher, *Washington Post*, September 5, 2020[1]

As we rounded the Labor Day turn and headed into the home stretch to November 3, POTUS needed a big win on the virus front to get that "Made in China" demon off his approval rating back. Delivering on his promise of a safe and effective vaccine before election day would be just the medicine he himself—along with the American public—desperately and urgently needed.

It was not just the Democrats who understood the high political stakes involved in delaying the Trump vaccine. Big Pharma clearly preferred Joe Biden to an incumbent president who was taking strong actions to dramatically reduce drug prices and bring home supply chains for the domestic manufacture of pharmaceuticals.[2] And a gaggle of anti-Trump bureaucrats at the FDA, inspired by Anthony Fauci, were clearly in on a manufactured slowdown of the vaccine ride and race.

Because there is so much blood on so many hands in the Curious Case of the Delayed Vaccine—as Perry Mason once noted, "Almost anyone is capable of a crime"[3]—we are going to treat this chapter as the description of a criminal investigation. Here are the unsolved mysteries: What happened to those Americans who lost their lives? Was it negligence, political gamesmanship, or soulless profiteering? You, the jury, shall decide.

MOVING IN WARP SPEED AND TRUMP TIME

My own role in the Curious Case of the Delayed Vaccine began with my previously referenced February 9, 2020, memo to the Coronavirus Task Force predicting a "workable vaccine" by October "if we act now."

When I made that In Trump Time prediction, the last thing I'd had on my mind was a politically potent October Vaccine Surprise to boost the Boss's chances of winning on November 3. It was just not on my radar at the time—and in all of my discussions with POTUS, he never once raised the issue. His only concern was for the American people. *Our only thought at the time was this: The faster we get the vaccine, the more lives we will save.*

As I write this now, with the benefit of both hindsight *and* a significant investigation undertaken by my own White House team, I can make this "blood on their hands" accusation without equivocation:

If not for the actions taken by Pfizer, the FDA, Anthony Fauci, the anti-Trump media, and the Biden-Harris campaign, my prediction of a vaccine being delivered to the American people by October or November would have been ***exactly*** *right, thousands of American lives would have been saved, and, yes, Donald Trump would have gotten an electoral boost.*

Here's the postmortem.

FROM ANTIGENS TO EFFICACY

The success of any vaccine depends on the *antigen*. It is the antigen in any vaccine that generates an immune response to a virus.[4]

A pharmaceutical company's search for such an antigen necessarily begins in a preclinical phase in which vaccine candidates are tested on animals. Once a candidate is found, it then undergoes a three-phase randomized clinical trial.

Phase One tests for safety and involves a very small number of human subjects. Phases Two and Three then test for "efficacy" or effectiveness with progressively larger pools of volunteers.

Of course, no one knows better than Big Pharma that a successful vaccine against a dangerous infectious disease can yield a profit bonanza. So it was that in late January 2020, as the crematoria in Wuhan, China, were sending up their smoke signals of an impending pandemic, a German pharmaceutical company named BioNTech began feverishly working on a possible vaccine. Its effort turned out to be very good news for Pfizer, as Pfizer had previously worked with BioN-Tech on flu vaccines.

For the uninitiated, Pfizer is a putatively American company headquartered in New York. Yet as the world's second largest drug company behind only Johnson & Johnson, with sales in more than a hundred countries around the world, the multinational Pfizer bleeds not red, white, and blue but Globalist dollar green.[5]

Nor does Pfizer any longer self-identify as an "American" company. Like many multinational corporations conceived and born in the United States with American labor and ingenuity, Pfizer now sees itself more like Switzerland or the Vatican.

As a corporate nation-state, Pfizer conducts its own quasi foreign policy with the broad goal of managing competing needs across its global empire rather than first serving the American people. It is not for nothing that the United Kingdom got a large allotment of the Pfizer vaccine to distribute to its citizens before the United States did.[6]

In my numerous interactions with Big Pharma executives during my White House years, I uniformly had bad experiences with these elites. They looked down on me as a dangerous "Buy American" nativist tasked by the president to bring their supply chains back home. And all I ever heard from those Globalist profiteers was that it would take too long or be too costly or both. Dismissive of any national security concerns, they simply and invariably dug in with both of their Gucci heels.

At any rate, on March 17, 2020, the sovereign state of Pfizer entered into a partnership with BioNTech and was literally off to the vaccine horse race—with a very healthy head start on much of the competition.

Fast-forward to June 30. The Food and Drug Administration announced some very good news for Pfizer as it set a relatively low effectiveness threshold of 50 percent.[7]

Of course, we would all like our vaccines to be closer to 100 percent effective, particularly against the deadly CCP Virus. But 50 percent is, you might say, not half bad, and after that announcement, Pfizer's stock price got a nice little bump.

The very next day, July 1, Pfizer's stock price got another nice little bump as it released promising early data from its Phase One and Phase Two studies.[8]

Clearly, at that point Pfizer's profit motive was aligning nicely with the public interest.

On July 13, the FDA took the critical step of granting fast-track designation for the Pfizer vaccine candidate.[9] So at least at that point, the FDA was very much playing along with the need for In Trump Time speed.

And speaking of speed, on July 22, Pfizer officially joined the Trump administration's Operation Warp Speed. It signed a contract worth almost $2 billion for the mass distribution of 100 million doses.[10] So far, it was so very good for the White House, for the millions of Americans fearful of becoming infected by the virus, for the FDA, and for Pfizer itself.

In fact, things were looking so good that Pfizer CEO Albert Bourla[11] proclaimed to the world on September 3 that the company would be able to announce the results of its Phase Three trial by the end of October. Said Bourla in no uncertain terms—and please remember this, as it is a key plot point—"We expect by the end of October, we should have enough [data] . . . to say whether the [vaccine] works or not."[12]

Of course, what Bourla did not explicitly say—but what the whole world understood—was that the Pfizer vaccine would likely be ready before election day!

You could almost hear the huzzahs, hallelujahs, and hosannas in the Oval Office and throughout the West Wing. Indeed, with the steady stream of positive vaccine news, there was an ebullient mood throughout the White House.

That manic mood lasted right up to the first presidential debate in Ohio on September 29. Then the politics of Pfizer's vaccine development hit the fan.

THE UNTOLD UNFORCED-ERROR DEBATE STORY

Let us stipulate here that the Boss's alpha-male performance at that first presidential debate got mixed reviews.[13] Yet the Boss's "house style" turned out to be of far less lasting political consequence than a brief exchange between him and Joe Biden at the twenty-six-minute mark of the debate.

That particular exchange about the vaccine approval trajectory would wind up poking both the Pfizer bear and the FDA rodent. It set into motion Newtonian forces that would, in turn, inflict significant political damage on the Trump Campaign. Here's that exchange:

> TRUMP: I spoke to the scientists that are in charge. They will have the vaccine very soon.
>
> BIDEN: Do you believe for a moment what he's telling you in light of all the lies he's told you about the whole issue of COVID. . . .
>
> TRUMP: Well I've spoken to the companies, and we can have it a lot sooner. It's a very political thing because people . . . would rather make it political and save less [lives]. . . . I've spoken to Pfizer, I've spoken to all of the people that you have to speak to . . . Moderna, Johnson and Johnson, and others. They can go faster than that by a lot. . . .

> He said it's a possibility that we'll have the answer before November 1.[14]

As I was sitting at home eating dinner and watching that particular exchange, my fork stopped in midair and my jaw clenched. Frozen in this time and space as I was, all I could think of was Newton's Third Law of Motion: every action has an equal and opposite reaction.

Clearly, Biden's debate prep team had instructed the suddenly Not So Sleepy Joe to hit POTUS square between the eyes on the issue of trust in a "Trump vaccine." If the Boss had simply said that he was hopeful we would soon have a safe and effective vaccine and quickly moved on—never mentioning election day as the deadline—he would never have triggered the deadly equal and opposite Newtonian reactions he got from both Pfizer and the FDA and the anti-Trump media. Instead, the issue would have been as dead and buried as truth at the *Washington Post*.

NEWTON'S THIRD LAW OF POLITICAL MOTION

Unfortunately, the Boss's debate performance gave Pfizer's anti-Trump CEO, Albert Bourla, a perfect opening to delay a vaccine that, as I have showed you, he had already promised would be ready by the end of October.

So it was that two days after the debate, Bourla sent out a Newtonian letter to all of Pfizer's US employees that was supposed to be an internal Pfizer document. Of course, Bourla or one of his Never Trump henchmen could have leaked it. The lucky winner was the Associated Press, which reported:

> The head of Pfizer, one of the drugmakers racing to develop a coronavirus vaccine, told employees on

> Thursday he was *disappointed* that its work was politicized during the presidential debate and tried to reassure U.S. staff that the company won't bend to pressure to move more quickly.
>
> CEO Albert Bourla told the employees that the company is "moving at the speed of science," rather than under any political timing . . . .
>
> "The only pressure we feel—and it weighs heavy—are the billions of people, millions of businesses and hundreds of government officials that are depending on us."[15] [Emphasis added.]

After I read that letter, I immediately wondered about whether Bourla had intentionally used the word *disappointed* to send a pointed and veiled personal message to the Boss. For those who know Donald J. Trump well, the worst thing he can say is that he is "disappointed" in you. If Bourla is that clever, he is even more evil than I believe him to be.

MEANS, OPPORTUNITY, BUT MOST OF ALL MOTIVE

Bourla's letter proved to be the pivotal point in President Trump's quest to deliver a vaccine to the American public before election day. Bourla all but said that Big Pharma Pfizer was going to delay the vaccine.

As to why Pfizer and Bourla would take such a action—the company and Bourla should have known that any delays would lead to loss of life. Bourla's Pfizer, along with Big Pharma, viewed President Trump's aggressive push to reduce drug prices and bring pharmaceutical manufacturing and supply chains back on shore as antithetical to their shareholders' interests.[16]

Need I point out here that depriving Big Pharma of the sweatshops and pollution havens of China, India, and the rest of the world would squeeze its bottom line? Just do the arithmetic; it would add up to tens of billions of dollars of forgone profits during a second Trump term. What's a few thousand American lives when set against that?

That Bourla and Pfizer strongly preferred Joe Biden to Donald Trump should not be in dispute. For every $1,000 that Pfizer employees donated to the Trump Campaign, they sent more than three times that to Biden.[17] As we say in economics, this spending pattern clearly reveals Pfizer's political preferences.

That Pfizer may have played slow and loose with its vaccine to help beat Donald Trump is likewise supported by this observation: the company played a key role in financing what would be a torrent of lie-filled anti-Trump Big Pharma commercials in the final months before election day.

There's no question that Big Pharma's Big Lies campaign got the Boss's attention. I was there more than once in the small dining room just off the Oval, where the Boss liked to watch the news and do his paperwork. When the Big Pharma ads came on, you could just see his blood boil.

The broader point, of course, is that Pfizer not only had the means and the opportunity to delay the vaccine past election day; it also had a huge *profit* motive.

WHAT THE HECK IS AN "INTERIM ANALYSIS"?

Of course, if we are to convict Pfizer of politically delaying the vaccine with something other than circumstantial evidence, it would be nice to have the proverbial "smoking gun." I cannot give you exactly that—but I can get pretty darn close.

This smoking gun revolves around the somewhat arcane phase of clinical trials known as "interim analyses." Work with me here.

An interim analysis is conducted when a certain threshold of "confirmed cases" is reached in the tested population, where a "confirmed case" is someone vaccinated who nonetheless comes down with the virus. So, if you have ten thousand confirmed cases in a trial with twenty thousand subjects taking the vaccine, the vaccine is only 50 percent effective. But if confirmed cases are only one thousand out of twenty thousand, the vaccine is 95 percent effective.

Now, here's the plot point in our murder mystery: when you hit the number of confirmed cases in an interim analysis, the data goes to an independent data-monitoring committee, and shortly thereafter, the findings are publicly released. This critical information not only enables a company to determine whether to continue with its vaccine candidate; it also provides important new information to the public as to whether the vaccine is likely to be viable.

With that as our background, let's cut to the Pfizer smoking-gun chase. On October 27, on the heels of both the presidential debate debacle and CEO Albert Bourla's anti-Trump letter, Pfizer announced that *it did not yet have the requisite thirty-two confirmed cases* to complete its first interim analysis. Ergo, there could not possibly be good news about the vaccine before election day.

In fact, Pfizer was playing a dangerous game. As reported in *Science* magazine, here's how it worked: to avoid hitting the thirty-two confirmed cases threshold, Pfizer stored, rather than immediately tested, the nasal swabs taken from participants who they suspected were infected. If they didn't test the swabs, they couldn't confirm cases.

Pfizer thereby avoided announcing that it had a highly effective Trump vaccine before election day. That fact is worth repeating: *Pfizer unilaterally decided to store rather than test swabs that would have certainly pushed it past the thirty-two confirmed cases mark. If it had instead immediately tested the stored swabs, we would have learned before election day that the company had a safe and highly effective vaccine—and gotten exactly the October Vaccine Surprise the Boss had been hoping for!*

If that is not at least a smoldering gun, I don't know what is, and based on the evidence presented, the only conclusion one can draw from Pfizer's means, motive, and opportunity in the Curious Case of the Delayed Vaccine is that there is significant American blood on Pfizer's hands.

Just how much blood am I talking about? Let's quickly look at one of the quickest ways to calculate the likely death toll from the vaccine delay. This is by using the so-called excess deaths measure, a staple of academia popularized during the pandemic.

The statistical conceit here is straightforward: compare the *predicted* number of deaths in the absence of a vaccine with the *actual* number of deaths once the vaccine is introduced over an appropriate time interval. When you use the excess-deaths yardstick, you don't have to calculate separate numbers for the various direct and indirect channels the virus kills through.

For example, there is the obvious *direct* channel, whereby a person who would otherwise have been vaccinated becomes infected and dies. But there are also more subtle *indirect* channels, such as a person who dies because he or she was infected by somebody who would otherwise have been vaccinated.

Using the data from the "excess deaths tracker" published by *The Economist*, you can easily get to more than fifty thousand excess deaths because of what turned into more than a two-month-long delay in introducing the Pfizer vaccine.[18] Of course, a good part of that delay can be laid right at Pfizer's doorstep. Yet the FDA would have a pair of very bloodied hands in that as well.

THE DEEP STATE FDA EMPIRE STRIKES BACK

Yes, indeed, the FDA's conduct unbecoming would be every bit as deadly and despicable as that of Pfizer. For it was the FDA—or more precisely a rogue unit within the FDA—that ended any hope of getting a vaccine into the arms of the American people before election day. Of course, every day of FDA delay meant that more Americans needlessly died.

To fully understand the FDA's rogue behavior, it is useful to first highlight the very different risk assessments used for the approval of therapeutic drugs versus vaccines. Whereas therapeutics help sick people like cancer patients who need help as quickly as possible, vaccines protect healthy people. Because of their different risk assessments, vaccine approvals generally take longer than therapeutic drug approvals do.

In the absence of an emergency such as a pandemic, the longer approval time for vaccines tends to be prudent. As history has painfully taught us, as many as eighteen months or longer after a pharmaceutical approval, patients may experience any number of autoimmune conditions ranging from abnormal blood clotting,[19] heart attacks, and liver failure to gastrointestinal bleeding and birth defects.[20]

So on its face, it's not unreasonable for the FDA to move more cautiously on vaccine approvals. That said, Congress, with the passage of the Project BioShield Act of 2004, put clear guardrails on the FDA's notorious risk aversion.

In particular, this act provides an important emergency bridge to rapid preapproval of vaccines by granting the FDA the authority to issue an Emergency Use Authorization (EUA). The clear legislative intent is that the FDA should err on the side of taking a greater risk rather than exerting undue caution under extraordinary circumstances such as a pandemic.

Given that legislative intent, it was fully expected that the FDA would quickly grant EUAs for the vaccines that would soon emerge from the clinical trial pipelines of Operation Warp Speed. What was totally unexpected was an out-of-left-field decision by the FDA's Center for Biologics Evaluation and Research (CBER) that would both flout Congress's intent and taunt the White House.

A DAY OF FDA INFAMY

On a fateful day, October 6, the CBER issued new guidelines requiring two months of safety data on at least half of the trial participants following the final dose of the vaccine before a company could get an EUA. As a matter of sheer calendar math, the practical effect of the FDA's announcement was to prevent Pfizer from even applying for an EUA until *a full two weeks **after** the election.* And here's the punch line: *That totally unnecessary **fait accompli** FDA decree* thereby *guaranteed there would be no good vaccine approval news for the Trump Campaign before the ballots were cast.*

Incredibly, officials in the Department of Health and Human Services—right up to Secretary Alex Azar—did not even learn of the new guidelines from the FDA or its commissioner, Stephen Hahn. Rather, they learned about the guidelines only from Pfizer and the pharmaceutical industry and only then after the news had been leaked to the press.

As a further gratuitous pile-on, after the FDA's October 6 kill shot, Pfizer took one more dance on the Trump vaccine grave. On October 16, Pfizer's Bourla published an open letter confirming his intent to wait until the third week of November to file for an EUA in accordance with the FDA's October 6 guidelines.

Of course, there was no need or requirement for Bourla to make any such statement. In point of fact, *an ethical Pfizer CEO who knew full well that the company was more than capable of delivering a vaccine well before the FDA's new deadline would have publicly protested the decision and mobilized the considerable lobbying power of Big Pharma to overturn it. Of course, that never happened, and Americans would die needlessly because of the FDA's delay.*

The question, of course, in the Curious Case of the Delayed Vaccine is: Why did the FDA take such a rogue action that would kill all hope of a Trump vaccine before election day? What might the agency's motive have been?

Certainly, within the FDA and the other alphabet-soup health care bureaucracies of the CDC, HHS, and NIH, there were deep rip currents of anti-Trump sentiment. I repeatedly saw this antipathy and partisanship up close and personal over the course of the pandemic.

Truth be told here, many of the health care bureaucrats simply despised us. Based on my numerous personal interactions, Stephen Hahn and Janet Woodcock at the FDA come immediately to my mind as virulent anti-Trumpers, as do Francis Collins and of course Anthony Fauci at the NIH.

Certainly, Bob Redfield at the CDC and the always arrogant Admiral Brett Giroir at HHS fall into the Deep Administrative State category as well. They both often wore their Never Trumpism on their sleeves and appeared to take no small amount of satisfaction in publicly contradicting the president.

In such ways, Hahn, Woodcock, Collins, Redfield, Giroir, and always Fauci created a permissive anti-Trump climate within their respective bureaucracies. In such a permissive climate—a particularly pernicious version of the "broken window theory"—DC's health care bureaucrats well knew that rogue anti-Trump decisions such as that made by the CBER and its director, Peter Marks, would be welcomed and applauded rather than punished or denounced.

In support of this assessment of a poisonous anti-Trump organizational culture within our health care bureaucracies, there is also this: when Fauci—the public face of these bureaucracies—was asked in early September whether the FDA should approve an EUA for Pfizer that might result in a vaccine before election day, the predictably passive-aggressive Fauci said this:

> If an EUA was granted before we had established that the vaccine was truly safe and effective, I would be disappointed. An EUA for a vaccine should be based on a considerable degree of safety and efficacy. . . . I would be against an EUA if it were issued without sufficient data to establish a strong signal of efficacy and safety.[21]

Note that nothing in this statement refers directly to the president. That is the passive aspect of the attack. Yet the statement, with its pointed use of the words "disappointed" and "against an EUA," suggests a highly aggressive move by Fauci to block President Trump's efforts to deliver a vaccine before election day. In effect, Fauci is clearly signaling to the

FDA and all its minions "If you want to stab Trump in the back, I've got *your* back."

BLOOD ON THE DEMOCRATS' HANDS

Of course, both the Biden camp and the anti-Trump media had a field day reporting all of the evil vaccine-delaying deeds of both the FDA and Pfizer—deeds that were in many ways the deadly fruit of a highly effective Democrat communications strategy.

That strategy had begun in earnest in the summer of 2020. Its goal had been to sow fear about and mistrust in the Trump vaccine so as to pressure both Pfizer and the FDA to delay the vaccine. It was a line of attack that clearly worked. In July, fully two-thirds of the American people trusted the vaccine. However, by the end of September and the eve of the first presidential debate, that number had fallen to an anemic 50 percent.[22]

This Labor Day weekend headline from *People* magazine in anticipation of the stretch run to election day perfectly encapsulates the Democrat strategy. Blared the headline, "Kamala Harris Says 'I Would Not Trust Donald Trump' with Coronavirus Vaccine as Death Toll Rises."[23]

Nor was that a one-and-done slip of the Harris tongue; she doubled down on the exact same message during the vice presidential debate on October 8, warning shrilly, "If the public health professionals, if Dr. Fauci, if the doctors tell us that we should take it, I'll be the first in line to take it, absolutely. But if Donald Trump tells us that we should take it, I'm not taking it."[24]

That, then, was the broader "blood on their hands" Biden-Harris playbook: elevate Anthony Fauci, trash Donald Trump, and make the public distrust the Pfizer vaccine. Never mind the impact that brass-knuckles strategy might have in delaying and suppressing the acceptance of the Pfizer vaccine—and thereby needlessly killing Americans. The whole point was to pressure both Pfizer and the FDA to delay approval until after election day—and that strategy, with the willing complicity of Pfizer and the FDA, worked like a deadly charm.

JEFF ZUCKER'S CNN ASSASSINS

For an anti-Trump media likewise intent on delaying the vaccine, the dilatory actions of Pfizer and the FDA provided a deliciously dizzying and seemingly unending combination of chum in the shark-infested Trump waters and manna from spin heaven.

- The *New York Times* would describe the Boss's pedal-to-the-metal quest as a "reckless obsession" that could "jeopardize safety, further erode public confidence in vaccines—and possibly kill."[25]
- Zucker's CNN opined, "If rushed, the likeliest result of October vaccinations . . . will be November fevers and sore arms and headaches—and perhaps even lawsuits and actual harm."[26]

Did those pontificators not understand this abiding fact of pandemic life: for every day that an otherwise safe and effective vaccine was delayed, thousands of Americans would die?

I think it is safe to say here that at least some journalists in the anti-Trump media did not carefully think through the consequences of their actions and were just behaving like obedient drone soldiers. At CNN, in particular, the word had come down from on high from the network's president, Jeff Zucker, that CNN's reporters and on-air talent were to do everything possible to defeat Donald Trump.[27] Clearly, selling fear and anxiety about a possibly rushed vaccine was squarely within the bull's-eye of that Trump Derangement Syndrome remit.

That said, I think it is equally safe to say that many journalists in the anti-Trump media—and certainly Jeff Zucker himself—knew *exactly* what they were doing. But like the brass-knuckled operatives in the Democrat Party pushing the "Do not trust the Trump vaccine" mantra, those journalists made a classic "the ends justify the means" choice: *it was better to defeat Orange Man Bad and be rid of him over the long second-term run than it was to save thousands of American lives in the short run.*

Mind you, the anti-Trump journalists who applauded Pfizer and its CEO for their prudence were the very same journalists who, under other circumstances, would have pilloried Pfizer, and more broadly Big Pharma, as profit-maximizing predators prone to price gouging senior citizens, cancer patients, and Third World countries.

It would all have been too funny if there had not been so much blood on so many hands: Pfizer and its CEO, Bourla; Big Pharma and its political action committees; the FDA and its rodent apparatchiks; Fauci, always Fauci; the Democrat Party, right up to its standard-bearers, Biden and Harris; and an anti-Trump media with CNN's General Zucker constantly leading a Pickett's Charge against ethical journalism.

THE BLOOD-ON-THEIR-HANDS BOTTOM LINE

If one takes the long view, the whodunit questions raised in the Curious Case of the Delayed Vaccine are much broader than any lost presidential campaign. They are questions that ultimately need to be answered, most likely by a truly bipartisan congressional committee.

Here, we would do well to recall the Spanish American philosopher George Santayana's famous admonition that those who cannot remember the past are condemned to repeat it. In this case, if we do not get fully to the bottom of the Curious Case of the Delayed Vaccine, such a delay may well happen again with equal, or perhaps even more, deadly consequences.

Of course, the other thing we need to get to the bottom of as a republic if this great and grand union called the United States of America is ever to stand again united is this: Was the 2020 presidential election stolen?

It is to this third rail of American journalism and the verboten Voldemort subject of our cable news networks that we now turn. Get ready for a rough ride, at least on Air Force One.

SEVENTEEN

SURFING ON AIR FORCE ONE AND BUGS ON A HARLEY WINDSHIELD

We may be entering one of the most chaotic periods in American history. It is very clear the Democrats are going to try to steal the election with absentee ballots and vote harvesting.

—Peter Navarro, journal entry, September 20, 2020

On the morning of November 1, I was looking forward to some comic relief—a big badass of a two-day barnstorming trip with the Boss on Big Bird One for ten "close the deal" rallies across seven battleground states. It doesn't get much better than that in Trump Land.

I knew, of course, that I wouldn't get to bed until four or five in the morning each day, and after the blitz was over I wouldn't just be dragging derriere, I'd be in the mumble tank. But it was history, I was going along for the ride, and we were on a glide path that I thought might even take us all the way home to a soft landing and second term.

A DRAG RACER ON NITRO

The worst part of any trip with the Boss was always the last, one-toke-over-the-fatigue-line, forty-minute bus ride from Joint Base Andrews back to the White House. That was the worst part *unless* you got one of the coveted few seats on POTUS's Marine One helicopter. That elegant bird would fly like an eagle seemingly within inches of the Washington Monument and get us back to home base in a quarter of the time.

Of course, one of the best parts of any trip on Air Force One was the takeoff. It is sudden, without much preparation, as you instantly rumble down the runway. There's no soothing voice telling you to "please take your seat," no martinet demanding that you put your seat belt on.

Nope. It's just slam-bam and off we go with Air Force One's "fly at the speed of sound" engines performing like a drag racer on nitro.

A GRIP AND GROAN WITH KIM JUNG-UN

Normally, on Air Force One, guests at the top of the influence chain are seated in the big conference room in the middle of the plane. It's got a nice long table with beautiful leather swivel chairs, a long couch on the left side of the room, and big-screen TVs at both the front and back of the table.

Then there is the soft carpet. It doubles as a decent bed to lie down on during the interminably long transcontinental red-eye trips I sometimes got to take with the Boss.

These were G20 trips such as the 2018 Buenos Aires and 2019 Osaka summits. That Osaka adventure, by the way, included an incredible leg to the Korean demilitarized zone and the Boss's grip and groan with Kim Jong-un. As the Nighthawks headed to our rendezvous with history flying low and loud over the South Korean landscape, I felt like an extra in *Apocalypse Now.*

THE BOSS AND I SURF BIG BIRD ONE

Though as senior staff I always had an assigned seat in one of the smaller executive cabins or among the seats immediately behind the conference room, I never used that seat. Instead, as soon as I got to the plane, I would hang out at the top of the stairs and get some sun and fresh air until the Boss's Marine One chopper landed. Then I would move inside the plane and make a beeline for the conference room, where I would remain for much of the journey.

I did that for two reasons. First, I quickly discovered that the conference room was a great place to do a little networking with whatever grand pooh-bahs might be on the plane that day—from captains of industry and cabinet officials to congressional leaders.

In fact, I met some of my very best allies and connections in that conference room. They include one of my all-time favorites, the now-retired congressman Sean Duffy, a true-blue MAGA man from the Badger State who would help me try to advance the Boss's beloved Reciprocal Trade Act on Capitol Hill.

Of course, the second reason I would make a beeline for the president's conference room was that it was always the very first place the Boss would go to when he boarded the plane. Ever the gracious host, he wanted to make sure that his guests felt comfortable.

One of the fun things I loved to do in that conference room during takeoffs was to crouch hands free like a surfer as the plane headed down the runway and up into the air and see how long I could hold my balance. Truth be told, the Boss liked to do something akin to the same thing.

As the Big Bird would shake, rattle, and roll down the runway and up into the red, white, and blue yonder, the leader of the Free World would just stand there holding court without holding on to anything. If the plane lurched a bit, it wouldn't faze him. It just showed me both how strong he is and why he's such a good golfer. With that kind of balance and his kind of build, it's pretty damn easy to hit the ball long, hard, and true.

At any rate, I'd like to tell you that I wound up on the Boss's Big Bird on November 1. But if I told you that, I'd be lying. Because sometime around noon that day, I got a curt email alert from the travel team that I had been scratched from the manifest.

Of course, I was molten lava hot when I got this news. So I immediately walked from my corner office in the Eisenhower Executive Office Building down the long hallway to where the folks on the advance team hung out. They were all very good folks, so I wasn't about to shoot the messenger. I just wanted to see who had elbowed me out of the way on what I knew to be a very crowded flight and whether my grounding might be fixable with a quick call to the Oval Office.

When I found out what had happened, my anger immediately melted into an outright laugh. I had been bumped by the last-minute addition of none other than Corey Lewandowski. Thought I, *if I had to get bumped by somebody, it might as well be one of my best buddies.*

As it turned out, it was a very good thing Corey went on the plane instead of me because he and his frequent coauthor, Dave Bossie, would become part of an absolutely priceless vignette, one that perfectly sets the stage for our discussion of the most sophisticated theft of an election in US history. So take it from here, Brother Corey, and tell us that tale.

> So Dave and I are stuffed like sardines in the back of the plane with none other than Jared Kushner, [Campaign Manager] Bill Stepien, and [Deputy Campaign Manager] Justin Clark. So at one point in the conversation, Bossie tells Kushner and Company point-blank, "You guys better be prepared for what's coming on election day."
>
> But all Jared said was how great everything was, how Stepien had done a perfect job since [Brad] Parscale had left twelve weeks ago, that they had everything under control, and things were beautiful.
>
> When Dave tried to press his case, Jared dismissed him with a pat on his head and said, "Hey, Dave, we've got it covered. If election day is our biggest problem, we're gonna be fine."
>
> Now, if you know Dave, he's not the kind of guy to take that kind of crap or give up. So Dave says, "Look, I'm telling you guys, I've done this, but you don't want to listen to me. I was a chief investigator for Congress, and I know what's coming, and you guys aren't ready." And Justin [Clark] was like "We've got more attorneys than we could ever use, and we are prepared."
>
> That night, as Dave and I walked off the plane. I said, "Dude, this thing is a f***ing shit show." And he asked me, "Do you want to go on the [Air Force One] trip tomorrow?" I said, "Hey, man, we've gone this far, so we gotta go."
>
> So we jumped on the plane for that last day and watched all of these guys congratulate themselves on

the campaign they ran. There's people dancing at the events and hugging each other, and saying "It's amazing what we've pulled off," etc., etc.

Nobody had any reality of what was coming. . . . They believed that the data indicated that they were in better shape than they were in 2016, that the absentee and mail-in ballot efforts were not going to impact them negatively, and they bought the messaging from the Republican National Committee spinmeisters who boasted, "We've knocked on more doors this cycle than ever in RNC history," and "We've transitioned the campaign from knocking on doors to online because we had to." Of course, come shortly after midnight on November fourth, reality would hit these Trump Campaign masterminds like they were bugs on a Harley-Davidson windshield.

EIGHTEEN

WE'VE GOT THIS! THEY STOLE IT!

I start the work day with a 7:10 AM radio hit with Bobby Gunther [Walsh] in Allentown Pennsylvania. Bobby's been around for 35 years, he has a perfect radio voice, he's pure Trump, and he understands exactly how his town has been screwed over by bad trade deals.

It's a cordial conversation and I get through to him by talking about the Philly shipyard and how all job creation is local. It is a great theme.

Once I get into the sweatshop, I do another radio hit [in] Gainesville Florida. . . . From there, I go out on the White House North Lawn and do a CBS live stream for something like 20 minutes. They let me run, no bad questions, and it's a good solid conversation. Nice.

That's about it for the day. I'm a burnt out case. I've left it all on the floor.

—PETER NAVARRO, JOURNAL ENTRY, DAY BEFORE ELECTION

I do a five minute hit on [Fox Business'] Charles Payne as my [TV] swansong for the election. Biden is in Scranton to beg forgiveness for destroying the manufacturing base in Pennsylvania with NAFTA and China. I joke with Charles that if Biden wins, you should [buy] Plexiglas, guns, and antidepressant stocks. . . .

I have a nice talk with Johnny Mac [John McEntee, the White House director of personnel]. We're just waiting to see how this goes but Johnny is ready to clean house . . . [FBI director] Chris Wray, [Secretary of Defense Mark] Esper, Fauci, Mnuchin [all gone]. . . .

At the 11th hour, Deborah Birx leaks one of her memos to the Washington Post *whining about how serious the crisis is. She might as well be [campaigning for] the Democrats. . . .*

At the East Wing [reception] . . . I see Rudy Giuliani crunching numbers and have a nice brief talk with Laura Ingraham. . . . I see [former acting attorney general] Matt Whitaker—a good guy who should be inside the building, not out. . . . The shining knight and light is Florida.

I see Pam Bondi and have a nice chat with her and [Florida campaign chair] Susie Wiles. [Both] did a great job down there [and] we cruised to a win.

There is indeed much at stake in this election—maybe for the country. The media once again did a great disservice to the president and this country by getting it so wrong. The question is whether this was hubris or intention.

—Peter Navarro, journal entry, election day

Election day, November 3, 2020, is also officially Pizza Night in the Roosevelt Room for the junior staff and communications team, courtesy of National Security Advisor Robert O'Brien. Starved as I am after working the phones and media all day, I drop by for a couple of thick-crust slices and a chat with Robert. Then, with heartburn on deck and heartache on the way, I leave the Roosevelt Room and head out the doors of the West Wing for a short stroll to the East Wing along the beautiful Colonnade.

This haunting historic corridor runs alongside the effervescent Rose Garden, and it was from the Colonnade that my favorite photo in presidential history was snapped: President John F. Kennedy in deep consultation with his brother Robert outside the Oval Office during the Cuban Missile Crisis.

Today I am walking in the footsteps of this history over to the East Wing of the White House. There I will watch the evening's election returns and schmooze with the star-studded throng.

POPS ON MY MIND, A FOX BACK STAB

My favorite feature of any East Wing social event is always the US Marine Band. Maybe it is because my father was a bandleader himself and I have fond memories of him on ballroom stages with his clarinet and sax directing his swing band ensemble, which usually included a drummer, a big stand-up bass, a waw-waw trumpeter (Frankie was the best), and an always beautiful female vocalist—I had my first crush on one of Pops' beauties after she sang her sultry version of "On the Street Where You Live" one very serene night in Lake George.

Though Pops' Glenn Miller style of music was as far from the playlist of the US Marine Band as the Waldorf Astoria ballroom is from the halls of Montezuma, there is just something about this supremely talented uniformed group of musicians that triggers memories. Like Marcel Proust's madeleine, this band always makes me drift back to my childhood days and remembrances of venues past, such as the Eden Roc, Fontainebleau, and Mount Washington Hotel—and Pops before he left Mom and Brad and me.

That night, as I walk up the stairs to the gala in the East Room and am greeted at the top by the sight and sounds of the Marine Band, I immediately see one of my favorite peeps, Judge Jeanine Pirro. She's holding court with a group of friends and admirers so I just give her a big smile and howdy wave. Then, as I walk past the band and into the crowded hallway, there's Brother Corey. I stop for a quick man hug and high five to his wife and kids.

Down the hall, Sarah Sanders pops up as though it is a college reunion. In one of the ante rooms, Kellyanne Conway looks as if she never left. There are Matt Whitaker, Pam Bondi, Director of Operations for Political Affairs Caroline Wiles, the first lady's chief of staff, Stephanie Grisham, and the Cipollone clan (all dozen of them). And strolling through the crowd, I can smell more than a little Big Money in the room as a gaggle of donors have earned one last return on their investment with front-row seats to history.

As the polls close and the returns begin to roll across the TV screens scattered around the rooms, the mood is all nerves, and the down-home sliders, chicken tenders, and fries all come with nervous chatter. I've got a pit in my own stomach—from either O'Brien's pizza or nerves. Hell, let's not kid ourselves. It's nerves.

And let's not kid ourselves about this, either: by midnight, the Boss is very well on his way to winning a second term. He's an absolute lock to take Ohio and Florida. And he has huge, seemingly insurmountable leads in the Blue Walls of Michigan, Pennsylvania, and Wisconsin.

The only off-key note in this second-term song is a far-too-early call at 11:20 p.m.[1] of Arizona for Joe Biden by Fox News. As groans and boos ripple through the East Wing crowd, you can almost hear the Boss over in the residence bellowing at the TV. And you can almost see Roger Ailes do a triple spin in his grave.

As soon as I see Fox's pissant move, I know that it will cost us votes in Arizona, where the polls are still open and at least some discouraged Trump voters are likely to stay home. I think to myself as I watch this sacrilege—one not even justified by the voting patterns we are witnessing—*With Ailes in the ground, no true Trump Republican is on guard in one heckuva divided Fox henhouse.*

Shortly before midnight, my phone rings above the din, and it's Steve Bannon. He's doing an Election Special on his *War Room: Pandemic* podcast broadcasting live from the rooftop of 101 Constitution Avenue—hands down the best view in town, at least of the US Capitol, National Mall, and Washington Monument. Says Steve with barely contained ebullience, "We've got this!"

And that's my cue to head home. If Steve says we've won, we've won—no one crunches electoral vote numbers better than Steve. And in 2016, he had gotten it exactly right early on election night, when everyone else had been moaning that the sky was falling.

So I leave the East Wing, backtrack along the Colonnade and past the Rose Garden, wend my way through the labyrinth of the West Wing basement, and head over to my office in the Eisenhower building. There, like Clark Kent, I pull off my suit and change into my workout clothes.

I then throw my coat and gloves on, grab my bike propped up against a wall in my office, walk down the stairs and out the door, and pedal to the metal home in the brisk night air.

At 6:00 a.m., Bannon wakes me from a fitful sleep with a second phone call and this outrage: "They stole it!"

NINETEEN

A WEST WING SURRENDER AND A WHITE-SHOE REBUFF

My sober assessment of the effort is that we are a day late and about 20 lawyers short—20 good lawyers short of an effort that could actually undo this election in favor of the president.

—Peter Navarro, journal entry, November 21, 2020

For the first week after the election, I go about my business at the White House. My mission is to get a six-pack of additional "Buy American" executive orders to the finish line in what is now effectively a lame-duck administration.

One EO would swiftly bring the US Postal Service into conformance with our tough "Buy American" government procurement rules. It would help ensure that a pending $6 billion contract for delivery vehicles would go to American manufacturers rather than the Indians or Turks.[1] MAGA forever!

A second EO would prohibit government departments such as Interior, Justice, and Homeland Security from using US tax dollars to procure or fly Chinese drones.[2] It is insane that we have high-tech Communist drone spies swarming American skies, particularly over sensitive government lands. This must end!

Still a third "Buy American" EO would end a government procurement deal signed in 1995 under the umbrella of POTUS's bête noire, the World Trade Organization. The Agreement on Government Procurement[3] requires US government agencies to treat more than fifty foreign countries *as if they are on US soil* for the purpose of awarding "Buy American" contracts.

So under the agreement, "Made in Germany" equals "Made in America"—yet more frigging insanity that we've vowed to do away with.

A point to note: these kinds of Globalist provisions that deprive the United States of its manufacturing rights are hidden in the fine print of many government contracts signed by past administrations. Do you see the value of a second Trump term?

NOT MY LANE, NOT MY JOB

As I pursue my executive order end game, my assumption is that Jared Kushner and Campaign Manager Bill Stepien are moving into high gear to challenge election results that appear sketchy at best and stolen at worst. Under this assumption, working on any election challenge is not my lane and not my job.

Yet as I go about my White House business this first week after the election, there are all manner of troubling signs that there may not be either the will or the means to fight what may well turn out to be the last battle of Donald J. Trump's political life.

One warning sign comes two days after the election at a senior staff meeting on November 5. While the meeting is scheduled as a video conference call, I schlep over to the chief of staff's office in the West Wing. Surely, Mark Meadows must be in the building working with the Boss, and I want to grab a little face time with him to discuss my executive orders.

No such luck. Instead, like much of the senior staff, Meadows is phoning the meeting in—both literally and figuratively. Wherever the heck he is, he sounds like Napoleon after Waterloo getting ready to be shipped out to Elba.

As Ivanka Trump and acting director of the Domestic Policy Council Brooke Rollins wistfully prattle on at the virtual meeting about how much good we have done over the last four years, I almost gag on their defeatist rhetoric.

Duly alarmed, I have a long phone call that night with the Hassett Man. Kevin Hassett let me know earlier in the day that he has picked up enough anomalies in his preliminary analysis to suggest that chicanery is indeed in the air. According to a very concerned Kevin, as I would note in my journal before going to bed that night:

> *Across the broad swath of battleground states, there appears to have been a cookie-cutter . . . effort to steal the election.*
>
> *Commonalities include: Halting of the vote count to determine just how big a margin would have to be erased by fraud; the appearance of large quantities of [harvested] bundled votes with questionable provenance; the inability of poll watchers to observe possible fraud; [and] the rejection of lawsuits based on the Catch-22 of an inability to provide evidence of fraud. Thus far, this is The Immaculate Deception.*

Two days later, on November 7, war officially breaks out between the Kushner-led Trump Campaign and a team led by the president's lawyer, Rudy Giuliani. On a phone call with

Matt Morgan, one of the Trump Campaign lawyers, all I hear are complaints about alleged "grandstanding" by Giuliani. Yet when pressed, Morgan can provide no assurances that the Trump Campaign will fully engage in the legal fight.

With my mother on her deathbed, I am in absolutely no mood for this kind of bull ship and backbiting. As I noted in my journal about my mother's now rapidly accelerating march to the grave:

> *So much pain. And morphine. Florida really needs a euthanasia law. This is unacceptable.*

She would be gone two days later. One of her last dying acts was to call up and cancel her subscription to the *Palm Beach Post* newspaper so as not to squander our inheritance. She was, as they might have said in her time, "one helluva broad."

THE CCP VIRUS STRIKES AGAIN

On Sunday, November 8, bad luck and CCP Virus trouble once again hit the West Wing. Keenly aware of the internecine warfare between the Kushner and Giuliani forces, the Boss has called up Dave Bossie and told him to take charge. The long-overdue transfer of power is supposed to take place this afternoon in the Oval Office at a big powwow with all concerned.

As I walk down the steps of the Eisenhower Executive Office Building that afternoon to head over to the West Wing, I see none other than Bossie himself. He has the most forlorn look on his face I have ever seen, and I am frankly perplexed.

Usually this burly bear of a man has a perpetual snarling grin on his face—as though he is about to have a big burger and a beer or eat a Democrat for lunch. But as I approach my good brother Dave, he puts up both of his boxer's hands to stop me in my tracks and says, "I just got tested before the POTUS meet, and the doc says I've got the virus."

I'm speechless. All I can think is *The trials of Job were jollier*, and this is indeed a bitter blow.

For all practical purposes, Bossie, the one guy with the experience from the Bush v. Gore election fight who might be able to save us, is now out of both the Oval Office meeting and the legal defense game. Bad luck and trouble indeed.

The next day, November 9, more dumb manure rolls downhill. During a drop-by at the Oval Office, I catch the Boss in the dining room off the Oval being egged on by a small gaggle of sycophants urging him to announce a run for president in 2024. I tell him flat out that it is a dumb idea because it will serve as a tacit admission that the 2020 election is over and done.

Say I in no uncertain terms, "What you damn well need to do right now is fight!"

Four days later, on November 13, I have another important opportunity to reiterate this message. That afternoon, I am summoned by Austin Ferrer, one of the Outer Oval gatekeepers, for a private POTUS meet. As I will note that night in my journal:

> *The Boss is in good spirits. I tell him right off the bat that he needs to fight hard to the end, get himself a crack legal team, and raise the money necessary to win this battle. Either by coincidence or by some contribution I may have made to his thinking, Steve [Bannon] tells me later in the day that the Boss called the campaign and issued a decree for a major shakeup.*

> *Justin Clark and Bill Stepien are out. Rudy's [team] is in charge [and] Jason Miller will report to them. This is all good news.*

And it would have been good news if Jared Kushner, Bill Stepien, and Justin Clark hadn't still been holding the purse strings for the effort. As we shall see, these three will do everything they can to sabotage Rudy's efforts even as they drag their heels on their own efforts.

RIDING TO THE SOUND OF THE GUNS

As this bad luck and trouble are unfolding, and to support the challenge effort, I allow several members of my staff to help out in the battleground states on their own time.

Joanna Miller and her mother join Corey Lewandowski and Pam Bondi in the Pennsylvania ring. No patriotic deed apparently goes unpunished, however, as Corey would wind up coming down with a bad case of the CCP Virus.

The young and always earnest Garrett Ziegler rides to the sound of the guns in Nevada. He will soon find himself crisscrossing an Indian reservation investigating outrageously illegitimate bribes for Biden votes.

Back at the White House, as the disquieting reports begin to filter in from the field, it is becoming increasingly clear that the Trump Campaign has indeed been caught with its legal pants down—just as Corey and Dave Bossie and others including attorney Cleta Mitchell warned.

Though Jared Kushner, Bill Stepien, and Justin Clark have all boasted about having thousands of lawyers ready to roll in every state where there might be even a hint of a challenge, the woefully underlawyered Trump campaign is now doing its best impression of General George Custer at Little Big Horn.

Cleta Mitchell, by the way, is as pro-Trump as it comes, and for her Trumpism, she will soon be canceled by the firm for whom she worked. Just disgusting stuff.

In one of the most revealing phone conversations I have ever had, Cleta tells me that as far back as May 2019, she put out a full alert to both the Trump Campaign and the Republican National Committee that the Democrats were getting ready to steal the election. In one instance, she met with Brad Parscale and told him that the campaign could use soft money from donors to finance the kind of legal counterstrike that was going to be necessary. To show you how out of touch with reality Brad the computer geek often is, he told Cleta, an election law specialist, that her idea was illegal.

Cleta also tells me that she put out an SOS to both Mark Meadows at the White House and Justin Clark at the Trump Campaign in September 2020. When she asked Meadows why the campaign had never acted on her advice, all Meadows had to say was, "It just didn't happen."

As for Justin Clark, Cleta does not mince words. She tells me flat out that Clark is unforgivably incompetent. Seems that Clark hired several attorneys for the Trump Campaign in Georgia but by definition, they could not now help on election fraud issues. This is because they are also working for the Georgia secretary of state and therefore conflicted out.[4] Talk about wasted money.

GLOBALIST WHITE SHOE HARDBALL IN THE SWAMP

A second fact increasingly in evidence is equally troubling. As the now-desperate Trump Campaign begins to send urgent pleas for help to legal firms across Washington, DC, none is ready to step up to the plate. Moreover, the problem is all the more acute in the so-called white-shoe prestigious law firms, where the top election law talent resides.

The poster child for the Big Trump Rebuff is Jones Day, the fifth largest law firm in the United States. Jones Day represented the Trump campaigns in both 2016 and 2020 as outside counsel. Yet when it comes time to help challenge the election results, Jones Day goes out of its way to announce to the world that it is "not representing President Trump, his campaign, or any affiliated party in any litigation alleging voter fraud."[5]

So why are the DC Legal Swampists suddenly abandoning President Trump in droves? The reason has nothing to do with personal feelings toward individuals or even the legal merits of any case. Rather, it is the hardball Globalist Swamp reality of Washington, DC.

It is both a simple and stark fact that the vast majority of the billable hours for firms such as Jones Day are paid for by large multinational corporations such as General Motors and Wall Street's Goldman Sachs. As a matter of profit-maximizing practice, these Globalist elites love to offshore their supply chains. And they hate just about everything about the Trump trade, "Buy American," and "America First" policies.

But with Jones Day in particular, I see the frozen legal shoulder as both a form of "Karma is a bitch" and a big F-U from one of the major partners in Jones Day, former White House legal counsel Don McGahn.

We have talked earlier about McGahn's lack of loyalty to both the president and his agenda along with Don's rough trade firing. So it should come as no surprise that Jones Day might want to help McGahn get some measure of Humpty Trumpty revenge.

Yet Jones Day is but the tip of the white-shoe, cold-shoulder iceberg. More than one lawyer I know who had worked at the White House urgently wants to help POTUS. Yet, these Trump Loyalists are not only being forbidden to do so by their law firms upon penalty of being fired; they are also being told that if they help the Boss, they will be canceled—they will never work in the Swamp again. These are Republicans, mind you, being threatened by other Republicans in law firms traditionally aligned with the Republican Party.[6]

Note to self: The Washington Nationals are not the only ones playing hardball in the nation's capital.

By the way, in another big F-U to the Boss, McGahn lists on the Jones Day website a nice little testimonial from another Trump bête noire, Senate Majority Leader Mitch McConnell. Swoons Mitch the Turtle, Don concluded his tenure "not only as the best White House Counsel I've seen on the job, but more broadly, as one of the most successful and consequential aides to any President in recent memory."[7]

Between God and Mammon, you just gotta love how these Swamp Creatures stick together like pigs in a velveteen blanket.

A FLAG OF SURRENDER OVER THE WEST WING

Ultimately, what is bothering me most in these several weeks after the election is the white flag of surrender that seems to have settled over the West Wing. Whenever I see Dan Scavino, he tells me how angry the Boss is about an election that both he and Dan know full well was stolen.

Yet in the same breath, Dan grouses about all the people who want the Boss to accept the loss gracefully, including the vice president (and that should have been a warning).

Mostly, what bothers me about the whole flag-of-surrender situation is that I simply cannot get my hands or head around what exactly has happened—much less any straight answers from anybody.

So it is that heading into the Thanksgiving holiday, I decide to put my Big Boy Harvard Researcher Pants on and get to the bottom of all this.

Definitively answering the question of whether the election was in fact stolen will now be not just my lane; it will also be my most important mission, not just for the Boss but for the Republic.

TWENTY

DUMB SONS OF BITCHES AND THE IMMACULATE DECEPTION

Sidney Powell remains a rogue cipher. If she truly has no evidence, she will have single-handedly destroyed our credibility. It is shameful how she is refusing to cooperate.

—Peter Navarro, journal entry, November 22, 2020

When I was learning how to write journal articles and eventually my Harvard PhD thesis, I used to spend long days and longer nights over at the MIT library. I liked to hang over in Geek Land rather than the button-down, bow-tie Widener Library at Harvard because MIT's library was quieter and less crowded. MIT also had the added benefit of more laissez-faire librarians who wouldn't wake me up when I took naps on the floor or bug me if brought food to sustain my quest.

At the library, the first thing I did was photocopy one or two seminal articles about the subject I was looking into and then read them carefully three or four times. Then I would read every journal article cited in these seminal articles along with *all* of the articles cited in *those* articles. Eventually, through that ever-expanding net, I would complete what they call in my trade the "literature review."

As I conducted the lit review, I would take copious notes and yellow-highlight relevant passages. But far more important, I would also begin to connect the threads of the broader tapestry of my investigation.

As I wove these threads together, I would begin to recognize various patterns. Those patterns would in turn lead me to hypotheses along with possible empirical lines of attack to test those hypotheses.

This is still pretty much my process. And it was that process I brought into the White House over the Thanksgiving weekend to investigate the November 3 presidential election.

My initial focus was on Arizona, Georgia, Michigan, Nevada, Pennsylvania, and Wisconsin. Each of these six battleground states appeared to be rife with fraud and election irregularities and riddled with statistical anomalies, and it had been in these six states where Biden had allegedly won the election.

If we simply clawed back Arizona with its 11 electoral votes and Georgia with its 16 votes, that would take Biden down from 306 Electoral College votes to just 279. In that scenario, all we would need do is pick up just one Blue Wall state to achieve the Trump victory: Michigan, Pennsylvania, or Wisconsin.

If, however, we were unable to successfully challenge Arizona and Georgia, successful reversals in Michigan and Pennsylvania plus a clawback of Nevada would still keep the Boss in the White House. And so the various scenarios went.

That was not wishful thinking; it was a strategy based on facts, evidence, and a reversal of errors.

And so when I arrived at my office early Thanksgiving morning, I was pleased to see on my conference table and an adjacent table a veritable mountain of three-ring binders that several volunteers from my staff had compiled.

One set of binders included literally thousands upon thousands of affidavits and declarations that had been collected across the battleground states. Another contained all the relevant legal filings, rulings, and judgments. Still another contained all of the various newspaper articles and cable news transcripts about the election.

Of course, all of the binders had digital analogues on my computer. But I am old school and much prefer printed pages, a yellow highlighter, a red pen for marginal notes, and a legal pad for other notes.

And so the process began as I started to pour through the mountain of information. By the end of Thanksgiving weekend—no turkey, no football, no problem—my hypotheses had crystallized around the broad concept of "election irregularities" rather than the more one-dimensional issue of election fraud. In fact, one of the most important results of the investigation was this: *There was no single "silver bullet" the Democrats had shot to kill the Trump campaign. Rather, it was "death by a thousand cuts." Or, more precisely, "death by a thousand election irregularities."*

KUSHNER & COMPANY PLAY "HIDE THE MONEY"

My investigation would go on for several weeks, and as I got deeper and deeper into the nitty and stolen gritty, I had to change my initial working assumption that Jared Kushner, Campaign Manager Bill Stepien, and Deputy Campaign Manager Justin Clark were simply incompetent.

Yes, they had been caught unprepared despite repeated warnings dating back months. The historical marker of Bush v. Gore should, in and of itself, have been enough motivation to have a massive legal team ready.

Yet slowly but surely, I began to see a possibly more malignant set of motives behind the failure of these key Trump campaign operatives to mount an aggressive postelection legal challenge.

With the election over, Kushner, Stepien, and Clark—each for his own specific reasons—seemed to simply want President Trump to pull a General MacArthur or Cincinnatus and either fade away or simply go back to his private-sector plow. That suspicion would arise in two ways.

First, the campaign was sitting on what I was told was over $70 million. Yet Kushner and Company not only refused to spend any substantial money on the investigation and legal defense. They refused to help fully fund the effort of the two guys trying to lead an aggressive charge: "America's mayor," Rudy Giuliani, and his field general, Bernie Kerik.

My thought was that the more money that was left in the Trump Campaign kitty, the more would be available for Stepien and Clark as political consultants for what already looked like a possible 2024 run by the Boss. "So why burn that money now on lawyers?" might be their thinking.

Second, Kushner and Company were withholding something more valuable than money, which is to say information. And the most important information they were withholding was what I was hearing were "blockbuster results" from a comprehensive investigation conducted by a fraud specialist, Berkeley Research Group.

The Berkeley Research Group—with forty offices on six continents, including an office in Beijing—received more than half a million dollars for its investigative efforts on behalf of the Trump Campaign.[1] Yet to this day, as far as I can gather, virtually none of their research has seen the light of day.

As it turned out, a good part of the problem in getting any smoking-gun analytics from the Berkeley Group might well be traced back to the fate of an expert witness named Charles Cicchetti. I actually knew Charlie from the days when I was heavily involved in the law and economics of electric utility regulation while at Harvard. He was a frequent expert witness in utility cases, and his star reputation had only grown since then.

Yet what happened to Charlie for having the temerity to challenge the election results was a cautionary tale in American fascism's new Cancel Culture environment. Charlie's alleged "sin" was to provide testimony in a case filed by Texas attorney general Ken Paxton before the US Supreme Court challenging the election results.[2]

The case, filed on December 8, 2020, argued that four defendant states—Georgia, Michigan, Pennsylvania, and Wisconsin—had all ignored both federal and state election laws behind the shield of the pandemic. Their illegal acts thereby had helped elect Joe Biden instead of Donald Trump, thereby in turn disenfranchising Texas voters.

The Cicchetti testimony turned out to be the star of the Texas AG show, as Charlie opined in a statistical shot heard round the daily news cycle that "The probability of former Vice President Biden winning the popular vote in the four Defendant States . . . given President Trump's early lead in those States as of 3 a.m. on November 4, 2020, is less than one in a quadrillion."[3]

Translation for the statistically disinclined: the election was stolen beyond any shadow of a shadow of probabilistic doubt.

In the wake of his testimony, Cicchetti was tossed like a Caesar salad by the anti-Trump media.[4] He was also repeatedly strafed by a large squadron of anti-Trump academic elites.[5]

My guess based on the intel I was receiving is that the folks at the Berkeley Research Group had taken one look at the public gutting of Cicchetti and decided that the chance of it happening to them if they continued to help Donald J. Trump was considerably more than one in a quadrillion.

Then there was this additional possible disincentive: the social media oligarch Google canceled a major contract with the Berkeley Research Group allegedly because of its association with the Trump election fraud fight—this according to one deeply placed source who I have no reason to doubt. If true—and Google has been extremely aggressive in promoting its Cancel Culture tactics across its many platforms—there may have been a logical fear within the Berkeley Group that it would lose even more business if it continued to help Donald Trump.

Of course, the other big fly in the data analytics ointment that I had to keep banging my head against was the highly counterproductive antics of the attorney Sidney Powell. To her credit, she had fought a long, slow battle to liberate former national security advisor General Michael Flynn from the clutches of the Russia Hoax FBI sting that had illegally engulfed him. Yet I must confess that anytime I saw Sidney on Fox News—or for that matter in the Fox studio greenroom in DC—she never impressed me as the Second Coming of Clarence Darrow.

Ever since election day, Powell had repeatedly gone on television to make extravagant claims about election fraud. It all came to a head on November 20 when Fox's Tucker Carlson rightly ripped into her for failing to put up but not shut up.[6]

The problem with Powell's claims was not so much the statements themselves but her abject refusal to provide even a scintilla of evidence that they were true—much less provide the infamous "Kraken"[7] that Powell claimed would crack the case wide open. Moreover, in her competition to be the Top Legal Dog for the Boss in the election fraud fight, she refused to hand over any documents to either the Trump Campaign or the Rudy Team.

Let me be crystal clear for the historical record: *Damn Dame Powell did incalculable harm to the battle against election fraud with her zaniness. Through guilt by association, she enabled the anti-Trump media to tar us all with her Gone to Crazy Town brush.*

That Powell's ultimate defense against a slap-suit lawsuit filed to shut her up was that the stuff she had said was so crazy that nobody would ever believe her was in and of itself zany.[8]

Let the history books, then, assign Sidney Katherine Powell to an appropriate dust bin. She more than earned it.

MITCH THE TURTLE'S TWISTED MISCALCULATION

There was, of course, one other possible source of data that would have been invaluable to any investigation: the Republican National Committee (RNC). Yet that would turn out to be a dry analytical hole as well—and the primary reason was Senate Majority Leader and all too Traditional Republican Mitch McConnell.

True to his Never Trump form, McConnell began doing everything possible behind his politically obscene scenes both to pressure President Trump into accepting the election result and to put the RNC off the election fraud scent.[9]

Of course, Mitch the Turtle is always playing a game within a game within a game. In this game, McConnell believed that with Trump out of the way, he—not Speaker of the House Nancy Pelosi, Senate Minority Leader Chuck Schumer, or even Joe Biden—would become the most powerful politician in the United States.

Here is how the Turtle's twisted calculus went: with the Democrats controlling both the White House and the House of Representatives, a Republican Senate would represent a secure life raft in a treacherous sea of progressive policies that would otherwise sink the Republic.

In the midst of this progressive craziness, Mitch's life raft would be boarded by those Republicans who were worried about massive tax hikes and a rapid expansion of the regulatory state. Think here (as Mitch certainly did) equally massive infusions of cash into GOP Senate coffers from frantic and freaked-out large corporate donors and the Globalist Koch Money Network.

At the same time—and Mitch found this absolutely delicious—both Pelosi and Schumer would have to go to Mitch hat in hand, knees on the ground, to get anything done. And in those negotiations, the likes of Elizabeth Warren and Bernie Sanders would be left-winged out in the Mitch McConnell righteous and right-winged cold—just like, I might add, during the Obama years of divided government, when Mitch had often reigned supreme.

Of course, McConnell's strategy all hinged upon the Republicans hanging on to the Senate. But his strategy quickly became unhinged in what may well be both one of the most massive miscalculations in US politics *and* the single best example of an American politician hoisted on his own petard. Let's connect those dots now.

For the Republicans to maintain control of the Senate, they would have to win at least one of the two Senate seats up for grabs in an upcoming January 5, 2021, runoff election in Georgia, where Republican incumbents David Perdue and Kelly Loeffler were facing off against two Democrat radicals, Jon Ossoff and Raphael Warnock. *If Mitch could keep just one of those Senate seats in the GOP column, he'd have a 51–49 majority.*

If not, there would be tie votes in the Senate, and the tie-breaker would be none other than Democrat Kamala Harris, the president of the Senate and vice president of this country. In that scenario, Chuck Schumer would become Senate majority leader and McConnell would go from the penthouse of power straight to the outhouse of irrelevance.

Of course, what McConnell should have done to ensure his path to power was join hands with President Trump in the battle against election chicanery, at least in Georgia. Here, any damn fool could see that Perdue and Loeffler were likely to have their elections stolen in the runoff unless the severe and systemic election fraud and irregularities in Georgia were addressed prior to that election.

In fact, the damn fool writing this book even went on TV in late December to warn of this possibility and to call for a postponement of the January 5 election pending a full investigation of the "cesspool" of fraud and irregularities otherwise known as Georgia's election system.[10]

By the way, on March 25, 2021, Republican governor Brian Kemp signed into law a sweeping election reform bill.[11] Though the anti-Trump media and liberal elites spun it as new "Jim Crow" restrictions on voting rights, all the legislation really did was help ensure that all *legal* votes are counted.

If that legislation had been in place prior to January 5—or if the runoff election had been postponed until the reforms were put in place—both Perdue and Loeffler would almost certainly have been elected, Republicans would be in control of the US Senate, and Mitch McConnell would still be King of the Washington Swamp.

Of course, rather than find common cause with President Trump, Mitch McConnell waged a behind-the-scenes war against the Boss within both the Senate and the RNC. As to why he did so, look no further than the Democrats' most useful idiot, Republican strategist Karl Rove.

For those of you who do not watch a lot of Fox News, Rove made his bones as the campaign mastermind for George W. Bush's 2000 and 2004 victories. Fast-forward to 2021, and Rove was the campaign guru for Perdue, Loeffler, and the Georgia Senate runoff elections.[12]

It is hardly a secret in Washington that Karl Rove despises Donald Trump, as the Boss has never turned down an opportunity to dump on Rove and Bush, along with Dick Cheney, for turning the Middle East into a giant Endless War sinkhole for American treasure, severed limbs, and corpses. As to why this matters, Karl Rove counseled candidates Loeffler and Perdue to put Trump at a distance during the runoff election rather than embrace Trumpism and thereby consolidate and energize the Republican base.

The perverse result of Rove's anti Trump strategy was that Georgia voters elected two Democrat senators to the left of Karl Marx in a state that leans heavily center right.

In April 2021, Donald Trump called Mitch McConnell a "dumb son of a bitch."[13] There are certainly a lot of reasons why the Boss got *that* exactly right. But the biggest reason must surely be McConnell's role—with a Karl Rove assist—in losing Republican control of the Senate. The McConnell-Rove Brainless Trust thereby turned America the Beautiful over to the Band of Sandinistas now controlling both the House and

Senate as well as the White House; at least Mark Levin's latest opus, *American Marxism*, will sell a lot of copies.

BILL BARR'S BUSHIE WHACKING

Though Mitch McConnell and Karl Rove may rightly be called "dumb sons of bitches," no one would dare apply that moniker to former Bush and Trump administration attorney general Bill Barr. Yet Barr would do every bit as much dumb damage as McConnell and Rove in his own Traditional Republican way.

After the November 3 election, as signs continued to mount that Democrat mischief had indeed been done, I fully expected Barr's Justice Department to step into the investigative breach. Weeks went by, however, and neither the FBI nor DOJ got off the investigative dime. Finally, on November 24, I called Bill on his private cell phone to plead my case for him to man up, lawsuit up, and get onto the damn playing field.

I must confess that when the Boss appointed Barr attorney general on December 7, 2018, to replace Jeff Sessions, I found his choice inexplicable. Once again, we had a Traditional, non-Trumpian Republican and confirmed Bushie put into yet another ultraimportant position of power.

My trepidations notwithstanding, Bill and I forged a strong bond over the next several years, primarily because we were at least sometimes Brothers and Hawks in Arms in the Situation Room on the topic of Communist China. It was one thing for me to take on Steve Mnuchin and Larry Kudlow alone; it was quite another when Bill Barr stepped up to the Sit Room plate and got into Mnuchin's and Kudlow's grills.

Because of that bond, Bill was always happy to take my calls—although in this case, he may have regretted it. Here is my journal entry for November 24:

> *The big event of the day was a 20-minute conversation with Bill Barr who totally rejects the idea of any Federal Justice Department intervention in the case. He reminded me that Bush v. Gore was done entirely by private sector lawyers representing the campaign.*

After I got off the phone with Bill, I felt disappointed, but I respected his difference of opinion. Yes, Bill, maybe you are right. Maybe it should be just the Trump Campaign and the Republican National Committee that fight this fight.

But here is where Bill Barr went off the Trumpian rails—or perhaps back to his Bush Loyalist roots. In an interview with the Associated Press barely a week after our phone call, he asserted that "we [in the Justice Department] have not seen fraud on a scale that could have effected a different outcome in the election."[14]

Oh, really, Bill, thought I. *How the bleep can you say that there is no evidence of widespread fraud when by your own admission to me, your own Justice Department has refused to investigate such fraud. And may I remind you, Bill, that you refused to investigate because, again by your own words during our phone conversation, you insisted that that is the job of the "private sector."*

Of course, Barr's Bushie-Whacking of the president on December 1 went viral across the anti-Trump media. The obligatory spin that spun like a whirling dervish was this: See Trump, even your own Attorney General thinks you are a liar.[15]

Yes, I was hotter than a Rolex in a Shanghai street market. The only person hotter was the Boss himself.

So bleep you, Bill Barr, not once but twice. That was just wrong, and that Bill Barr Bushie-Whack was yet one more piece of bitter fruit falling from the bad personnel tree of the Trump White House.

THE BIRTH OF *THE IMMACULATE DECEPTION*

It would take me another few weeks after Thanksgiving weekend to actually finish the report that I would title *The Immaculate Deception.* I released the report on December 17, and after holding a press conference by phone with a couple of hundred reporters, I was pleased to walk over a copy to the Oval Office and hand it to the Boss.

As part of the package, I also brought a big poster board that had the proverbial money shot and smoking gun from the report. This was a six-by-six matrix that showed how all six battleground states had been plagued by most or all of the six categories of election irregularities I had uncovered. The categories, which range from outright fraud, ballot mishandling, and contestable process fouls to Equal Protection Clause violations, voting machine irregularities, and significant statistical anomalies—were prominently featured in all of the six battleground states.

2020 Presidential Election Irregularities

	ARIZONA	GEORGIA	MICHIGAN	NEVADA	PENNSYLVANIA	WISCONSIN
Outright Voter Fraud	✓	✓		✓		✓
Ballot Mishandling		✓	✓	✓	✓	✓
Contestable Process Fouls	✓	✓	✓	✓	✓	✓
Equal Protection Clause Violations	✓	✓	✓	✓	✓	✓
Voting Machine Irregularities	✓	✓		✓	✓	
Significant Statistical Anomalies	✓	✓	✓	✓		

SOURCE: The Navarro Report, Volume One, The Immaculate Deception

After carefully studying this "one picture is worth a thousand steals" matrix, the Boss called Molly Michael into the Oval office and told her to make sure that every member of the House of Representatives and Senate had a copy on their desks by tomorrow morning. "Sir, yes, sir," was her reply, and within the hour, my staffer Joanna Miller was working with Molly to send digital copies of the report to Capitol Hill.

Now, I am not going to burden you here with the deepest of dives into what my investigation found. Instead, I'm going to end this chapter with just a very brief overview of the six dimensions of fraud and irregularities that I identified along with some of the most important findings.

If you are not convinced by the time you finish this brief overview that the 2020 election was likely stolen, please go to my website at www.peternavarro.com and read the full three-volume Navarro Report.

I can tell you without equivocation that the winner of the 2020 election is not sitting in the White House today—and that should give all of us pause.

A SURFEIT OF VOTER FRAUD

Let's start with the problem of *outright fraud.* Here the categories range from bribery, fake ballots, and dead voters to ballots counted multiple times and ineligible voters such as illegal aliens and out-of-state voters.

The most brazen bribery occurred in the Silver State of Nevada, where Native Americans traded their Joe Biden votes for Visa gift cards along with jewelry and other "swag."[16] According to the *Epoch Times*, such vote-buying schemes may also have occurred in Arizona and Wisconsin.[17]

One of the most disturbing examples of possible fake ballots involved a truck driver who picked up large crates of ballots in New York and delivered them in the dead of night to a polling location in the battleground of Pennsylvania.[18] To this day, neither the suspect tractor-trailer nor the mysterious ballots—likely measuring in the tens of thousands—have been run to ground.

Still a third fraud, which played an outsized role in Wisconsin, involved so-called *indefinitely confined voters*. This category, which requires a much lower level of voter identification check, is normally restricted to the elderly and disabled. However, after Wisconsin election officials broadened that definition to include pretty much anybody, the number of indefinitely confined voters surged in the Badger State from just under 70,000 voters in 2019 to over 200,000 in 2020.[19]

Note that the 130,000-vote increment of new indefinitely confined voters was more than five times the alleged Biden victory margin in Wisconsin. And yes, all of those votes were counted despite the fact that the Wisconsin Supreme Court ruled the expanded definition of indefinitely confined voters to be legally incorrect.[20]

Oh, did I mention—and I buried the lead—this surge of indefinitely confined voters was observed only after election officials in the Democrat strongholds of "Dane and Milwaukee counties offered illegal advice that encouraged individuals to use indefinite confinement as a way to ignore the state's photo I.D. requirement."[21] And today, stories and pictures abound of "indefinitely confined" Wisconsin voters during the election season at weddings, riding their bikes, going on vacation, and definitely being anything but indefinitely confined.[22]

Perhaps the most interesting category of fraud that came up in my investigation was that of *dead voters* and so-called *ghost voters*, a ghost voter being a person who votes under the name of a voter who does not reside at the address where that ghost voter is registered.

For example, in Georgia more than twenty thousand ghost voters may well have cast ballots in the 2020 election after having moved out of state.[23] That's about twice the alleged Biden victory margin—and just the tip of the fraud and election irregularities iceberg in the cesspool of Georgia.

As for dead voters, they were so very alive across all six battleground states that one wag quipped, in reference to a classic Bruce Willis movie, that the 2020 election was the "Sixth Sense" election: "I see dead people voting."

BALLOT MISHANDLING

My investigation also uncovered five distinct flavors of so-called ballot mishandling. These ranged from the lack of adequate voter ID checks, signature matching abuses, and so-called *naked ballots* lacking an outer envelope to broken chains of custody and ballots without postmarks.

Here it must be said that it is critical for election integrity that ballot counters legally verify absentee and mail-in ballots by checking if the signatures on the outer envelopes match the voters' registration records.[24] Yet signature-matching abuses ran rampant in Nevada, Pennsylvania, and especially Georgia, where a secret consent decree effectively gutted signature-matching procedures.[25]

As for the titillating problem of naked ballots, it is illegal, perhaps for obvious reasons, to accept any ballot lacking an outer envelope, as that is the only way to verify a voter's identity. Yet the problem was particularly acute in Pennsylvania as a result of illegal "guidance" issued by Secretary of State Kathy Boockvar that naked ballots be counted.

This incident is especially egregious because when the Pennsylvania Supreme Court rejected this guidance, Boockvar, a registered Democrat put into office by the George Soros political machine,[26] refused to issue new guidance.[27]

Equally egregious, the increased use of unsupervised drop boxes across several battleground states dramatically enhanced the risk of a broken chain of custody. So, too, did the increased practice of so-called *ballot harvesting*, whereby private third parties pick up ballots from voters and deliver them to drop boxes or election officials.

Wisconsin election officials added a particularly fraudulent twist to this ballot harvesting problem, which is an open invitation to stuff-the-ballot-box fraud. They illegally and disproportionately located hundreds of drop boxes in heavily Democrat urban areas, thereby encouraging ballot harvesting to the benefit of Joe Biden.

And did I mention this? Again, I buried the lead: *any* use of a drop box in Wisconsin is illegal. Therefore, the votes cast through them should not be legally counted in any certified election result—yet they were.[28]

It is likewise against state law for ballots to be backdated so as to meet an election deadline. Yet in Wisconsin alone, the US Postal Service may have backdated as many as 100,000 ballots.[29] That is roughly five times the alleged Biden victory margin in Wisconsin.

CONTESTABLE PROCESS FOULS

The outsized impact of a third dimension of election irregularities—so-called *contestable process fouls*—cannot be overstated. This is because central to the fairness and integrity of any election is the unfettered ability of observers to monitor the receipt, opening, and counting of the ballots.

Such observers seek to answer questions such as: Is a signature-matching process being conducted? Does each ballot have an outer envelope, or is it a naked ballot? Are ballots being run through the tabulation machines more than once?

Yet in Michigan—arguably the "first among equals" in the battleground states when it came to abusing Republican observers—election officials in Democrat strongholds such as Detroit covered the windows of rooms where ballots were being processed and counted so as to block the view from the outside.[30] In Pennsylvania, similar observer abuses ran rampant as tens of thousands of ballots were processed in back rooms.[31]

EQUAL PROTECTION CLAUSE VIOLATIONS

As yet another important dimension of election irregularities, there were numerous violations of the Equal Protection Clause of the Constitution's Fourteenth Amendment. Most egregious, across all six battleground states, Republican voters were often treated in ways that were tantamount to voter suppression.

As a prime example, in-person voters were often subjected to higher standards of voter identification and certification than were absentee and mail-in-ballot voters. That decidedly unequal treatment disproportionately benefited Joe Biden because President Trump had a much higher percentage of in-person voters. In some states, three out of four absentee and mail-in ballots cast went into the Joe Biden column.

I could go on and on, but I think you get the picture. Both fraud and election irregularities were rife in the six battleground states in the 2020 presidential election. Regardless of your political party, these findings should be troubling. At a minimum, every US citizen should want to get to the bottom of what happened.

Yet to this day, if you try to plumb those depths, you will face the Cancel Culture wrath of the anti-Trump media; a censoring, deplatforming, and fascist social media, and intense political and social pressure—even the threat of lawsuits and the loss of your job—from just about every corner and angle imaginable.

My view here is that the only thing worse than the theft of the 2020 election from President Trump and the more than 74 million Americans who voted for him has been the abject refusal of key institutions such as our courts, the Fourth Estate, state legislatures, and Congress to fully investigate this matter. Yet here are the wages of this Cancel Culture, See-No-Election-Evil sin:

If the greatest democracy in world history this side of ancient Athens and Rome cannot run a free and fair election, how can we as a people and republic collectively look the rest of the world in the eyes—especially Communist China—and lecture them on the virtues of democracy and our own now obviously deeply flawed institutions?

And if, on our home shores, nearly half of American citizens continue to have troubling questions about the fairness of the 2020 presidential election, is that not a recipe for a Cold Civil War, particularly in what increasingly appears to be a fifty-fifty country ideologically split right down the middle?

In fact, it was just such a Cold Civil War that Steve Bannon, the Boss, and I were hoping to avert with our Green Bay Sweep on January 6, 2021, and its broader mission of getting to the truth about November 3 for the American people.

TWENTY-ONE

THE DEMOCRATS' UNRESTRICTED LAWFARE AND ART OF THE STEAL

I follow him to serve my turn upon him . . . not I for love and duty but seeming so for my peculiar end.

—Iago in *Othello*, Act I, Scene 1

I hope Mike is going to do the right thing. I hope so. . . . Because if Mike Pence does the right thing, we win the election. He has the absolute right to do it. . . . All Vice President Pence has to do is send it back to the states to recertify, and we become president, and you are the happiest people.

—Donald J. Trump, January 6, 2021[1]

D-DAY. GREEN BAY SWEEP. ZERO DARK THIRTY. As dawn breaks on a raw and windy Washington, DC, and as the sun tries in vain to fight its way through the gathering storm clouds hanging low over the National Mall, the last three people on God's good Earth who want to see violence erupt on Capitol Hill this sixth day of January are Stephen K. Bannon, myself, and President Donald John Trump.

To pull off an operation Bannon has dubbed the Green Bay Sweep—and thereby keep President Trump in the White House for a second term—we must have only peace and calm on Capitol Hill. This Green Bay Sweep will be our last, best chance to snatch a stolen election from the Democrats' jaws of deceit, and the last thing we want is to hand Congress an excuse to abort the operation.

If you are a football fan, you know Coach Vince Lombardi's original 1960s version of this sweep. With the deftness of a magician, Green Bay quarterback Bart Starr handed the ball off to halfback Paul Hornung, who, with the subtlety of a hammer seeking a five-pound nail, headed for the end zone behind a phalanx of blockers.

In Steve Bannon's political version of this sweep, Vice President Mike Pence will play the role of Team Trump's designated quarterback. And on this sixth day of January, after the US Congress convenes sometime around 1:00 p.m. to certify the presidential election results, Pence, as president of the Senate, will hand the ball off to various pro-Trump members of Congress—more than a hundred have signed up for the fight.

The goal is *not* to get the election overturned today. The goal is to subject the ballots—the *legal* votes of American citizens along with what we believe to be a flood of *illegal* ballots—to careful scrutiny and investigation.

Of course, for all this to work, Pence must assert his constitutional power as Senate president. He must put certification of the election on ice for at least another several weeks while Congress and the various state legislatures involved investigate all of the fraud and election irregularities that will be raised today on Capitol Hill.

On this cold, momentous day, I shiver as I think to myself, "January 6 will be either Mike Pence's finest hour or the traitorous 'Et u, Brute?' end of both his and Donald Trump's political careers."

It has certainly been no secret around the West Wing that the vice president is under tremendous pressure from his own chief of staff, Marc Short, to throw in the Trump towel. If today does indeed end in Shakespearean tragedy, Short will play the role of Iago.

Marc Short's "peculiar end" will be as it always has been in his lobbying career, to advance the interests of a Globalist Koch Network[2] that staunchly opposes the Populist Trump.[3] This is a Koch organization from which Marc Short has drawn so many paychecks.[4]

THE ART OF THE STEAL AND HOW THEY DID IT

On this raw and windy day, I wake with the dawn and immediately jump into my cold tub for a ten-minute soak in fifty-degree water. Like some Mad Russian, I've been doing this cold-plunge routine for almost ten years now. And I can't think of a better way to jump-start one's day.

I check my messages and am pleased to see Steve Bannon has us fully ready to implement our Green Bay Sweep on Capitol Hill. Call the play. Run the play.

I spend the next hour on my laptop computer reviewing yesterday's media coverage of the release of volume 2 of my election irregularities report. In homage to the Boss's most famous opus—and as a spot-on description of what the Democrats have actually done—I have named this new report *The Art of the Steal.*

As with volume 1, *The Immaculate Deception*, the media coverage of *The Art of the Steal* is scant. Since the November 3 election, the anti-Trump media have ruthlessly suppressed any news or analysis questioning the integrity of the 2020 presidential election. No surprise there—just dog bites man.

But Silicon Valley's social media oligarchs—principally Twitter's Jack Dorsey, Facebook's Mark Zuckerberg, and Google's Sundar Pichai—have also been biting and barking like the censoring dogs they are. With the advent of ever-more-sophisticated artificial intelligence algorithms, these Three Kings of Cancel Culture are quickly plumbing new depths of Orwellian control while giving the fascism of the Great Firewall of China a run for its money.

As to why I felt the need to write a follow-up to *The Immaculate Deception*, there was this obvious lacuna: *The Immaculate Deception* only identified *what* the Democrats had done to steal the election. What I really needed to do in *The Art of the Steal* was describe exactly *how* they did it. How did a large army of Democrat operatives steal an election right out from under the noses of the American people?

This excerpt from *The Art of the Steal* provides the topline answer to that question: "The Democrat Party used a two-pronged Grand 'Stuff the Ballot Box' Strategy to flood six key battleground states . . . with enough illegal absentee and mail-in ballots to turn a decisive Trump victory into a narrow and illegitimate Biden alleged 'win.'"[5]

In effect, the Democrats weaponized the absentee and mail-in ballot process, and it is not like we weren't warned. In their landmark 2005 election integrity report, former president and Democrat Jimmy Carter and former secretary of state and Republican James A. Baker, III, were blunt in their assessment: "Absentee ballots remain the largest source of potential voter fraud."[6]

Here's how *The Art of the Steal* describes the two perniciously effective and complementary prongs of the Democrats' Grand Stuff the Ballot Box Strategy:

> Prong One dramatically INCREASED the amount of absentee and mail-in ballots in the battleground states [while] Prong Two dramatically DECREASED the level of scrutiny of such ballots—effectively taking the election "cops" off the beat. This pincer movement resulted in a FLOOD of illegal ballots into the battleground states which was more than sufficient to tip the scales from a decisive legal win by President Trump to a narrow and illegitimate alleged "victory" by Joe Biden.[7]

In a landmark *Time* magazine cover story by Molly Ball, the Democrats have all but confessed to this Grand Stuff the Ballot Box Strategy. And Molly Ball is neither a right-wing hack nor a Fourth Estate slouch; she was the 2019 winner of the Gerald R. Ford Journalism Prize for Distinguished Reporting on the Presidency.

In her "kiss and tell" article, Ball highlighted a long list of operatives who have openly boasted about how they gamed America's election system to overthrow a sitting president. That she portrayed these smug zealots as saviors of the election rather than as thieves is yet another Big Reveal—not just of Ball's own Progressive ideology but also of the much deeper rot eating away at our election system and our broader Republic.

In this Big Reveal, we bare stark witness to an "ends justify the means" mentality that has gripped far too many Americans on the left. As Corey Lewandowski once put it, these Machiavellian cadres apparently hate Donald Trump more than they love their country.[8]

Memo number one to Molly's Merry Band of Democrat Thieves: Destroying the integrity of our election system to topple a sitting president you loathe is no Devil's bargain. It's national suicide.

Now, here's the *real* money-shot quote from Molly Ball's exposé. This quote is a perfect fusion of my description in *The Art of the Steal* of how the Democrats stuffed the ballot box with what Ball described in her own Booklet of Revelations. Wrote Ball, "In the end, nearly half the electorate cast ballots by mail in 2020, practically a revolution in how people vote. . . . Only a quarter of voters cast their ballots the traditional way: in person on Election Day."[9]

Memo number two to Good Golly, Ms. Molly herself: Stuffing the ballot box with illegal absentee and mail-in ballots as the Democrats did is ***not a revolution****. Rather, it is a* ***counterrevolution*** *and* ***coup*** *that runs against the grain of everything we stand for in this country.*

Of course, in the real world, one must expect political parties to engage in strategic gaming of the system regardless of whether that tramples on the founding principles of our nation. So, yes, I am a "men are no angels" Madisonian realist here.

Yet what bothered me most about the Democrats' Grand Stuff the Ballot Box Strategy as I got deeper and deeper into my investigation was this: the Democrats had begun implementing their strategy *years* before the November 3 election,[10] and it had indeed been carried out under our very noses.

Here, the conventional wisdom is that the Democrats simply hid behind the pandemic to push forward their massive absentee and mail-in ballot campaigns. Yet—and this is the real scoop— ***the pandemic simply served as an accelerant*** *for all manner of election integrity fires set by Democrats across the battleground states dating back almost to the minute that Donald J. Trump was inaugurated as the United States' forty-fifth president.*

DAMN CHAIN OF CUSTODY, FULL SPEED AHEAD

So how exactly did the Radical Democrats pull off their Grand Stuff the Ballot Box Strategy? As with *The Immaculate Deception*, you can read the full report at my website www.peternavarro.com. But here's the Cliffs Notes version of *The Art of the Steal.*

First and foremost, the Democrats significantly relaxed all manner of absentee and mail-in ballot rules.

Register to vote after the deadline? No problem, at least for the 150,000 people casting ballots in Arizona, where the alleged Biden victory margin was just over 10,000 votes. Proven.

Request an absentee ballot before or after a statutory deadline? No problem at all, at least in Georgia. More than 300,000 absentee ballots fell into that category in the state where the alleged Biden victory margin was less than 12,000 votes. Proven.

And how about counting absentee ballots postmarked after 8:00 p.m. on election day? Just bring it on, at least in Pennsylvania. Proven.

As a second major boost to the absentee and mail-in ballot counts, the Democrats pushed aggressively forward with so-called *universal* voting. This is a practice extraordinarily vulnerable to fraud, yet the Democrats altered laws in both Nevada and Wisconsin so mail-in ballots could be sent automatically to every single individual on the voter rolls. It didn't matter if those voters were dead. It didn't matter if they had moved out of state long ago. Again, proven.

And as Civil War admiral David Farragut rolled over in his grave, it was "Damn any chain-of-custody issues ahead" as the Democrats dramatically increased the use of drop boxes to boost mail-in voting—even in states such as Georgia and Michigan where it is explicitly illegal to do so. As the drop boxes proliferated, so, too, did the practice of ballot harvesting in fully four of the six battleground states. Proven.

TAKING THE ELECTION COPS OFF THE BEAT

Even as the Democrats engineered an unprecedented flood of absentee and mail-in ballots—many of questionable provenance—they used Prong Two of their strategy to dramatically *decrease* any scrutiny of these ballots. At the tip of this particular "take the election cops off the beat" spear was a dramatic relaxation of *signature matching.*

Signature matching is one of the most critical elements of election integrity. It is one of the best ways to ascertain *whether the person casting the ballot in a registered voter's name is one and the same person.*

Not surprisingly, Democrats went straight for the signature-matching jugular, and once again, it was the cesspool of Georgia, with its illegal and secret consent decree, that led the way. And by the way, the most corrosive clause in Georgia's consent decree was this poison signature-matching pill: *If an election worker found a signature* ***not*** *to match, it still could* ***not*** *be rejected unless a majority of the registrars, deputy registrars, or absentee ballot clerks reviewing the signature agreed.*

As a second blatant way the Democrats took the election cops off the beat, there was the state-mandated *illegal counting of naked ballots.* Recall, here, that a naked ballot is one for which there is no outer envelope containing the voter's information.

As a key tenet of election integrity, naked ballots should *never, ever* be tallied and for obvious reasons. Yet in the electoral bordello otherwise known as Pennsylvania, Secretary of State Kathy Boockvar brazenly issued guidance that such naked ballots be counted.[11]

Yet, it gets worse. After getting her hand caught in that particular cookie jar, Boockvar doubled down on her renegade and reprehensible behavior by ignoring an explicit direction from the Pennsylvania Supreme Court to amend that unauthorized guidance.

Boockvar's breathtakingly brazen breaking of the election rules is instructive because it illustrates more broadly one of the most clever and diabolical games the Democrats played to take the election cops off the beat. That was to politically capture the offices of the secretaries of state in both Michigan and Pennsylvania in the corporal forms of Jocelyn Benson in the Wolverine State and the aforementioned Boockvar.[12]

Though secretary of state is generally considered a "down-ballot" post lacking the prestige of governor or lieutenant governor, secretary of state is the chief election officer—the top election cop—in most of the fifty states. So it was a particularly diabolical long-range move to capture that office in the key battleground states of Michigan and Pennsylvania. Together, these states have a combined total of 36 electoral votes, which is plenty enough to swing a presidential election.

Just how did the Democrats pull off that capture? Enter here, stage far left, the billionaire Wall Street oligarch and notorious anti-Trump Globalist George Soros.

Soros was first seen in the 1990s breaking the backs of Britain's blue-collar working classes by shorting, and thereby breaking, the British pound. Since then, the billions of dollars he has accumulated have been used to finance all manner of Globalist and Democrat causes.

What is truly scary about Soros is the length of his strategic gaming horizon. Globalist George and his operatives literally spent *years* seeking to capture secretaries of state around the country.

As far back as 2006, Soros helped fund a political action committee known eponymously as the Secretary of State Project.[13] Its goal was to build a "Democrat firewall" for presidential elections in key battleground states. The Soros strategy was to place progressive extremists such as Benson and Boockvar in positions of authority where they might be willing to bend, and at times break, the law.[14] Of course, that was *exactly* what happened in the 2020 presidential election.

Consider, for example, Kathy Boockvar's highly questionable guidance in Pennsylvania on September 11, 2020. She directed local election officials *not* to perform on-the-spot signature analysis for absentee and mail-in ballots.[15] In effect, mail-in ballots could *not* be rejected even if election officials deemed that there was an improper signature match.[16]

When it comes to outrageousness, this is about as outrageous as it gets in terms of *decreasing* the scrutiny of mail-in and absentee ballots.

More broadly, Boockvar would exhibit a total disregard for the sanctity of our legal system when she submitted clearly unauthorized guidance a few days before the November 3 election. This misguidance missile would allow voters lacking proof of identification to have their mail-in ballots cured until November 12—fully nine days *after* the election.

Here is what should really trouble anyone concerned about election integrity: though the Pennsylvania Supreme Court would later rule Boockvar had clearly lacked the statutory authority to take that step, the election fraud horse was already out of the barn.[17]

Not to be outdone, Boockvar's brazen twin, Jocelyn Benson, would issue equally brazen guidance in early October that instructed Michigan election cops *cum* clerks to *simply assume that all absentee ballot signatures were accurate.*[18] Oh, really? Yes, *really*!

Like Boockvar, Benson, too, would get slapped down by a judge for making a wild presumption that was found "nowhere in state law."[19] Yet, as with Boockvar's breaking of the rules, the legal decision to overturn Benson's guidance would come too late to alter the outcome of the November election.

That was the modus operandi of Benson and Boockvar: to bend or break the law and see if they could get away with it. On the basis of this behavior alone, one could easily argue that Michigan and Pennsylvania, and therefore the 2020 presidential election, were stolen from Trump voters.

ZUCKERBERG PRIVATIZES OUR PUBLIC ELECTIONS

The same harshly accurate assessment can be made about Mark Zuckerberg's massively pernicious contributions—both financially and strategically—to the theft of the 2020 election. It was, after all, Zuckerberg's Big Facebook Bucks—nearly *half a billion* dollars—that helped engineer what was effectively a hostile private sector takeover of our public election system.

Zuckerberg's gambit was to use a Trojan horse front group known as the Center for Tech and Civic Life (CTCL), which would target primarily Democrat strongholds in three key Blue Wall states. The prime targets included Wayne County, Michigan, where Detroit is located; Dane County, Wisconsin, where the state capital, Madison, is located; and Philadelphia County, Pennsylvania.

As Breitbart noted about the effectiveness of the Zuckerberg gambit in the Keystone State, "Seventy-three percent of Joe Biden's more than 125,000 vote margin gain in Pennsylvania . . . came from the seven counties and one city . . . that received more than $18 million from the Mark Zuckerberg–funded Center for Technology and Civic Life."[20]

Note that there is only one degree of separation between George Soros and Mark Zuckerberg. Zuckerberg's CTCL would be staffed by many of the very same people that had worked for Soros's Open Society Foundation.[21]

Now as much as Mark Zuckerberg kisses me off for his role in stealing the 2020 election and censoring and canceling all manner of conservatives and Republicans on Facebook—including President Trump himself—what ultimately frosts me about him is his open sympathy for a totalitarian prison-state that is jailing and torturing its people on a scale not seen since the 1930s.

Mr. Zuckerberg, what is the difference between concentration camps in Auschwitz and the Chinese Communist Party's reeducation death camps in Tibet and Xinjiang province? *Nothing.*

And please tell me how you can possibly condone the kind of live organ harvesting now being performed by Chinese butchers on Falun Gong and Uighur prisoners, who are often buried alive once they are bereft of their kidneys, hearts, and corneas.[22]

Then there is this: Zuckerberg has despicably hired Chinese Communist Party members to increase Facebook's capabilities to censor Trump supporters and the conservative movement, and Zuckerberg himself has expressed sympathies for Chinese Communist Party ideology.[23]

THE POLITICAL BEAUTY OF THE GREEN BAY SWEEP

While my role in challenging the election outcome had been to carefully document the fraud and myriad election irregularities, Steve Bannon's role was to figure out how to use this information—what he called the "receipts"—to overturn the election result. That's how Steve had come up with the Green Bay Sweep idea.

The political and legal beauty of the strategy was this: by law, both the House of Representatives and the Senate must spend up to two hours of debate per state on each requested challenge.[24]

For the six battleground states, that would add up to as much as twenty-four hours of nationally televised hearings across the two chambers of Congress. Through these televised proceedings, we would finally be able to short-circuit the crushing censorship of the anti-Trump media and take our case directly to the American people.

Of course, to quote the great John Steinbeck quoting the very good Scottish poet Robert Burns, the best laid plans of mice and Trump's men often go awry.

Truth be told here, today's operation is as much a Hail Mary as it is a Green Bay Sweep. It is President Trump's best, and perhaps final, shot at shining a blaring spotlight on all of the election irregularities and fraud we had uncovered in our investigation. Yet its success or failure will all hinge on Quarterback Mike.

In assessing the odds of a Pence betrayal, my thoughts turn to the trajectory of my own relationship with VPOTUS over the last four years. From the very first day I met Mike, he was always kind and complimentary to me.

He particularly liked my feistiness on TV and would often remark positively on my verbal jousts with anti-Trump antagonists like Jake Tapper and Chris Wallace. One time, the VP even did a pretty spot on impression of me and my hand gestures, and it was warmly hilarious.

During the first several years of the administration, I often met with Mike in the vice president's office in the West Wing. There, as I would sit forward on one of his couches with my notes and charts, VPOTUS would sit ramrod straight in his chair. I would then brief him on anything from China's Seven Deadly Unfair Trade Sins to my progress on rebuilding the Philly shipyard.

To his credit, VPOTUS would always have read whatever material I had sent him the night before at his Naval Observatory residence. And he was always a quick study.

My relationship with Michael Richard Pence would turn, however, on a thin Koch dime as soon as Marc Short walked back into the building on March 1, 2019, to take over the job as the vice president's chief of staff from Nick Ayers. Short had been fired from his job as White House legislative affairs director for incompetence just a year earlier.*

With Short's second coming, it was like the Soviet Union taking over Eastern Europe. As an Iron Koch Curtain fell over the vice president, the only way you could speak to VPOTUS was to go through Short, and in this particular West Wing version of a catch-22, Short would never allow you to speak to him.

My anxiety over Pence's possible disloyalty had been heightened over the last week by the fact that the vice president had refused to take my repeated phone calls about the raft of election irregularities, *despite a direct request from President Trump to do so.*

In what was the single most bizarre sixty seconds of my tour at the White House, I had gotten a call from the Situation

* He says he quit, but generally the way it worked in the Trump White House was that you got your walking papers and then you were allowed to claim that you were resigning as a face-saving measure.

Room several days earlier informing me the vice president was on the line, and they wished to connect me. When I said "of course," the connection was made and I heard "Mr. Vice President, Mr. Navarro is now on the line."

Then, to my bewilderment and chagrin, it was crickets as the connection was immediately broken. When I called back to the Sit Room to get Mike back on the line, I was informed that VPOTUS would get back to me. He never did.

Now Donald Trump's best chance to take back an election that was almost certainly stolen is in the hands of a man he thought he could trust who is increasingly the odds-on favorite to betray him.

Earlier in the week, the president's tweetmeister, Dan Scavino, had invited me to join the Boss on stage for today's rally on the Ellipse. POTUS had loved my election fraud reports and had personally directed Molly Michael, his executive assistant, to make sure those reports were sent to every congressman and senator.

Scavino's invitation notwithstanding, as January 6 approached, as celebrities and congressmen and senators jostled for podium time, and as key fifth columnists within the White House were increasingly pressuring the Boss to drop his election challenge and go gently into that good night, I, along with any possibility of a motivational speech from me about election fraud, was unceremoniously dropped from the program.

"Trouble not," said I to Brother Scavino when he sheepishly delivered the news to me. I thought "Better that I stay home that morning anyway to coordinate with Bannon to make sure we had our Green Bay Sweep ducks in a row. Then I'd go take a run on the National Mall at noon to go watch the festivities from the cheap seats."

AS COLD AS A CNN ANCHOR

Among the most awe-inspiring places to run a five-mile loop, Washington's National Mall certainly must rank at the top of the list. This loop runs with equal grandeur and grace from the US Capitol to the Lincoln Memorial through the Washington Monument. Yet these three stunning landmarks and paeans to American patriotism are not my favorite scenic features on the Mall.

That honor belongs to the hauntingly beautiful red and Romanesque sandstone Smithsonian "Castle." This architectural icon is roughly midway between Capitol Hill and the Washington Monument and just a half-mile walk from my home near—and yes there is some irony here—Chinatown.

Just before noon on this bitterly cold January 6 day, I lace up my running shoes and, for my warm-up, I briskly walk down 7th Street and onto the Mall. Once I hit the Mall's soft gravel path, I turn West and begin running in the direction of the Lincoln Monument and towards the Ellipse and the Boss's speech.

Despite my wool layering, the bitter wind off the Potomac River bites right through every piece of clothing I have on. It is as cold as a CNN anchor interviewing Kellyanne Conway.

My first thought while looking into the faces of the various Trump supporters scattered along the way is that this feels like neither a protest nor a wake. Rather, it is much more like a festival.

With nothing but smiles on their faces, and even in the bitter cold, these Merry Bands of Deplorables are walking peacefully along in their classic Trump gear—MAGA hats, Trump 2020 banners, and no shortage of American flags.

Soon, as I drift off into my own inner runner's world, I begin to think about how it had all begun during the 2016 campaign, and about all of the great things that had been accomplished in the last four years.

During the 2016 campaign, as Candidate Trump's top economic and trade advisor, I had developed a "four points of the policy compass" mantra that would become the guiding policy light of our administration. As I had described it on CNN:

> You have to understand the DNA of the Trump campaign to understand our economic plan. The president gets up every morning trying to grow the economy and create jobs for the American people. And dating back to the campaign . . . we pushed four points of the policy compass.
>
> . . . [T]ax cuts to stimulate investment and productivity here in America, deregulation to increase our global competitiveness, unleashing our coal, oil and natural gas resources again for competitive purposes but also to increase the purchasing power of consumers, and to have fair, balanced and reciprocal trade.
>
> This is what drives our economic policy. It's clear as a bell in results.[25]

And clear as a bell the results were: By January of 2020, and three years into the administration, the Boss had built the strongest economy in modern American history. Of course, it had all gone to *Sturm und Drang* and seed and dung once the Chinese Communist Party Virus hit our economy and society like a Category Five hurricane.

And so now, rather than getting ready to settle in for a second term, I am running toward a rally being held by a lame-duck president who is mounting one last procedural challenge to an election that has been stolen not just from him but also from the more than 74 million Americans who voted for him.[26]

AN UNDULATING SWARM OF DEPLORABLES

As I run in easy rhythm toward 12th Street and the Ellipse beyond, the distant roar of the crowd begins to pull me out of my reverie and back into the moment. I focus on the Washington Monument majestically before me with its ring of American flags flowing in the stiff nor'easter breeze. Next, my eyes move right to the slope that runs down from the Monument and toward the Ellipse.

Normally an open green knoll, this slope is jammed with a teeming mass of humanity stretching from the Washington Monument all the way to the foot of the Ellipse stage where POTUS is holding court. As I watch the swarm of Deplorables undulating with the rhythms of the Boss's speech, the now *not*-so-distant roar is music to my ears.

At this point, I stop and just take it all in. Gathered before me is the power of Trumpism in all its might and glory—and peacefulness!—for all the world to see. Think I, *Maybe, just maybe, we can pull this Green Bay Sweep off today.*

I don't know whether it was for two minutes or twenty minutes, but at one point of sharp clarity, I realize I am freezing. I quickly do a 180-degree turn and start back East in the direction of Capitol Hill.

While good thoughts had pleasantly filled my mind as I had run toward the Trump rally, a flood of bad "elections have consequences" thoughts now plague me. In this new and darker moment, nobody knows better than I that Donald Trump needs a second term to finish what he had started.

We need first and foremost to continue reshoring, rebuilding, and strengthening our manufacturing base. To do so, we necessarily need to significantly up our tariff game on China and decouple from that cruel Communist regime once and for all—and nobody is more ready to do that than POTUS himself in a second term. After the massive damage his no longer "good friend" Xi Jinping has wrought with a demon virus unleashed from Wuhan, the Boss is itching to finish our China fight.

I have my own second-term priorities as well: as the director of the Office of Trade and Manufacturing Policy, I started a number of key initiatives that are still in midstream, from the rebuilding of my beloved shipyards in blue-collar towns like Panama City, Florida, and Marinette, Wisconsin, to putting an end forever more to the massive importation of counterfeit goods from Communist China.

If, however, our Green Bay Sweep fails today, it will not just be a second term and a Populist Economic Nationalist president we will be losing; the Great United States will be saddled with a figurehead president who will be nothing more than a pliant puppet of the Socialist wing of a Democrat Party that long ago turned its Globalist back on working-class America.

The greatest fear haunting me as I now run toward Capitol Hill is this: in that very same Oval Office where I had stood at the shoulder of the Boss as he signed so many executive orders that had done so much good for the working men and women of America, Joe Biden will, with repeated strokes of his own Party of Davos pen, undo everything President Trump accomplished.

AN EERIE CALM BEFORE A BIZARRE STORM

When I reach the Capitol Hill perimeter, it is only lightly guarded by an improvised barrier knitted together with bike racks, loose fencing, and a smattering of Capitol Hill police.

In the cold mist, *nothing* seems amiss. There is no massive crowd. Nothing aggressive about anyone I see. If anything, it is eerily quiet, with nothing to foreshadow what is to come.

Convinced that all is well in Trump Land and that the Green Bay Sweep is ready to roll, I do not linger at the fence. Instead, I turn west once again, run back to 7th Street, and then walk north toward home and lunch.

At 1:15 p.m., National Public Radio issues this news update: "Republicans seeking to overturn President-elect Joe Biden's win in the November election have moved to challenge the results from Arizona, as Congress begins the usually pro forma process of counting each state's electors."[27]

I breathe a big sigh of relief: our Green Bay Sweep has begun *exactly* as planned.

But even as this Green Bay Sweep starts flawlessly, it is also all beginning to unravel.[28] As more and more protesters gather at the improvised fence around the Capitol, the Capitol Hill police inexplicably offer little resistance. Some of these police officers even open the gates to let protesters onto the grounds.[29] In the ensuing chaos, Pence will be whisked away by Secret Service agents. Congressmen and senators will scatter to the Capitol building subway tunnels that will take them to safety. And when this gaggle of conniving politicians all reconvene this night at 8:00 p.m.,[30] Pence, in league with Speaker of the House Nancy Pelosi, Senate Majority Leader Mitch McConnell, and House Minority Leader Kevin McCarthy, will use the excuse of the violence on Capitol Hill to halt any further attempt to challenge the election results.

In this inglorious way, the Green Bay Sweep will end with either a fumble, a sack, or an interception—choose your own football metaphor. But any way you phrase it, Michael Richard Pence will have secured his place in history as the Brutus most responsible both for the final betrayal of President Trump and the unceremonious burial of election integrity.

In the wake of the Capitol Hill riot, putative Trump "loyalists" such as Larry Kudlow, Steve Mnuchin, and Mick Mulvaney subsequently join a chorus of Democrats condemning the president.

And the Fall of the White House of Trump is complete—or so it looks at the darkest end of that grim day.

A FULL-FRONTAL LAWFARE ASSAULT

Given how these events unfolded, it should be clear, why Stephen K. Bannon, myself, and Donald John Trump were the last three people on God's good Earth who wanted to see violence erupt that January 6 day on Capitol Hill. For it was this violence that finally put an abrupt end to any hope the president had for taking back an election likely stolen from him and from the more than 74 million Americans who voted for him.

As I have pondered these events in the cold, clear light of the many dawns that have followed, the one analog to what the Democrats did that keeps coming hauntingly back to me is this:

In their chilling landmark 2002 book *Unrestricted Warfare*, two Communist colonels in China's People's Liberation Army provide a detailed battle plan to take down the United States of America without ever having to resort to hot *kinetic warfare*.[31] Instead, these high-ranking military officers call for the use of *economic warfare*, such as intellectual property theft to steal our technological seed corn; *information warfare*, which is nothing more than the use of traditional propaganda; and, most relevant here, a chillingly innovative weapon known as *lawfare*.

The central idea behind lawfare is to use the existing laws, rules, and norms of one's enemy and change, bend or break them in ways that allow you to press your own advantage. And that is exactly what the Democrat Party and its operatives did in their "ends justify the means" Never Trump fury to win the 2020 race.

The best I can say about the Democrat Party's unrestricted lawfare tactics in their takedown of Donald Trump is that they offer a master class in the cooptation and weaponization of our election system.

The worst I can say is that by stealing the election, the Democrats have completely and utterly shattered confidence in that very same election system. Tragically, what Robert A. Pastor, the executive director of the Commission on Federal Election Reform, had to say in 2005 is more true today than it ever was: "Polls indicate that many Americans lack confidence in the electoral system, but the political parties are so divided that serious electoral reform is unlikely without a strong bipartisan voice."[32]

In our now deeply divided American Republic, the Democrats' full-frontal *lawfare assault* on American democracy may not be a complete recipe for that insurrection the Democrats profess to be so fearful of. Yet the Democrats' conduct has certainly set a dangerous precedent and thereby laid a bloody predicate.

Until we get to the bottom of all of this—and get to the bottom of it we must—we will remain as we are now, a House Divided that has been brought to our knees by the Fall of the White House of Trump.

DJT, we hardly knew ye.

But you'll be back. We know it. And they know it.

EPILOGUE

SOLDIERING ON

As I write these words on a hot, muggy August morning in the nation's capital, I remain a man on a mission. Cincinnatus and his plow will have to wait. Dylan Thomas had it exactly right: "Do not go gentle into that good night."

As an assistant to the president for trade and manufacturing policy in the Trump White House, my mission was to help the president create high-paying jobs for blue-collar Americans. And that was exactly what I did. I did it through everything from the drafting of tough "Buy American" executive orders and the rebuilding of our shipyards to defending this country against Communist China's economic aggression through strong sanctions and fair trade tariffs. It was an honor and privilege to serve my country and the man whom I regard as the greatest president in a generation.

After the plague from China hit, my mission abruptly morphed into helping President Trump save American lives and lives around the world. As this book documents, we were able to do just that through actions ranging from the president's courageous travel ban on China to his delivery of ventilators and a suite of vaccines in warp speed—and in Trump Time. I never let up, and I left everything on the floor.

In normal times, following such White House service, I would have been courted by traditional publishing houses such as Simon & Schuster and HarperCollins and have a long list of lucrative speaking engagements. I would likely be on the board of directors of a major corporation or philanthropic institution, helping to guide its strategy. I might also be a research fellow at Harvard or Stanford or a prestigious think tank—even perhaps president of a major academic institution. And I most certainly would be a well-compensated analyst for a major television network such as ABC, CNN, or Fox.

But these are not normal times. These are anything but normal times. And in these times of toil and national trouble, rather than being invited to participate in any of the opportunities of post–White House service normally afforded to people of my experience, I have been canceled.

But that's okay. I have been canceled because I have freely chosen to speak this Big Truth to power:

- Truth One: The November 3, 2020, presidential election was stolen. That's my view based on my ongoing investigation and emerging evidence, and I continue to believe that a thorough state-by-state forensic audit of the ballots will show that Donald Trump and the more than 74 million Americans who voted for him won the 2020 election.
- Truth Two: The January 6, 2021, violence on Capitol Hill was *not* instigated by President Trump. POTUS 45 was the very last person to want such violence, precisely because it derailed his best chance to get a full and fair accounting of the flood of illegal ballots

cast in the November 3 election. And by no stretch of the imagination was January 6 an insurrection.

- Truth Three: The pandemic, which has killed more than six hundred thousand Americans and more than 4 million victims worldwide, was almost certainly genetically engineered in a bioweapons lab in Wuhan, China, using gain-of-function experiments funded in part by Anthony Fauci's vast Washington, DC, bureaucracy.

Until we as a nation fully confront this Big Truth and get to the bottom of what happened on November 3 and January 6 and in a Wuhan bioweapons lab, we will not be able to move forward either as a fully functioning democracy or as a proud republic.

Unless we confront this Big Truth, we are headed inexorably for massive civil unrest at best and civil war at worst.

Here's the spark that may ignite America's prairie fire: the illegitimate Biden regime and the academic, corporate, media, social media, and scientific elites that support this regime have embraced a set of extreme values and policies that are totally out of sync with the cultural, economic, political, and social fabric of the American nation.

To put this problem most simply and succinctly, most Americans who voted in the 2020 presidential election—regardless of their party—did *not* sign up for what the Biden regime is now delivering.[1]

And please hear me clearly: Main Street USA does not want to live in a world of economic lockdowns, forced vaccinations, and unreasonable mask mandates. Nor do we approve of open borders, the teaching of Critical Race Theory, or the defunding of our police. And we in this broad swath of Middle America strongly oppose profligate spending, crippling taxes, shuttered pipelines, soaring gasoline prices, and skyrocketing inflation.

A triumphant second-term President Trump would have been cracking down on all of this woke progressive madness and fiscal irresponsibility. Instead, the illegitimate Biden regime is enabling it.

As part of our growing national anger, the vast majority of us are also tired of being spoon-fed propaganda disguised as news. And we loathe bearing witness to the canceling and deplatforming of any thought that deviates from the nanny-state, progressive narrative.

CNN, MSNBC, the *New York Times*, and the *Washington Post* in particular are working hand in glove with the social media oligarchs running Facebook, Twitter, and Google to desecrate and all but destroy the First Amendment. A second-term President Trump would have had none of that, either.

The only way out of our ideological and partisan cul-de-sac is to turn around and confront the Big Truth now being swept under our national rug. The gulf between the phrases "elections have consequences" and "*stolen* elections have consequences" is now as big, wide, and dangerous as those now looming across America's partisan and ideological divides.

Today's crisis is as oddly un-American as it is ahistorical. At critical times in our nation's history—the patriotism of World War II is the gold standard—we have always been Americans first rather than partisans and ideologues. Today, the abomination we are witnessing is decidedly not that.

Because we cannot rely on our media and our elites to acknowledge, much less address, today's Big Truth, we must use our own human agency to advocate fiercely for freedom and democracy. As I have said many times in this book, it is time for Action, Action, Action.

We must first and foremost hold Communist China morally and financially accountable for the viral havoc it has wreaked on the world. As this book has demonstrated, the damages run into the tens of *trillions* of dollars.

We must get to the bottom of January 6. Was it simply an intelligence failure whereby government officials failed to heed the ample warnings of possible trouble?[2] What did the Capitol Hill police, the speaker of the House, the FBI, the Pentagon, and the Department of Homeland Security know, and when did they know it? And if they knew that trouble was coming, why didn't they arrange to better defend the Capitol?[3]

Troubling signs now point to the possibility that there was ample intelligence to act upon but the dangers were ignored. Was that purposeful? Was it perpetrated by those who sought to provoke an attack on our Capitol as a means of derailing what I have referred to in this book as the Green Bay Sweep? It's a fair question. It remains without a credible answer.[4]

We must continue to press for full forensic audits of the November 3 election results in all fifty states and insist upon the decertification of any results in which significant fraud and election irregularities are found. At the time of this writing, Arizona is leading the way in conducting a comprehensive recount and canvass of its election results, and preliminary evidence points to significant irregularities.[5]

Efforts are under way to conduct similar audits in numerous other states—including the cesspool of Georgia[6]—and there is a growing national movement to get to the bottom of November 3. Predictably, the Biden regime's Department of Justice has threatened state officials who engage in such audits with criminal prosecution,[7] while Twitter quickly suspended all election audit "war room" accounts.[8]

Despite these efforts of the jackbooted Biden regime and Silicon Valley's deplatforming oligarchs to suppress all efforts to uncover the Big Truth about November 3, the American people continue to hunger for such truth. We simply can't have faith in our election system when two-thirds of Republicans and more than a quarter of Independents believe that the 2020 presidential election was rigged and stolen from Donald Trump.[9]

FAUCI LIED, AMERICANS DIED

We also must relentlessly pursue Anthony Fauci and the bureaucrats of the National Institutes of Health until they come clean about the Wuhan lab and the role of gain-of-function experiments in creating the pandemic.

- Fauci first categorically denied that the virus could have come from the Wuhan Institute of Virology. He has since been forced to acknowledge that strong possibility.[10]
- Fauci denied unequivocally in congressional testimony that his agency had helped fund the Wuhan lab.[11] He was forced to retract that Big Lie as well.[12]
- And in the biggest of his lies, Fauci has repeatedly denied before Congress that his agency funded gain-of-function experiments at the Wuhan lab—this despite abundant and overwhelming evidence to the contrary.[13] Now senators Rand Paul and Ron Johnson both want Fauci charged with lying to Congress.[14] A conviction would carry a prison term of up to five years.[15]

Most broadly, Fauci and his Deep Administrative State henchmen along with Big Pharma must be held ethically and legally accountable for everything from the Wuhan lab gain-of-function catastrophe and suppression of low-cost therapeutics such as hydroxychloroquine and ivermectin to the political, partisan, and deadly delay in delivering the Trump vaccines to the American people.

As for America's social media and its Silicon Valley oligarchs, I see no hope for any epiphany and voluntary reformation. During the 1960s, Latin America was plagued by an epidemic of people "disappeared" by violent militia under the cover of government authority.[16] Today's social media oligarchs are committing the same kind of "disappeared" violence against anyone who dares to speak any Big Truth.

Facebook, Twitter, and Google, in particular, are so deeply embedded in the politics and organizational culture of censorship and correct woke thought that they and their fearful leaders with names such as Zuckerberg, Dorsey, and Pichai offer us only one choice: *This unholy Trinity of Silicon Valley's Great Wall of Censorship and De-Platforming must be broken up and turned into public utilities.*

THE BIG TRUTH WILL OUT

At this stage in my life, I am at peace with being canceled. I'd rather speak my Big Truth to power on alternative networks such as Newsmax, Real America's Voice News, and One America News Network and on alternative platforms such as Steve Bannon's *War Room* livestream and podcast, Raheem Kassam's podcast and website *The National Pulse*, Darren Beattie's website Revolver.News, John Solomon's website Just the News, and the Hoft brothers' website Gateway Pundit. I'd rather do that than become a silenced prisoner of the corporate media beholden to my own individual pursuit of money and fame.

Whether it takes a year or five years or several decades, there is no doubt in my mind that, as with the election stolen by Kennedy from Nixon in 1960, we will learn beyond any shadow of reasonable doubt that the Biden forces stole the election from Trump. My investigation to date has all but proved this.

Whether it takes a year or five years or several decades—again based on my investigation—we will also come to understand unequivocally that the worst pandemic in US history since 1918 was indeed spawned through gain-of-function experiments in a bioweapons lab in Wuhan, China. The truly *big* question is whether it was an act of war by Communist China designed to take Hong Kong, topple Donald J. Trump, and advance China's geopolitical and military agendas.

From this historical perspective, the US media and elites of our time now propping up the illegitimate Biden regime and protecting the likes of Anthony Fauci and Big Pharma will be seen as the fools and shills and threats to our republic that they have been, are now, and likely will continue to be, at least for the foreseeable future.

AN AMERICA BACK ON TRACK

If I could wave a magic wand, here are some of the additional actions that I would like to see taken to get this nation back on track.

- Stop the forced vaccination of our children and those already infected with the virus who have developed robust antibodies. To do otherwise is simply bad science,[17] and the forced vaccination of our children in particular puts an entire generation of Americans at needless, and potentially existential, risk.

- Swiftly integrate the use of safe, low-cost, effective therapeutics such as hydroxychloroquine and ivermectin into our national pandemic-fighting plan. The vaccines will never be 100 percent effective—companies such as Pfizer and agencies such as the Centers for Disease Control and Prevention have told us so—and we will need such low-cost therapeutics to take death off the table and turn the Chinese Communist Party's virus into nothing more threatening than the common cold.
- Cease the teaching of Critical Race Theory in our schools and the US military. This Marxist doctrine is inflaming racial tensions and dividing this country rather than healing us—even as it harms the combat readiness of our military forces.
- Close the southern border to illegal immigration. The economic burden associated with the opening of our southern border to *the single largest influx of illegal aliens in our history* is falling disproportionately on poor Black, Brown, and blue-collar Americans who are seeing their job opportunities and wages squeezed—while further seeding and spreading the virus.
- Cease the kind of reckless government spending never before seen in our history and understand that the road to prosperity in America is paved with blue-collar manufacturing. We must at all costs stop the offshoring of our jobs. We must manufacture as much of what we buy as possible right here on US soil.
- Finally, decouple our economy and financial markets from Communist China and staunchly defend

> America against its economic aggression. And we must not blink when Communist China comes calling for Taiwan. Peace never comes through weakness.

On the political front, the Democratic Party must decide between woke progressive extremism versus a return to its roots as the party of blue-collar and working-class Americans. By the same token, the Republican Party must decide whether it is going to be the Party of Davos and the traditional Globalist Koch Network or the party of working-class America and Donald John Trump.

Whichever party seizes the blue-collar, working-class, Deplorables high ground will rule the United States for decades to come. I'm betting on Donald John Trump and a Republican Party built in his image and built to last.

I thank you with all my heart for reading this book. If you have gotten this far, I can be assured that you have carefully considered my facts and arguments, and I appreciate that.

I want nothing more than a strong and prosperous America, yet I deeply fear we are moving in the opposite direction.

So thanks for listening and reading. I'd love to hear from you at www.peternavarro.com. Peace. Out.

ACKNOWLEDGMENTS

This book would not have been possible without the stellar editorial assistance of Kate Hartson, together with Elaine and her team. I was truly in the best of hands and editing pens.

I want to also thank Kate along with Louise Burke for having the courage under fire to launch All Seasons Press. They are doing so against the stiff and bitter headwinds of a cancel culture, deplatforming, virtue-signaling corporate media, social media, and publishing world. We in MAGA land—and America—should wish them all the best of luck in providing a voice to those of us who would surely otherwise be silenced.

A big MAGA thanks also must go to my team at the White House for all their good work during America's plague year. Chris Abbott and Hannah Robertson were brave soldiers during even the darkest days of the pandemic, and they laid it all on the line for our country. Garrett Ziegler, Brendan McCommas, and Joanna Miller went far beyond the extra mile after November 3.

It was an honor, pleasure, and privilege serving in the trenches with 2016 campaign veterans such as Dan Scavino, Stephen Miller, Johnny McEntee, and Kellyanne Conway. In addition, Robert O'Brien, Matt Pottinger, Catherine Keller, and Pat Cipollone were always there to help punch through any West Wing walls.

Doc Hatfill remains an inspiration, and Steve Bannon remains on top of his "listen to the signal, not the noise," truth to power messaging. Steve's admonition to always "show, not tell" was ever most in my mind during the drafting of the manuscript.

All errors and omissions are my own.

NOTES

ONE: THE SKINNY DEAL, EAST WING, RED, WHITE, AND BLUES

1. Office of the Historian, “Foreign Relations of the United States 1950–1955,” US Department of State, accessed February 10, 2021, https://history.state.gov/historicaldocuments/frus1950-55Intel/d192.
2. President Trump, “Remarks by President Trump at Signing of the U.S.-China Phase One Trade Agreement,” White House, January 15, 2020, https://trumpwhitehouse.archives.gov/briefings-statements/remarks-president-trump-signing-u-s-china-phase-one-trade-agreement-2/. The Chinese Communist Party propaganda organs had a much more muted view of a treaty viewed by hardliners on the mainland as yet another humiliation by a foreign power.
3. “5 Reasons Dow Will Finish the Week on an Incredible High,” CCN, January 17, 2020, https://www.ccn.com/5-reasons-dow-will-finish-the-week-on-an-incredible-high/.
4. “Unemployment Rates in 15 States Were Lower than the 3.5-Percent U.S. Rate in December 2019,” U.S. Bureau of Labor Statistics, January 29, 2020, https://www.bls.gov/opub/ted/2020/unemployment-rates-in-15-states-were-lower-than-the-3-point-5-percent-u-s-rate-in-december-2019.htm. See also Catherine Thornbecke, “US Adds Solid 145K Jobs in December, Unemployment Remains at 50-Year Low,” ABC News, January 10, 2020, https://abcnews.go.com/Business/us-adds-solid-145k-jobs-december-unemployment-remains/story?id=68193958.
5. James Pethokoukis, “3 Charts Showing Good News about American Wage Growth,” American Enterprise Institute, January 7, 2020, https://www.aei.org/economics/3-charts-showing-good-news-about-american-wage-growth/. See also Ernie Tedeshi, “Pay Is Rising Fastest for Low Earners. One Reason? Minimum Wages,” *New York Times*, January 3, 2020, https://www.nytimes.com/2020/01/03/upshot/minimum-wage-boost-bottom-earners.html.
6. Pam Key, “Navarro: ‘Everyone Who Wants a Job Can Get a Job’ in the Trump Economy,” Breitbart, December 29, 2019, https://www.breitbart.com/clips/2019/12/29/navarro-everyone-who-wants-a-job-can-get-a-job-in-the-trump-economy/.
7. Tom Ozimek, “Pentagon: Border Wall Going up at about 1 Mile Per Day, and Rising,” *Epoch Times*, September 20, 2019, https://www.theepochtimes.com/pentagon-border-wall-going-up-at-about-1-mile-per-day-and-rising_3089137.html.

8. "Mexico Deploys Almost 15,000 Troops to US Border," Newsy, June 15, 2019, https://youtu.be/0VocQ4YVQskh.
9. "Border Numbers Fall for Third Month in a Row, but Remain High," US Department of Homeland Security, September 10, 2019, https://www.dhs.gov/news/2019/09/10/border-numbers-fall-third-month-row-remain-high.
10. Ibid.
11. Stephen Walt, "Barack Obama Was a Foreign-Policy Failure," *Foreign Policy*, January 18, 2017, https://foreignpolicy.com/2017/01/18/barack-obama-was-a-foreign-policy-failure/.
12. Mark Hyman, "Wag the Dog: Bill Clinton Unleashed," *American Spectator*, November 19, 2019, https://spectator.org/wag-the-dog-bill-clinton-unleashed/.
13. Philip Rucker and Robert Costa, "'It's a Hard Problem': Inside Trump's Decision to Send More Troops to Afghanistan," *Washington Post*, August 21, 2017, https://www.washingtonpost.com/politics/its-a-hard-problem-inside-trumps-decision-to-send-more-troops-to-afghanistan/2017/08/21/14dcb126-868b-11e7-a94f-3139abce39f5_story.html.
14. "Presidential Approval Ratings—Donald Trump," Gallup, https://news.gallup.com/poll/203198/presidential-approval-ratings-donald-trump.aspx. This number reflects the Gallup Poll result for January 16 through January 29, 2020. The previous two weeks the approval rating was at 44 percent, suggesting a possible bump from the phase one China deal. Trump's approval rating hit a low of 35 percent in August 2017.
15. "Presidential Ratings—Issues Approval," Gallup, https://news.gallup.com/poll/1726/presidential-ratings-issues-approval.aspx. For the period January 16–29.
16. "Presidential Ratings—Issues Approval," Gallup, https://news.gallup.com/poll/1726/presidential-ratings-issues-approval.aspx.
17. See, for example, "2024 US Presidential Odds Tracker," Sports Betting Dime, updated August 17, 2021, https://www.sportsbettingdime.com/politics/us-presidential-election-odds/.
18. "Why Voting Matters: Supreme Court Edition," Axios, June 28, 2018, https://www.axios.com/hillary-clinton-2016-election-votes-supreme-court-liberal-justice-1b4bc4fc-9fad-44b4-ab54-9ef86aa9c1f1.html.
19. The square miles for each state are 56,539 for Michigan, 44,820 for Pennsylvania, and 54,314 for Wisconsin. The total is 155,673.
20. There are 538 votes in the Electoral College, and it normally takes at least 270 to win. In 2016, there were seven faithless electors, two for Trump and five for Clinton. Colin Powell received three votes. John Kasich, Rand Paul, Bernie Sanders, and Faith Spotted Eagle each received one.

21. "Donald Trump Favours High Tariffs on Chinese Exports," BBC News, January 7, 2016, https://www.bbc.com/news/business-35258620.
22. Tim Hains, "Chris Wallace Grills WH Trade Advisor Peter Navarro on New China Tariffs: Are Costs Passed on to Customers?" Real Clear Politics, August 4, 2019, https://www.realclearpolitics.com/video/2019/08/04/chris_wallace_grills_ustr_peter_navarro_on_new_tariffs_.html.
23. Hans A. von Spakovsky and Peyton Smith, "China Is Poisoning America with Fentanyl," Heritage Foundation, March 5, 2019, https://www.heritage.org/crime-and-justice/commentary/china-poisoning-america-fentanyl. "US Drugs Bust Uncovers Enough Chinese Fentanyl to Kill 14 Million People," *South China Morning Post*, August 30, 2019, https://www.scmp.com/news/world/united-states-canada/article/3024993/us-drugs-bust-uncovers-enough-chinese-fentanyl-kill.
24. Peter Navarro, *The Coming China Wars: Where They Will Be Fought and How They Can Be Won*, rev. and exp. ed. (Upper Saddle River, NJ: FT Press, 2008).
25. Peter Navarro and Greg Autry, *Death by China: Confronting the Dragon—a Global Call to Action* (Upper Saddle River, NJ: FT Press, 2011).
26. Peter Navarro, *Crouching Tiger: What China's Militarism Means for the World* (Amherst, NY: Prometheus Books, 2015).
27. "President Obama and the President of the People's Republic of China Hold a Joint Press Conference," YouTube, September 25, 2015, https://www.youtube.com/watch?v=4lhQjsbkAPI. Julie Hirschfeld Davis and David E. Sanger, "Obama and Xi Jinping of China Agree to Steps on Cybertheft," *New York Times*, September 25, 2015, https://www.nytimes.com/2015/09/26/world/asia/xi-jinping-white-house.html.
28. Charlie Spiering, "Steve Bannon: 'Original Sin' of Team Trump Was Embracing the Establishment," Breitbart, September 10, 2017, https://www.breitbart.com/politics/2017/09/10/steve-bannon-original-sin-team-trump-embracing-establishment/.
29. Hunter (Daily Kos staff), "White House Loses Top-Level Staffer: Deputy Chief of Staff Kate Walsh Abandons Ship," Daily Kos, March 30, 2017, https://www.dailykos.com/stories/2017/3/30/1648756/-White-House-loses-top-level-staffer-deputy-chief-of-staff-Katie-Walsh-abandons-ship.
30. Mara Hvistendahl, "Films Financed by Steven Mnuchin Were Tailored to Appeal to China," The Intercept, September 22, 2020, https://theintercept.com/2020/09/22/films-steve-mnuchin-china-hollywood-censorship/.
31. Howard Gleckman, "TaxVox: Campaigns, Proposals, and Reforms," Tax Policy Center, October 13, 2016, https://www.taxpolicycenter.org/taxvox/clinton-and-trump-advisers-display-wide-differences-tax-policy-debate.

32. 1,104 days.
33. "China Backtracked on Nearly All Aspects of US Trade Deal: Sources," CNBC, May 8, 2019, https://www.cnbc.com/2019/05/08/china-backtracked-on-nearly-all-aspects-of-us-trade-deal-sources.html.
34. "Billionaires of Las Vegas," *Dreams* Magazine, https://ladreams.com/billionaires-of-las-vegas/
35. Devin O'Connor, "Las Vegas Casino Tycoon Sheldon Adelson Biggest US Political Donor over Past 20 Years," Casino.org, July 4, 2020, https:// www.casino.org/news/las-vegas-casino-tycoon-sheldon-adelson-usbiggest- political-donor/.
36. Peter Navarro, *The Coming China Wars*, p. 150. "China has become the world's prime breeding ground for new and exotic strains of influenza and other viruses, including both the deadly SARS virus and avian flu. The primary reason…is that so many different farm animals live in such close proximity to humans and other species. The resultant 'cross-pollution' creates a 'soup of chemicals and viruses' that now threaten the world with new and exotic influenza and other viruses and the possibility of a pandemic in which tens of millions of people may die."
37. Franklin D. Roosevelt Presidential Library and Museum, "Pearl Harbor: Why Was the Attack a Surprise?" Google Arts and Culture, https://artsandculture.google.com/exhibit/pearl-harbor-why-was-the-attack-a-surprise-u-s-national-archives/QRVzV65K.
38. Amy Qin, "China's Leader, under Fire, Says He Led Coronavirus Fight Early On," *New York Times,* February 15, 2020, https://www.nytimes.com/2020/02/15/world/asia/xi-china-coronavirus.html. "In an internal speech published on Saturday, Mr. Xi said he had 'issued demands about the efforts to prevent and control' the coronavirus on Jan. 7, during a meeting of the Politburo Standing Committee, the highest council of the Communist Party, whose sessions are typically cloaked in secrecy. Xi Jinping, "Speech during the Meeting of the Standing Committee of the Political Bureau of the Central Committee Study the Work of Responding to the Novel Coronavirus Pneumonia Epidemic," QSTheory.com, February 15, 2020, http://www.qstheory.cn/dukan/qs/2020-02/15/c_1125572832.htm.

TWO: FEAR, LOATHING, AND SAINT FAUCI IN THE SITUATION ROOM

1. Warren Fiske, "Did Fauci Tell U.S. 'Not to Worry About' Coronavirus?," Politifact, April 29, 2020, https://www.politifact.com/factchecks/2020/apr/29/steve-bannon/did-fauci-tell-us-not-worry-about-coronavirus/.
2. White House Situation Room, January 28, 2020.

3. Anthony S. Fauci, H. Clifford Lane, and Robert R. Redfield, "Covid-19—Navigating the Uncharted," *New England Journal of Medicine* 382 (March 26, 2020): 1268–69, https://www.nejm.org/doi/full/10.1056/NEJMe2002387.
4. Justine Coleman, "White House Releases Photo of Trump, Advisers Monitoring al-Baghdadi Raid in Situation Room," The Hill, October 27, 2019, https://thehill.com/policy/international/middle-east-north-africa/467641-white-house-releases-photo-of-trump-and.
5. James Gordon Meek et al., "Kayla Mueller in Captivity: Courage, Selflessness as She Defended Christian Faith to ISIS Executioner 'Jihadi John,'" ABC News, August 25, 2016, https://abcnews.go.com/International/kayla-mueller-captivity-courage-selflessness-defended-christian-faith/story?id=41626763.
6. Liji Thomas, "Cremation Numbers Reveal Possible Suppression of True COVID-19 Data in China," Newsmedical.net, June 8, 2020, https://www.news-medical.net/news/20200608/Cremation-numbers-reveal-possible-suppression-of-true-COVID-19-data-in-China.aspx.
7. Associated Press, "Five MILLION People Were Able to Flee Wuhan Before It Was Put Under Quarantine and Head to Neighbouring Chinese Province—Taking the Deadly Coronavirus with Them," *Daily Mail*, February 9, 2020, https://www.dailymail.co.uk/news/article-7983311/Mapping-app-location-data-shows-virus-spread-China.html.
8. John Catsimatidus, "Dr. Anthony Fauci 1-26-20," *The CATS Roundtable*, January 25, 2020, https://soundcloud.com/john-catsimatidis/dr-anthony-fauci-1-26-20.
9. Bruce Nussbaum, *Good Intentions: How Big Business and the Medical Establishment Are Corrupting the Fight Against AIDS* (New York: Penguin, 1990), https://www.scribd.com/document/111129786/Good-intentions-Bruce-Nussbaum, 123.
10. Ibid., 121.
11. Sean Strub, "Whitewashing AIDS History," HuffPost,February 21, 2014, https://www.huffpost.com/entry/whitewashing-aids-history_b_4762295.
12. Jocelyn Kaiser, "NIH lifts 3-year ban on funding risky virus studies," Science, December 19, 2017. https://www.sciencemag.org/news/2017/12/nih-lifts-3-year-ban-funding-risky-virus-studies.
13. Glenn Kessler, "Fact-checking the Paul-Fauci flap over Wuhan lab funding," Washington Post, May 18, 2021. https://www.washingtonpost.com/politics/2021/05/18/fact-checking-senator-paul-dr-fauci-flap-over-wuhanlab-funding/. See also: Reality Check Team, BBC News, "Coronavirus: Was US money used to fund risky research in China?" BBC News, August 2, 2021. https://www.bbc.com/news/57932699
14. These emails were released in response to a Freedom of Information Act request by BuzzFeed. See Natalie Bettendorf and Jason Leopold, "Anthony Fauci's Emails Reveal the Pressure That Fell on One Man,"

BuzzFeed News, June 2, 2021, https://www.buzzfeednews.com/article/nataliebettendorf/fauci-emails-covid-response.

15. Samuel Chamberlain, Mark Moore, and Bruce Golding, "Fauci Was Warned That COVID-19 May Have Been 'Engineered,' Emails Show," *New York Post*, June 2, 2021, https://nypost.com/2021/06/02/fauci-was-warned-that-covid-may-have-been-engineered-emails/.
16. The entire memo and other documents from my White House years can be found at https://peternavarro.com.
17. Bob Woodward, *Rage* (New York: Simon & Schuster, 2020), 235–36.

THREE: THE WHITE HOUSE VIRUS DENIER COUNCIL AND TASK FORCE OF DOOM

1. "Past Seasons Estimated Influenza Disease Burden," Centers for Disease Control and Prevention, https://www.cdc.gov/flu/about/burden/past-seasons.html?web=1&wdLOR=c88B120D1-08B1-2F46-A689-65664EB3ED63.
2. Blair Shiff, "Coronavirus Will Have 'Minimal Impact' on US Economy, Larry Kudlow Says," Fox Business, January 29, 2020, https://www.foxbusiness.com/healthcare/coronavirus-minimal-impact-us-economy-larry-kudlow.
3. "First on CNBC: CNBC Transcript: National Economic Council Director Larry Kudlow Speaks with CNBC's 'Squawk on the Street' Today," CNBC, March 6, 2020, https://www.cnbc.com/2020/03/06/first-on-cnbc-cnbc-transcript-national-economic-council-director-larry-kudlow-speaks-with-cnbcs-squawk-on-the-street-today.html.
4. Ibid.
5. David Moye, "'Morning Joe' Host Gets Personal, Calls Melania Trump 'Absolutely Shameless,'" HuffPost, August 26, 2020, https://www.huffpost.com/entry/morning-joe-host-scarborough-melania-trump-shameless_n_5f468527c5b6cf66b2b1a8a8. See also Aaron Rupar, "The RNC Keeps Referring to Covid-19 in the Past Tense. 1,147 American Deaths Were Reported Tuesday," Vox, August 26, 2020, https://www.vox.com/2020/8/26/21402124/rnc-coronavirus-past-tense-larry-kudlow; Andrew Solender, "Trump Adviser Refers to Coronavirus in Past Tense in RNC Speech as He Claims 'Successful' Fight," *Forbes*, August 25, 2020, https://www.forbes.com/sites/andrewsolender/2020/08/25/trump-adviser-refers-to-coronavirus-in-past-tense-in-rnc-speech-as-he-claims-successful-fight/?sh=79b076a22bcb; Adam Kelsey, "3 Key Takeaways from Night 4 of the Republican National Convention," ABC News, August 28, 2020, https://preprod.abcnews.go.com/Politics/key-takeaways-night-republican-national-convention/story?id=72577773.
6. Russell Berman, "Remember the Pandemic?," *The Atlantic*, August 25, 2020, https://www.theatlantic.com/politics/archive/2020/08/larry-kudlow-pandemic/615676/.

7. Ibid.
8. Michael Bender and Rebecca Ballhaus, "How Trump Sowed Covid Supply Chaos. 'Try Getting It Yourselves,'" *Wall Street Journal*, August 31, 2020, https://www.wsj.com/articles/how-trump-sowed-covid-supply-chaos-try-getting-it-yourselves-11598893051?mod=searchresults_pos2&page=1. The article reported this remark almost correctly as "Do whatever you have to do, and I'll do whatever I have to do."
9. John Binder, "Peter Navarro to Coronavirus Price Gougers: 'We're Going to Come for You,'" Breitbart, March 22, 2020, https://www.breitbart.com/politics/2020/03/22/peter-navarro-price-gougers-hoarders/.

FOUR: A PEACE CORPS MARTIAN IN THE WHITE HOUSE

1. Dino-Ray Ramos, "The Best Quotes from 'The Martian,'" Bustle, October 1, 2015, https://www.bustle.com/articles/114396-7-martian-quotes-from-the-book-that-luckily-made-it-into-the-movie.
2. Sarah Ellison, "The Inside Story of the Kushner-Bannon Civil War," *Vanity Fair,* April 14, 2017, https://www.vanityfair.com/news/2017/04/jared-kushner-steve-bannon-white-house-civil-war.
3. Tony Pierce, "Donald Trump Has Read a Lot of Books on China: 'I Understand the Chinese Mind,'" *Los Angeles Times,* May 3, 2011, https://latimesblogs.latimes.com/washington/2011/05/donald-trump-i-understand-the-chinese-mind.html.
4. Margot Roosevelt, "One of Trump's Biggest Economic Supporters? It's a UC Irvine Economist," *Orange County Register,* August 16, 2016, https://www.ocregister.com/2016/08/16/one-of-trumps-biggest-economic-supporters-its-a-uc-irvine-economist/.
5. Editorial Board, "All Hail the Lobster King," *Wall Street Journal*, June 28, 2020, https://www.wsj.com/articles/all-hail-the-lobster-king-11593381414.
6. Kelly Riddell, "No, Obama, You Presided over a Loss of Manufacturing Jobs, and Failed to Deliver on Exports," *Washington Times*, November 30, 2016, https://www.washingtontimes.com/news/2016/nov/30/no-obama-you-presided-over-loss-manufacturing-jobs/.
7. "Databases, Tables, & Calculators by Subject," U.S. Bureau of Labor Statistics, July 28, 2021, https://data.bls.gov/timeseries/CES3000000001.
8. Rebecca Savransky, "Obama to Trump: 'What Magic Wand Do You Have?,'" The Hill, June 1, 2016, https://thehill.com/blogs/blog-briefing-room/news/281936-obama-to-trump-what-magic-wand-do-you-have.
9. Eric Weiner, "In Thailand, 'Sanuk' Has Been Elevated to an Ethos, a Way of Life—Which Perhaps the West Could Learn From," BBC, November 24, 2015, http://www.bbc.com/travel/story/20151119-can-thailand-teach-us-all-to-have-more-fun.
10. Phil Carroll, "Nakhon Phanom Royal Thai Air Force Base in the Vietnam War," Vietnam Security Police Association, Inc., https://vspa.com/pdf/k9-nkp-doghandlers-perspective-carroll.pdf.

11. The United States Army Equipment and Optical School (USAMEOS) at Fitzsimons Army Medical Center (FAMC) in Aurora, Colorado, to be exact. See "Biomedical Equipment Technician," LiMSwiki.org, https://www.limswiki.org/index.php/Biomedical_equipment_technician.
12. "HHS Office of the Assistant Secretary for Preparedness and Response," U.S. Department of Health and Human Services, https://www.phe.gov/about/aspr/Pages/default.aspx.
13. Anne P. Mitchell, "Full Text of Dr. Rick Bright Whistleblower Complaint Against DHHS over Coronavirus Handling and Pushing of Hydroxychloroquine," The Internet Patrol, May 5, 2020, https://www.theinternetpatrol.com/full-text-of-dr-rick-bright-whistleblower-complaint-against-hhs-in-coronavirus-handling/.
14. Ibid.
15. Ebony Bowden, "White House Sends Protective Gear to NYPD in 'Operation Blue Bloods,'" *New York Post*, April 2, 2020, https://nypost.com/2020/04/02/white-house-sends-nypd-protective-gear-in-operation-blue-bloods/.
16. "'This Week' Transcript 5-17-20: Peter Navarro, Sen. Bernie Sanders," ABC News, May 17, 2020, https://abcnews.go.com/Photos/week-transcript-17-20-peter-navarro-sen-bernie/story?id=70728796.

FIVE: AN UNLOST FEBRUARY AND OFF TO THE VACCINE HORSE RACE

1. For such a critique, see, e.g., Cameron Peters, "A Detailed Timeline of All the Ways Trump Failed to Respond to the Coronavirus," Vox, June 8, 2020, https://www.vox.com/2020/6/8/21242003/trump-failed-coronavirus-response
2. *New Day*, transcript, CNN, February 28, 2020, http://transcripts.cnn.com/TRANSCRIPTS/2002/28/nday.05.html.
3. Ibid.
4. *Fareed Zakaria GPS*, transcript, CNN, May 3, 2020, http://transcripts.cnn.com/TRANSCRIPTS/2005/03/fzgps.01.html.
5. "Fact Sheet for Recipients and Caregivers," U.S. Food and Drug Administration, June 25, 2021, https://www.fda.gov/media/144414/download, 4.

SIX: TAKING DEATH AND FEAR OFF THE THERAPEUTICS TABLE

1. Fahim Abed, "Afghan War Casualty Report: February 2020," *New York Times*, February 6 , 2020, updated October 29, 2020, https://www.nytimes.com/2020/02/06/magazine/afghan-war-casualty-report-february-2020.html.
2. Lisette Voytko, "Fauci Says Remdesivir Reduces Recovery Time for Coronavirus Patients," *Forbes*, April 29, 2020, https://www.forbes.com/

sites/lisettevoytko/2020/04/29/fauci-says-remsdesivir-reduces-recovery-time-for-coronavirus-patients/?sh=39906c6f3755.

3. Adam Andrzejewski, "Dr. Anthony Fauci: The Highest Paid Employee in the Entire U.S. Federal Government," *Forbes*, January 25, 2021, https://www.forbes.com/sites/adamandrzejewski/2021/01/25/dr-anthony-fauci-the-highest-paid-employee-in-the-entire-us-federal-government/?sh=7cc18674386f.
4. Lauren Hirsch, "Trump Signs $8.3 Billion Emergency Coronavirus Spending Package," CNBC, March 6, 2020, https://www.cnbc.com/2020/03/06/trump-signs-8point3-billion-emergency-coronavirus-spending-package.html.

SEVEN: THE SCURRILOUS CASE OF HYDROXY HYSTERIA

1. Associated Press, "'Anecdotal Evidence,' Dr. Fauci Says of Malaria Drug Claim," *New York Times*, March 20, 2020, https://www.nytimes.com/video/us/politics/100000007046134/trump-fauci.html.
2. Veronika Kyrylenko, "Fauci Brushed Off E-mail Suggesting Hydroxychloroquine Was Effective Against COVID-19: 'Too Long for Me to Read,'" The New American, June 5, 2021, https://thenewamerican.com/fauci-brushed-off-email-suggesting-hydroxychloroquine-was-effective-against-covid-19-too-long-for-me-to-read/.
3. "Hydroxychloroquine can be prescribed to adults and children of all ages. It can also be safely taken by pregnant women and nursing mothers." "Medicines for the Prevention of Malaria While Traveling: Hydroxychloroquine (Plaquenilä), Centers for Disease Control and Prevention, https://www.cdc.gov/malaria/resources/pdf/fsp/drugs/Hydroxychloroquine.pdf.
4. See my report on hydroxychloroquine at my website, https://peternavarro.com, for a broad overview of the literature and extended discussion of the science behind the medicine. At the time of this writing, countries representing at least one-fourth of the world's population are aggressively using hydroxychloroquine to fight the pandemic; they range from France, Italy, Spain, and Turkey to Brazil, Panama, Saudi Arabia, and Switzerland. There are literally hundreds of studies showing the effectiveness of hydroxychloroquine, and one meta-analysis of more than two hundred of these studies from around the world involving over three thousand authors and almost two hundred thousand patients has shown a 64 percent improvement in rates of hospitalization and mortality when hydroxychloroquine is administered in early treatment used. Tragically, almost 80 percent of the extant studies have yielded results in favor of the use of hydroxychloroquine. Yet the public perception stoked by Hydroxy Hysteria is just the opposite. Yes, there is blood on CNN's hands.
5. See, e.g., Xuesong Chen and Jonathan D. Geiger, "Janus Sword Actions of Chloroquine and Hydroxychloroquine Against COVID-19," *Cellular Signalling 72* (September 2020): 109706, https://www.sciencedirect.com/science/article/pii/S0898656820301832.

6. Martin J. Vincent et al., "Chloroquine Is a Potent Inhibitor of SARS Coronavirus Infection and Spread," *Virology Journal* 2, article 69 (August 22, 2005), https://virologyj.biomedcentral.com/articles/10.1186/1743-422X-2-69.
7. This landmark study examined the antiviral effects of chloroquine a medicine very similar to hydroxychloroquine with more side effects. Hydroxychloroquine was developed precisely because chloroquine had such side effects. Ibid.
8. Ibid.
9. See, e.g., Deba Prasad Dhibar et al., "Post-exposure Prophylaxis with Hydroxychloroquine for the Prevention of COVID-19, a Myth or a Reality? The PEP-CQ Study," *International Journal of Antimicrobial Agents* 56, no. 6 (November 6, 2020), 106224, https://www.sciencedirect.com/science/article/abs/pii/S0924857920304350?via%3Dihub; Özlem Polat, Ramazan Korkusuz, and Murathan Berber, "Hydroxychloroquine Use on Healthcare Workers Exposed to COVID-19—A Pandemic Hospital Experience," *Medical Journal of Bakirkoy* 16, no. 3 (2020): 280–86, http://cms.galenos.com.tr/Uploads/Article_47752/BTD-16-280-En.pdf; Juan M. Luco, "Hydroxychloroquine as Post-exposure Prophylaxis for Covid-19: Why Simple Data Analysis Can Lead to the Wrong Conclusions from Well-Designed Studies," *Trends in Medicine*, February 12, 2021, Open Access Text, https://www.oatext.com/hydroxychloroquine-as-post-exposure-prophylaxis-for-covid-19-why-simple-data-analysis-can-lead-to-the-wrong-conclusions-from-well-designed-studies.php; Sun Hee Lee, Hyunjin Son, and Kyong Ran Peck, "Can Post-exposure Prophylaxis for COVID-19 Be Considered as an Outbreak Response Strategy in Long-Term Care Hospitals?," *International Journal of Antimicrobial Agents* 55, no. 6 (June 2020), 105988, April 17, 2020, https://pubmed.ncbi.nlm.nih.gov/32305587/; Milan Sharma, "STUDY: Four Hydroxychloroquine Doses Works to PREVENT Coronavirus in Healthcare Workers," Fort Russ News, June 6, 2020, https://fort-russ.com/2020/06/study-four-hydroxychloroquine-doses-works-to-prevent-coronavirus-in-healthcare-workers/.
10. See, e.g., "HCQ for COVID-19," www.c19study.com.
11. Please visit https://peternavarro.com and read my report on hydroxychloroquine authored with Dr. Steven Hatfill.
12. See "HCQ for COVID-19," an analysis of all 313 studies.
13. U.S. Food and Drug Administration, letter to Dr Rick Bright, March 28, 2020, https://www.fda.gov/media/136534/download.
14. Jonathan Swan, "Scoop: Inside the Epic White House Fight over Hydroxychloroquine," Axios, April 5, 2020, https://www.axios.com/coronavirus-hydroxychloroquine-white-house-01306286-0bbc-4042-9bfe-890413c6220d.html.
15. Matthieu Mahévas et al., "No Evidence of Clinical Efficacy of Hydroxychloroquine in Patients Hospitalised for COVID-19 Infection

and Requiring Oxygen: Results of a Study Using Routinely Collected Data to Emulate a Target Trial," medRxiv, April 14, 2020, https://www.medrxiv.org/content/10.1101/2020.04.10.20060699v1.

16. Minali Nigam and Elizabeth Cohen, "French Study Finds Hydroxychloroquine Doesn't Help Patients with Coronavirus," CNN, April 15, 2020, https://www.cnn.com/2020/04/15/health/new-french-study-hydroxychloroquine/index.html.
17. Katie Thomas and Knvul Sheikh, "Small Chloroquine Study Halted over Risk of Fatal Heart Complications," *New York Times*, April 12, 2020, updated September 14, 2020, https://www.nytimes.com/2020/04/12/health/chloroquine-coronavirus-trump.html.
18. Jessica Glenza, "Brazilian Chloroquine Study Halted After High Dose Proved Lethal for Some Patients," *The Guardian*, April 24, 2020, https://www.theguardian.com/world/2020/apr/24/chloroquine-study-coronavirus-brazil.
19. Joseph Magagnoli et al., "Outcomes of Hydroxychloroquine Usage in United States Veterans Hospitalized with Covid-19," medRxiv, April 21, 2020, https://www.medrxiv.org/content/10.1101/2020.04.16.20065920v1.full.pdf.
20. Case fatality rates vary considerably across countries. The rate was above 7.7 percent in Italy, while at least one study showed a range across countries of 0.25 to 10 percent. See "Mortality Risk of COVID-19," Our World in Data, https://ourworldindata.org/mortality-risk-covid.
21. "HCQ For COVID-19." www.c19study.com.
22. In Italy, for example, the case fatality rate is only 1 percent in the 50-to-59-year age bracket but jumps to 3.5 percent in the 60-to-69-year age bracket and then to 12.8 percent in the 70-to-79-year age bracket. By the time one reaches the age of 80, there is a one in five chance of dying, at least in Italy. See "Mortality Risk of COVID-19," Our World in Data, https://ourworldindata.org/mortality-risk-covid.
23. Rashawn Ray, "Why Are Blacks Dying at Higher Rates from COVID-19?," Brookings, April 9, 2020, https://www.brookings.edu/blog/fixgov/2020/04/09/why-are-blacks-dying-at-higher-rates-from-covid-19/.
24. Samia Arshad et al., "Treatment with Hydroxychloroquine, Azithromycin, and Combination in Patients Hospitalized with COVID-19," *International Journal of Infectious Diseases* 55 (August 2020): 396–403, https://www.sciencedirect.com/science/article/pii/S1201971220305348.
25. Fauci's beef focused on the fact that some of the patients in the study had also been taking corticosteroids, which may have provided an added benefit. It was a red herring, as the Ford study had statistically controlled for that. See Beth LeBlanc, "Fauci: Henry Ford Health's Hydroxychloroquine Study 'Flawed,'" *Detroit News*, July 31, 2020, https://www.detroitnews.com/story/news/local/michigan/2020/07/31/anthony-fauci-henry-ford-health-hydroxychloroquine-study-flawed/5559367002/.

26. Jessie Hellmann and Peter Sullivan, "Five Takeaways from Fauci's Testimony," The Hill, July 31, 2020, https://thehill.com/policy/healthcare/510037-five-takeaways-from-faucis-testimony.
27. "Reviving the US CDC," *The Lancet*, May 16, 2020, https://www.thelancet.com/journals/lancet/article/PIIS0140-6736(20)31140-5/fulltext.
28. "Our data has very convincingly shown that across the world in a real-world population that this drug combination [of hydroxychloroquine and the antibiotic azithromycin] . . . does not show any evidence of benefit, and in fact, is immutably showing a signal of grave harm." Jamie Gumbrecht and Elizabeth Cohen, "Large Study Finds Drug Trump Touted for Covid-19 Is Linked to Greater Risk of Death and Heart Arrhythmia," CNN, May, 22, 2020, https://edition.cnn.com/2020/05/22/health/hydroxychloroquine-coronavirus-lancet-study/index.html.
29. Mandeep R. Mehra et al, "Retraction - Hydroxychloroquine or chloroquine with or without a macrolide for treatment of COVID-19: a multinational registry analysis," The Lancet, June 13, 2020. https://www.thelancet.com/journals/lancet/article/PIIS0140-6736(20)31324-6/fulltext
30. *New Day*, transcript, CNN, July 29, 2020, http://transcripts.cnn.com/TRANSCRIPTS/2007/29/nday.05.html.
31. David R. Boulware et al., "A Randomized Trial of Hydroxychloroquine as Postexposure Prophylaxis for Covid-19," *New England Journal of Medicine 383* (August 6, 2020): 517–25, https://www.nejm.org/doi/full/10.1056/nejmoa2016638.
32. Barack Obama, *A Promised Land* (New York: Crown, 2020), 389.
33. Victor Davis Hanson, "Will Biden Give In to the Hydroxy Effect?," PJ Media, December 9, 2020, https://pjmedia.com/columns/victor-davis-hanson/2020/12/09/will-biden-give-in-to-the-hydroxy-effect-n1198503.

EIGHT: KILL THE GM CHICKEN, SCARE THE VENTILATOR MONKEY

1. Carrie MacMillan, "Ventilators and COVID-19: What You Need to Know," Yale Medicine, June 2, 2020, https://www.yalemedicine.org/news/ventilators-covid-19.
2. Associated Press, "'Where Are the Ventilators?': Cuomo Pleads for More Help for New York," *New York Times*, March 24, 2020, https://www. nytimes.com/video/us/politics/100000007051271/cuomo-coronavirusupdate.
3. Ibid.
4. "Gov. Andrew Cuomo Admits Stockpile of Thousands of Unused Ventilators," Elite Feed. March 28, 2020, https://elitefeed.com/2020/03/28/

gov-andrew-cuomo-admits-stockpile-of-thousands-of-unused-ventilators/.

5. Kaylee McGhee White, "Andrew Cuomo, Admit Your Nursing Home Policy Killed Seniors," *Washington Examiner*, May 11, 2020, https://www.washingtonexaminer.com/opinion/andrew-cuomo-admit-your-nursing-home-policy-killed-seniors.
6. Mariah Kreutter, "9 Women Have Now Accused Gov. Andrew Cuomo of Sexual Harassment," MSN, March 30, 2021, https://www.msn.com/en-us/news/us/nine-women-have-now-accused-gov-andrew-cuomo-of-sexual-harassment/ar-BB1eGLB3.
7. John Binder, "Shuttered Lordstown Plant to Reopen with 600 U.S. Jobs Making Electric Trucks," Breitbart, May 22, 2020, https://www.breitbart.com/politics/2020/05/22/shuttered-lordstown-plant-to-reopen-with-600-u-s-jobs-making-electric-trucks/.
8. Chris Anderson, "GM Closing Lordstown Assembly Plant, Cutting 14,700 Jobs in North America," 19 News, November 26, 2018, https://www.cleveland19.com/2018/11/26/gm-closing-lordstown-assembly-plant-cutting-jobs-north-america/.
9. Ibid.
10. "GM-UAW 'Catalyst' Peter Navarro Helped Seal Deal," Fox Business, October 16, 2019, https://www.foxbusiness.com/politics/gm-uaw-talks-included-peter-navarro.
11. Gavin Bade, "'GM Was Wasting Time': Trump Invokes DPA to Force GM to Make Ventilators," Politico, March 27, 2020, https://www.politico.com/news/2020/03/27/trump-slams-gm-over-ventilator-production-delays-costs-151885.
12. Ebony Bowden and Julia Marsh, "NYC Garment District to Begin Producing Surgical Gowns Amid Coronavirus Crisis," *New York Post*, April 20, 2020, https://nypost.com/2020/04/20/nyc-garment-districts-to-produce-surgical-gowns-amid-coronavirus/.

NINE: SWEET ON HONEYWELL, HIGH ON PERNOD, AND A PPE MISSION

1. Honeywell's production went from 20 million masks per month in March 2020 to 32 million masks per month by November. See "Honeywell Delivers 225 Million N95 and Surgical Masks in December for Health Care and Government Use," Honeywell, January 11, 2021, https://www.honeywell.com/us/en/press/2021/1/honeywell-delivers-225-million-n95-and-surgical-masks-in-december. See also "DOD Details $133 Million Defense Production Act Title 3 COVID-19 Project," U.S. Department of Defense, April 21, 2020, https://www.defense.gov/Newsroom/Releases/Release/Article/2158351/dod-details-133-million-defense-production-act-title-3-covid-19-project/.

2. Nicole Randall, "PPE Manufacturers Take Action to Support Global Communities in Need," International Safety Equipment Association, June 5, 2020, https://safetyequipment.org/knowledge-center-items/ppe-manufacturers-take-action-to-support-global-communities-in-need/.
3. Jessica Glenza, "Fauci Thanks US Health Workers for Sacrifices but Admits PPE Shortages Drove Up Death Toll," *The Guardian*, April 8, 2021, https://www.theguardian.com/us-news/2021/apr/08/anthony-fauci-thanks-us-healthcare-workers-true-heroes.
4. Juliet Linderman and Martha Mendoza, "US Medical Supply Chains Failed, and COVID Deaths Followed," AP News, October 6, 2020, https://apnews.com/article/virus-outbreak-pandemics-ap-top-news-global-trade-fresno-4354f8e8026cf8135b74fa19f0d0f048.
5. Andrea Shalal, "WTO Report Says 80 Countries Limiting Exports of Face Masks, Other Goods," Reuters, April 23, 2020, https://www.reuters.com/article/us-health-coronavirus-trade-wto-idUSKCN2253IX.
6. "COVID-19 Impact Assessment and Outlook on Personal Protective Equipment," UNICEF, May 4, 2020, https://www.unicef.org/supply/stories/covid-19-impact-assessment-and-outlook-personal-protective-equipment. See also https://macmap.org/content/images/static/trademeasure/Covid19-Measures.pdf.
7. "COVID-19 Response," Pernod Ricard USA, https://www.pernod-ricard-usa.com/covid19-response.
8. "UPS Promotes Laura Lane to Chief Corporate Affairs and Communications Officer," Globe Newswire, July 28, 2020, https://www.globenewswire.com/news-release/2020/07/28/2068823/0/en/UPS-Promotes-Laura-Lane-To-Chief-Corporate-Affairs-And-Communications-Officer.html.
9. "FEMA Phasing Out Project Airbridge," Federal Emergency Management Agency, June 18, 2020, https://www.fema.gov/press-release/20210318/fema-phasing-out-project-airbridge.
10. Jonathan Allen, Phil McCausland, and Cyrus Farivar, "Jared Kushner's Highly Scrutinized 'Project Airbridge' to Begin Winding Down," NBC News, May 11, 2020, https://www.nbcnews.com/politics/white-house/jared-kushner-backed-project-airbridge-be-largely-grounded-n1204646.
11. Kathryn Watson, "What Is Project Airbridge?," CBS News, March 30, 2020, https://www.cbsnews.com/news/coronavirus-what-is-project-airbridge/.

TEN: ROCKING WITH THE GODFATHER OF POLITICAL SOUL IN TEST SWAB LAND

1. Katie Kerwin McCrimmon, "The Truth About COVID-19 and Asymptomatic Spread: It's Common, So Wear a Mask and Avoid Large Gatherings," UCHealth Today, November 5, 2020, https://www.uchealth.org/today/the-truth-about-asymptomatic-spread-of-covid-19/.

2. Lena Sun, "CDC Director Warns Second Wave of Coronavirus Is Likely to Be Even More Devastating," *Washington Post*, April 21, 2020, https://www.washingtonpost.com/health/2020/04/21/coronavirus-secondwave-cdcdirector/. See also Joe Pinsker, "The Winter Will Be Worse," *The Atlantic*, August 5, 2020, https://www.theatlantic.com/family/archive/2020/08/winter-us-coronavirus-pandemic-dangerous-indoors/614965/.
3. Anthony Kuhn, "South Korea's Drive-Through Testing for Coronavirus Is Fast—and Free," NPR, March 13, 2020, https://www.npr.org/sections/goatsandsoda/2020/03/13/815441078/south-koreas-drive-through-testing-for-coronavirus-is-fast-and-free.
4. Shawn Boburg et al., "Inside the Coronavirus Testing Failure: Alarm and Dismay Among the Scientists Who Sought to Help," *Washington Post*, April 3, 2020, https://www.washingtonpost.com/investigations/2020/04/03/coronavirus-cdc-test-kits-public-health-labs/?arc404=true.
5. "2016 United States Presidential Election in Maine," Wikipedia, https://en.wikipedia.org/wiki/2016_United_States_presidential_election_in_Maine.
6. Celine Castronuovo, "Trump Wins Electoral Vote in Maine's 2nd Congressional District," The Hill, November 4, 2020, https://thehill.com/homenews/campaign/524507-trump-wins-electoral-vote-in-maines-2nd-congressional-district.
7. "HHS and DOD Award $11.6 Million Contract to Puritan Medical Products to Boost U.S. Production of Swabs for Cue Health COVID-19 Tests," U.S. Department of Health and Human Services, November 23, 2020, https://public3.pagefreezer.com/browse/HHS%20%E2%80%93%C2%A0About%20News/20-01-2021T12:29/https://www.hhs.gov/about/news/2020/11/23/hhs-dod-award-11-6-million-contract-puritan-medical-products-boost-us-production-swabs-cue-health-covid-19-test.html.

ELEVEN: A MORNING CNN PRAYER, A NIGHTLY MSNBC WAKE

1. *Fareed Zakaria GPS*, transcript, CNN, May 3, 2020, http://transcripts.cnn.com/TRANSCRIPTS/2005/03/fzgps.01.html.
2. Jeffrey Jones, "President Trump's Job Approval Rating Up to 49%," Gallup, March 24, 2020, https://news.gallup.com/poll/298313/president-trump-job-approval-rating.aspx?utm_source=alert&utm_medium=email&utm_content=morelink&utm_campaign=syndication.
3. Andrew Solender, "Trump's Approval Drops to 39% in Gallup Poll, Down 10 Points Since May," *Forbes*, June 10, 2020, https://www.forbes.com/sites/andrewsolender/2020/06/10/trumps-approval-drops-to-39-in-gallup-poll-down-10-points-since-may/?sh=43a0522e487b.
4. In March, his overall approval rating was at 48 percent while his job performance rating was at 49 percent. By July, those ratings had fallen to

39 percent and 42 percent, respectively. Jeffrey Jones "President Trump's Job Approval Up to 49%." Gallup. March 24, 2020. https://news.gallup.com/poll/298313/president-trump-job-approval-rating.aspx Andrew Solender. "Trump's Approval Drops To 39% In Gallup Poll., Down 10 Points Since May. Forbes. June 10, 2020. https://www.forbes.com/sites/andrewsolender/2020/06/10/trumps-approval-drops-to-39-in-gallup-poll-down-10-points-since-may/?sh=43a0522e487b. Jeffrey Jones, "Latest Trump Job Approval Rating at 42%." Gallup. August 5, 2019. https://news.gallup.com/poll/262694/latest-trump-job-approval-rating.aspx

TWELVE: A FAUCIAN GAIN-OF-FUNCTION BARGAIN WITH A WUHAN DEVIL

1. Trent Baker, "Trump: If Someone Hits Me, I Have to Hit Them Back Harder—'That's What We Want to Lead,'" Breitbart, April 3, 2016, https://www.breitbart.com/clips/2016/04/03/trump-if-someone-hits-me-i-have-to-hit-them-back-harder-thats-what-we-want-to-lead/.
2. Jerry Dunleavy, "Trump CDC Director Robert Redfield Says COVID-19 'Most Likely' Came from Wuhan Lab," MSN News, March 26, 2021, https://www.msn.com/en-us/news/politics/trump-cdc-director-robert-redfield-says-covid-19-most-likely-came-from-wuhan-lab/ar-BB1eZZVD.
3. Jane Berg, "Animals in Chinese Markets Carried SARS-like Virus," Center for Infectious Disease Research and Policy, September 9, 2003, https://www.cidrap.umn.edu/news-perspective/2003/09/animals-chinese-markets-carried-sars-virus.
4. Antonio Regalado, "No One Can Find the Animal That Gave People Covid-19," MIT Technology Review, March 26, 2021, https://www.technologyreview.com/2021/03/26/1021263/bat-covid-coronavirus-cause-origin-wuhan/.
5. "The Wuhan Lab at the Heart of the Pandemic Origin Theory," RFI, March 31, 2021, https://www.rfi.fr/en/the-wuhan-lab-at-the-heart-of-the-pandemic-origin-theory.
6. Marlene Lenthang, "State Department Warned in 2018 That Wuhan Lab Testing Bats for Coronavirus Had Sloppy Safety Precautions and Had the Potential to Cause a 'New SARS-like Pandemic," *Daily Mail*, April 14, 2020, https://www.dailymail.co.uk/news/article-8218817/State-Department-warned-2018-Wuhan-lab-cause-new-SARS-like-pandemic.html.
7. James Beal, "LAB 'CLOSED': Controversial Laboratory Studying Bats in Wuhan 'Shut Down After Hazardous Event in October,' Mobile Data Shows," The Sun, May 9, 2020, https://www.thesun.co.uk/news/11586875/wuhan-lab-studying-bats-shut-october/.
8. Edmund DeMarche, "US Learned Several Wuhan Lab Researchers Sickened Before COVID-19 Outbreak: Former State Department Official," Fox News, May 24, 2021, https://www.foxnews.com/world/wuhan-lab-covid-19-outbreak-china-researchers-sick-state-department.
9. ORIGINS-OF-COVID-19-REPORT.pdf (house.gov)

10. "Jon Stewart on Vaccine Science and the Wuhan Lab Theory," *The Late Show with Stephen Colbert*, June 15, 2021, https://www.youtube.com/watch?v=sSfejgwbDQ8.
11. "U.S. Government Gain-of-Function Deliberative Process and Research Funding Pause on Selected Gain-of-Function Research Involving Influenza, MERS, and SARS Viruses," U.S. Department of Health and Human Services, October 17, 2014, https://www.phe.gov/s3/dualuse/Documents/gain-of-function.pdf#:~:text=Gain-of-function%20studies,%20or%20research%20that%20improves%20the%20ability,and%20preparedness%20efforts,%20and%20furthering%20medical%20countermeasure%20development.
12. Rand Paul, "Americans Deserve the Truth about Gain-of-Function Research and the Wuhan Lab," *National Review*, August 4, 2021. https://www.nationalreview.com/2021/08/americans-deserve-the-truth-about-gain-of-function-research-and-the-wuhan-lab/. *See also:* Wendong Li et al, "Bats are natural reservoirs of SARS-like coronaviruses," PubMed.go, September 29, 2005. https://pubmed.ncbi.nlm.nih.gov/16195424/. John Cohen, "Wuhan coronavirus hunter Shi Zhengli speaks out," Science, July 31, 2020. https://science.sciencemag.org/content/369/6503/487.full
13. "The Wuhan Lab at the Heart of the 'Extremely Unlikely' Leak Theory," Medical Xpress, March 29, 2021, https://medicalxpress.com/news/2021-03-wuhan-lab-heart-extremely-leak.html.
14. "New Sars-like Coronavirus Discovered in Chinese Horseshoe Bats," EcoHealth Alliance, October 30, 2013, https://www.ecohealthalliance.org/2013/10/new-sars-like-coronavirus-discovered-in-chinese-horseshoe-bats.
15. Peter Daszak on C-SPAN, https://www.c-span.org/video/?404875-1/pandemics.
16. "Funding Pause for Certain Types of Gain-of-Function Research Projects," National Institutes of Health, October 17, 2014, https://grants.nih.gov/grants/guide/notice-files/NOT-OD-15-011.html.
17. Evita Duffy, "Lawmakers Demand Investigation of NIH 'Secretively' Funneling US Tax Dollars to Notorious Wuhan Lab," The Federalist, February 23, 2021, https://thefederalist.com/2021/02/23/lawmakers-demand-investigation-of-nih-secretively-funneling-us-tax-dollars-to-notorious-wuhan-lab/.
18. Kevin Loria, "The US Government Is Lifting a Ban on Engineering Deadly Viruses to Make Them More Dangerous," Business Insider, December 20, 2017, https://www.businessinsider.com/nih-lifts-ban-on-flu-mers-sars-virus-gain-of-function-research-2017-12.
19. Peter Navarro, "Tony Fauci's Cover-up Leaves Blood on His Hands," *Washington Times*, June 10, 2021, https://www.washingtontimes.com/news/2021/jun/10/tony-faucis-coverup-and-blood-his-hands/.

20. Raheem J. Kassam, "COVID 'Looks Engineered,' Govt-Funded Immunologist Told Fauci in January 2020," The National Pulse, June 2, 2021, https://thenationalpulse.com/news/covid-looks-engineered-govt-funded-immunologist-told-fauci-in-january-2020/.
21. Kristian G. Andersen et al., "The Proximal Origin of SARS-CoV-2," *Nature Medicine* 26 (2020): 450–52, https://www.nature.com/articles/s41591-020-0820-9.
22. Jenni Fink, "Timeline of What Dr. Fauci Has Said About the Wuhan Lab and COVID's Origins," *Newsweek*, May 25, 2021, https://www.newsweek.com/timeline-what-dr-fauci-has-said-about-wuhan-lab-covids-origins-1594698.

THIRTEEN: A CHINESE COMMUNIST PARTY TRAGEDY IN FIVE HEINOUS ACTS

1. Fareed Zakaria GPS, transcripts, CNN. May 3, 2020. https://transcripts.cnn.com/show/fzgps/date/2020-05-03/segment/01
2. Josh Feldman, "Jake Tapper Abruptly Ends Peter Navarro Interview After Clash on Trump Covid Response: 'You're Not Answering the Question,'" Mediaite, September 13, 2020, https://www.msn.com/en-us/news/politics/jake-tapper-abruptly-ends-peter-navarro-interview-after-clash-on-trump-covid-response-you-re-not-answering-the-question/ar-BB18Zok7.
3. Elaine Okanyene Nsoesie et al., "Analysis of Hospital Traffic and Search Engine Data in Wuhan China Indicates Early Disease Activity in the Fall of 2019," Harvard Library, Office for Scholarly Communication, August 6, 2020, https://dash.harvard.edu/handle/1/42669767.
4. Reuters Staff, "Chinese Officials Investigate Cause of Pneumonia Outbreak in Wuhan," Reuters, December 31, 2019, https://www.reuters.com/article/us-china-health-pneumonia/chinese-officials-investigate-cause-of-pneumonia-outbreak-in-wuhan-idUSKBN1YZ0GP.
5. "China Delayed Releasing Coronavirus Info, Frustrating WHO," Associated Press, June 1, 2020, https://apnews.com/article/united-nations-health-ap-top-news-virus-outbreak-public-health-3c061794970661042b18d5aeaaed9fae.
6. Lawrence Wright, "The Plague Year," *New Yorker*, December 28, 2020, https://www.newyorker.com/magazine/2021/01/04/the-plague-year. See also Jeremy Page and Natasha Khan, "On the Ground in Wuhan, Signs of China Stalling Probe of Coronavirus Origins," *Wall Street Journal*, May 12, 2020, https://www.wsj.com/articles/china-stalls-global-search-for-coronavirus-origins-wuhan-markets-investigation-11589300842.
7. "Seafood Market Closed After Outbreak of 'Unidentified' Pneumonia," *Global Times*, January 1, 2020, https://www.globaltimes.cn/content/1175369.shtml.
8. Chiara Fiorillo, "WU ONLY LIVE TWICE: World May NEVER Prove Wuhan 'Lab Leak' as China Will Have DESTROYED Evidence,

Warn ex-MI6 Boss," *The Sun*, June 3, 2021, https://www.thesun.co.uk/news/15150475/coronavirus-pandemic-lab-leak-theory-evidence-china/. See also Kim Sengupta, "China Deliberately Destroyed Evidence About Start of Coronavirus, Report Says," *Independent*, May 2, 2020, https://www.independent.co.uk/news/world/asia/coronavirus-cause-china-research-evidence-destroyed-a9495856.html.

9. Mark Hodge, "WHERE IS SHE? Hunt for 'Patient Zero' Scientist Who 'Disappeared' from Wuhan Lab After Coronavirus Outbreak," *The Sun*, August 23, 2020, https://www.thesun.co.uk/news/12476233/patient-zero-scientist-wuhan-lab/. See also Brittany Vonow, "WITHOUT A TRACE: Five Wuhan Whistleblowers Still Missing and One Is Dead After Exposing True Horrors of Coronavirus," *The Sun*, April 19, 2020, https://www.thesun.co.uk/news/11430712/wuhan-whistleblowers-missing-one-dead-coronavirus/; Michael R. Gordon, Warren P. Strobel, and Drew Hinshaw, "Intelligence on Sick Staff at Wuhan Lab Fuels Debate on Covid-19 Origin," *Wall Street Journal*, May 23, 2021, https://www.wsj.com/articles/intelligence-on-sick-staff-at-wuhan-lab-fuels-debate-on-covid-19-origin-11621796228.
10. Press Trust of India, "China Hoarded PPE, Selling It at High Rates: White House Official," Business Standard, April 21, 2020, https://www.business-standard.com/article/pti-stories/china-hoarded-ppe-selling-it-at-high-rates-white-house-official-120042100164_1.html.
11. *Fareed Zakaria GPS,* transcript, CNN, May 3, 2020, http://transcripts.cnn.com/TRANSCRIPTS/2005/03/fzgps.01.html.

FOURTEEN: A CCP VIRUS COMMISSION AND THE ULTIMATE INTERNATIONAL TORT

1. "Weekly Address: President Obama Establishes Bipartisan National Commission on the BP Deepwater Horizon Oil Spill and Offshore Drilling," The White House, May 22, 2010, https://obamawhitehouse.archives.gov/the-press-office/weekly-address-president-obama-establishes-bipartisan-national-commission-bp-deepwa.
2. See https://peternavarro.com for the entire document and other book-related documents.
3. Mary Hui, "Under the Cover of a Pandemic, China Is Dismantling Hong Kong's Last Freedoms," Quartz, April 20, 2020, https://qz.com/1841137/china-uses-coronavirus-as-cover-to-erode-hong-kong-freedoms/.
4. Dave Merrill, "No One Values Your Life More than the Federal Government," Bloomberg, October 19, 2017, https://www.bloomberg.com/graphics/2017-value-of-life/.
5. "Most Say China Should Pay Some of World's COVID Costs," Rasmussen Reports, July 28, 2020, https://www.rasmussenreports.com/public_content/politics/current_events/china/most_say_china_should_pay_some_of_world_s_covid_costs.

6. Office of Advocacy, "Small Businesses Generate 44 Percent of U.S. Economic Activity," U.S. Small Business Administration, January 20, 2019, https://advocacy.sba.gov/2019/01/30/small-businesses-generate-44-percent-of-u-s-economic-activity/.

FIFTEEN: THE LAST DAYS OF POMPEO AND THE THREE FEARS

1. Richard Sokolosky and Aaron Miller, "Qatar Crisis: Can Rex Tillerson Fix This Mess?," Carnegie Endowment for International Peace, July 10, 2017, https://carnegieendowment.org/2017/07/10/qatar-crisis-can-rex-tillerson-fix-this-mess-pub-71483.
2. Jess Stein, "Trump's Quest to Shatter GOP Economics Reached Its Culmination in 2019," *Washington Post*, December 27, 2019, https://www.washingtonpost.com/business/2019/12/27/trumps-quest-shatter-gop-economics-reached-its-culmination/.
3. Qiao Liang and Wang Xiangsui, *Unrestricted Warfare: China's Master Plan to Destroy America* (Beijing: China's People's Liberation Army, 1999).
4. Jordan Williams, "Pompeo, Mnuchin Among Trump Cabinet Members Who Discussed 25th Amendment: Report," The Hill, January 8, 2021, https://thehill.com/homenews/administration/533303-pompeo-mnuchin-among-trump-cabinet-members-who-discussed-25th.

SIXTEEN: THE CURIOUS CASE OF THE DELAYED VACCINE

1. Philip Rucker, "Trump Fixates on the Promise of a Vaccine—Real or Not—as Key to Reelection Bid," *Washington Post*, September 5, 2020, https://www.washingtonpost.com/politics/trump-vaccine-election/2020/09/05/c0da86d6-edf5-11ea-99a1-71343d03bc29_story.html.
2. Darragh Roche, "Big Pharma Backs Joe Biden, but People Don't Think He'll Fix Drug Pricing," *Newsweek*, September 29, 2020, https://www.newsweek.com/big-pharma-joe-biden-fix-drug-pricing-1534809.
3. "The Case of the Crying Comedian," *Perry Mason*, season 5, episode 5, October 14, 1961.
4. "Understanding How Vaccines Work," Centers for Disease Control and Prevention, July 2018, https://www.cdc.gov/vaccines/hcp/conversations/downloads/vacsafe-understand-color-office.pdf. As a fine point, alternatively, a viable vaccine contains a blueprint for the production of such an antigen.
5. Sandesh Archarya, "Largest Pharmaceutical Companies in the World in 2020," Explore Biotech, https://explorebiotech.com/largest-pharmaceutical-companies-in-the-world/.
6. Benjamin Mueller, "Why the U.K. Approved a Coronavirus Vaccine First," *New York Times*, December 2, 2020, https://www.nytimes.com/2020/12/02/world/europe/uk-covid-vaccine-pfizer.html.
7. "Development and Licensure of Vaccines to Prevent COVID-19," U.S. Food and Drug Administration, June 2020, https://www.fda.gov/

regulatory-information/search-fda-guidance-documents/development-and-licensure-vaccines-prevent-covid-19.

8. "Pfizer and BioNTech Accounce Early Positive Data from an Ongoing Phase 1/2 Study of mRNA-Based Vaccine Candidate Against SARS-CoV-2," Pfizer, July 1, 2020, https://www.pfizer.com/news/press-release/press-release-detail/pfizer-and-biontech-announce-early-positive-data-ongoing-0.
9. "Pfizer and BioNTect Granted FDA Fast Track Designation for Two Investigational mRNA-Based Vaccine Candidates Against SARS-CoV-2," Pfizer, July 13, 2020, https://www.pfizer.com/news/press-release/press-release-detail/pfizer-and-biontech-granted-fda-fast-track-designation-two.
10. Noah Weiland, Denise Grady, and David E. Sanger, "Pfizer Gets $1.95 Billion to Produce Coronavirus Vaccine by Year's End," *New York Times*, July 22, 2020, https://www.nytimes.com/2020/07/22/us/politics/pfizer-coronavirus-vaccine.html.
11. Bourla moved to the United States when he was thirty-four, according to Wikipedia. See "Albert Bourla," Wikipedia, https://en.wikipedia.org/wiki/Albert_Bourla. He told Margaret Hoover on PBS's *Firing Line* that he had become an American citizen. See "Albert Bourla," PBS, January 1, 2021, https://www.pbs.org/wnet/firing-line/video/albert-bourla-f24lvl/.
12. Berkeley Lovelace, Jr., "Pfizer CEO Confirms Late-Stage Coronavirus Vaccine Trial May Have Results in October," CNBC, September 3, 2020, https://www.cnbc.com/2020/09/03/pfizer-ceo-confirms-coronavirus-vaccine-trial-may-have-results-in-october.html.
13. Daniel Bush and Lisa Desjardins, "5 Takeaways from the First Trump-Biden Debate," PBS, September 30, 2020, https://www.pbs.org/newshour/politics/5-takeaways-from-the-first-trump-biden-debate.
14. USA Today Staff, "Read the Full Transcript from the First Presidential Debate Between Joe Biden and Donald Trump," *USA Today*, September 30, 2020, https://www.usatoday.com/story/news/politics/elections/2020/09/30/presidential-debate-read-full-transcript-first-debate/3587462001/.
15. Linda A. Johnson and Jonathan Lemire, "Pfizer CEO Pushes Back Against Trump Claim on Vaccine Timing," Associated Press, October 1, 2020, https://apnews.com/article/election-2020-virus-outbreak-donald-trump-business-elections-bba3859d8465c309311bb911af33780f.
16. Victor Reklaitis, "Pharma Stocks Fall as Trump Targets Drug Prices with Executive Orders," MarketWatch, July 25, 2020, https://www.marketwatch.com/story/pharma-stocks-fall-with-trump-set-to-sign-executive-orders-targeting-drug-prices-2020-07-24.
17. The contributions of individual Pfizer employees totaled $381,930 to the Biden campaign and $119,768 to the Trump campaign. See https://www.opensecrets.org/orgs/pfizer-inc/summary?id=D000000138.
18. Thanks to former Council of Economic Advisers staffer Joe Sullivan for grinding this out. See "Tracking Covid-19 Excess Deaths Across

Countries," *The Economist*, May 11, 2021, https://www.economist.com/graphic-detail/coronavirus-excess-deaths-tracker.

19. "Xeljanz, Xeljanz XR (tofacitinib): Drug Safety Communication—Due to an Increased Risk of Blood Clots and Death with Higher Dose," U.S. Food and Drug Administration, July 26, 2019, https://www.fda.gov/safety/medical-product-safety-information/xeljanz-xeljanz-xr-tofacitinib-drug-safety-communication-due-increased-risk-blood-clots-and-death.
20. Naveed Saleh, "10 Dangerous Drugs Recalled by the FDA," MDLinx, July 24 , 2019, https://www.mdlinx.com/article/10-dangerous-drugs-recalled-by-the-fda/lfc-4008.
21. Philip Rucker, Josh Dawsey, and Yasmeen Abutaleb, "Trump Fixates on the Promise of a Vaccine—Real or Not—as Key to Reelection Bid," *Washington Post*, September 5, 2020, https://www.washingtonpost.com/politics/trump-vaccine-election/2020/09/05/c0da86d6-edf5-11ea-99a1-71343d03bc29_story.html.
22. Megan Brenan, "Two-Thirds of Americans Not Satisfied with Vaccine Rollout," Gallup, February 10, 2021, https://news.gallup.com/poll/329552/two-thirds-americans-not-satisfied-vaccine-rollout.aspx.
23. Georgia Slater, "Kamala Harris Says 'I Would Not Trust Donald Trump' with Coronavirus Vaccine as Death Toll Rises," People, September 5, 2020, https://people.com/politics/kamala-harris-would-not-trust-donald-trump-coronavirus-vaccine/.
24. J. Clara Chan, "Kamala Harris Says She Wouldn't Trust a Vaccine Trump Recommended," MSN, October 8, 2020, https://www.msn.com/en-us/entertainment/news/kamala-harris-says-she-wouldnt-trust-a-vaccine-trump-recommended/ar-BB19O9k4.
25. Rick Perlstein, "Gerald Ford Rushed Out a Vaccine. It Was a Fiasco," *New York Times*, September 2, 2020, https://www.nytimes.com/2020/09/02/opinion/coronavirus-vaccine-trump.html.
26. Kent Sepkowitz, "Why Trump Should Worry About a Rushed Vaccine," CNN, September 10, 2020, https://edition.cnn.com/2020/09/10/opinions/trumps-rush-to-a-covid-vaccine-risks-this-danger-sepkowitz/index.html.
27. Joseph A. Wulfsohn and Brian Flood, "CNN Staffer Admits Network's Focus Was to 'Get Trump Out of Office,' Calls Its Coverage 'Propaganda,'" Fox News, April 13, 2021, https://www.foxnews.com/media/cnn-staffer-networks-trump-office-coverage-propaganda.

EIGHTEEN: WE'VE GOT THIS! THEY STOLE IT!

1. Sarah Ellison, "Trump Campaign Was Livid When Fox News Called Arizona for Biden—and Tensions Boiled Over On-air," *Washington Post*, November 4, 2020. https://www.washingtonpost.com/lifestyle/style/fox-news-election-night-arizona/2020/11/04/194f9968-1e71-11eb-90dd-abd0f7086a91_story.html. See also Stephen Battaglio, "Why Fox News Analyst Arnon Mishkin Called Arizona for Biden on Election Night," *Los Angeles Times*, November 5, 2020, https://www.latimes.com/

entertainment-arts/business/story/2020-11-05/fox-news-arnon-mishkin-election-2020-arizona-trump-biden.

NINETEEN: A WEST WING SURRENDER AND A WHITE-SHOE REBUFF

1. David Shepardson, "Oshkosh Defense to Build Next-Generation U.S. Postal Delivery Vehicles," Reuters, February 23, 2021, https://www.reuters.com/article/us-usa-postal-service/oshkosh-defense-to-build-next-generation-u-s-postal-delivery-vehicles-idUSKBN2AN2A1.
2. Dawn M. K. Zoldi, "The Latest Executive Order on Drones: The Ban on Chinese and 'Foreign Entity' UAS Expanded," Drone Life, January 21, 2021, https://dronelife.com/2021/01/21/the-latest-executive-order-on-drones-the-ban-on-chinese-and-covered-country-uas-expanded/.
3. "WTO Agreement on Government Procurement (GPA)," Department of Commerce, https://legacy.trade.gov/mas/ian/tradeagreements/multilateral/wto/tg_ian_002072.asp.
4. Mark Niesse, "Trump Hires Election Lawyers Who Were Supposed to Defend Georgia," *Atlanta Journal-Constitution*, November 11, 2020, https://www.ajc.com/politics/trump-hires-election-lawyers-who-were-supposed-to-defend-georgia/WNCZZOIDZFEF3PYKEV3IROORRI/.
5. "Jones Day Statement Regarding Election Litigation," Jones Day, November 2020, https://www.jonesday.com/en/news/2020/11/jones-day-statement-regarding-election-litigation.
6. Randall D. Eliason, "Opinion: Yes, Going After Trump's Law Firms Is Fair Game," *Washington Post*, November 12, 2020, https://www.washingtonpost.com/opinions/2020/11/12/yes-going-after-trumps-law-firms-is-fair-game/.
7. "Donald F. McGahn II (Don)," Jones Day, https://www.jonesday.com/en/lawyers/m/donald-mcgahn?tab=overview.

TWENTY: DUMB SONS OF BITCHES AND *THE IMMACULATE DECEPTION*

1. Caroline Spiezio, Disha Raychaudhuri, and Rick Linsk, "Trump Campaign's Post-election Legal Spending Topped $7M with Kasowitz in the Lead," Reuters, February 1, 2021, https://www.reuters.com/article/lawyer-trump-spend-idUSL1N2K8025.
2. "AG Paxton Sues Battleground States for Unconstitutional Changes to 2020 Election Laws," Ken Paxton, Attorney General of Texas, December 8, 2020, https://www.texasattorneygeneral.gov/news/releases/ag-paxton-sues-battleground-states-unconstitutional-changes-2020-election-laws.
3. Vivek Saxena, "Statistician in 2020 Election Lawsuit Lays Out Chances of Biden Winning as 'One in a Quadrillion,'" BizPacReview, December 9, 2020, https://www.bizpacreview.com/2020/12/09/statistician-in-2020-election-lawsuit-lays-out-chances-of-biden-winning-as-one-in-a-quadrillion-1003758/.
4. See, e.g., Eric Litke, "Lawsuit Claim That Statistics Prove Fraud in Wisconsin, Elsewhere Is Wildly Illogical," Politifact, December 9, 2020,

https://www.politifact.com/factchecks/2020/dec/10/facebook-posts/texas-lawsuit-statistics-fraud-wisconsin-michigan/; Peter Coy, "Understanding That 'One-in-a-Quadrillion' Claim About the Election," MSN News, December 11, 2020, https://www.msn.com/en-us/news/opinion/understanding-that-e2-80-98one-in-a-quadrillion-e2-80-99-claim-about-the-election/ar-BB1bR9df.

5. See, e.g., "Stanford Professor Explains Why the Statistics Quoted by Kayleigh McEnany in the Texas SCOTUS Lawsuit Are Wrong—twitchy.com," *The Spectator*, December 9, 2020, https://thespectator.info/2020/12/09/stanford-professor-explains-why-the-statistics-quoted-by-kayleigh-mcenany-in-the-texas-scotus-lawsuit-are-wrong-twitchy-com/.
6. Tucker Carlson, "Tucker Carlson: Time for Sidney Powell to Show Us Her Evidence," Fox News, November 19, 2020, https://www.foxnews.com/opinion/tucker-carlson-rudy-giuliani-sidney-powell-election-fraud.
7. Reality Check Team and BBC Monitoring, "What Is It and Why Has Trump's Ex-lawyer Released It?," BBC, November 28, 2020, https://www.bbc.com/news/election-us-2020-55090145.
8. Krista Kafer, "Kafer: Defense Strategy in Dominion Lawsuit Not 'Reasonable,'" *Denver Post*, March 27, 2021, https://www.denverpost.com/2021/03/27/dominion-lawsuit-election-fraud-sidney-powell/.
9. Marianne Levine and Melanie Zanona, "McConnell Warns Senate Republicans Against Challenging Election Results," Politico, December 15, 2020, https://www.politico.com/news/2020/12/15/mcconnell-gop-election-results-445524.
10. John Solomon, "Trump Adviser Peter Navarro Urges 'Cesspool' Georgia to Delay Senate Runoff until February," Just the News, December 23, 2020, https://justthenews.com/politics-policy/elections/trump-adviser-peter-navarro-urges-cesspool-georgia-delay-senate-runoff.
11. Quinn Scanlan, "Kemp Signs Sweeping Elections Bill Passed by Georgia Legislature. Here's What's in It," ABC News, March 25, 2021, https://abcnews.go.com/Politics/kemp-sign-sweeping-elections-bill-passed-georgia-legislature/story?id=76677927.
12. David Krayden, "Karl Rove Says the Georgia Senate Runoff Election Is 'the Last Line of Defense for Conservative Values,'" Daily Caller, November 19, 2020, https://dailycaller.com/2020/11/19/last-defense-conservative-values-karl-rove-georgia-senate-runoff-election/.
13. Alex Isenstadt, "'Dumb Son of a Bitch': Trump Rips McConnell at Mar-a-Lago," Politico, April 11, 2021, https://www.politico.com/news/2021/04/11/trump-mcconnell-dumb-son-of-a-bitch-rnc-480748.
14. Lauren Egan, "Barr Says No Evidence of Widespread Voter Fraud, Defying Trump," NBC News, December 1, 2020, https://www.nbcnews.com/politics/white-house/barr-says-no-evidence-widespread-voter-fraud-defying-trump-n1249581.
15. Evan Perez and Devan Cole, "William Barr Says There Is No Evidence of Widespread Fraud in Presidential Election," CNN, December 2, 2020,

https://edition.cnn.com/2020/12/01/politics/william-barr-election-2020/index.html.

16. Paul Bedard, "Pro-Biden Effort Offered Native Americans $25–$500 Visa Gift Cards and Jewelry to Vote," *Washington Examiner*, December 3, 2020, https://www.washingtonexaminer.com/washington-secrets/pro-biden-effort-offered-native-americans-25-500-visa-gift-cards-jewelry-to-vote.
17. Ivan Pentchoukov, "Illegal Money-for-Votes Raffles Conducted in Several States in 2020 Election," The Epoch Times, December 1, 2020, https://www.theepochtimes.com/illegal-money-for-votes-raffles-conducted-in-several-states-in-2020-election_3598915.html.
18. "A Truck Driver with USPS Says He Was Suspicious of His Cargo Load of 288,000 COMPLETED Ballots," December 1, 2020, https://www.youtube.com/watch?v=R0xaA4dYsbQ.
19. "WisGOP: Trump Lawsuit Highlights Indefinitely Confined Voter Increase," WisPolitics.com, https://www.wispolitics.com/2020/wisgop-trump-lawsuit-highlights-indefinitely-confined-voter-increase/.
20. "WisGOP: Some Indefinitely Confined Voters Are Not Indefinitely Confined," WisPolitics.com, https://www.wispolitics.com/2020/wisgop-some-indefinitely-confined-voters-are-not-indefinitely-confined/.
21. "WisGOP: Trump Lawsuit Highlights Indefinitely Confined Voter Increase."
22. "WisGOP: Some Indefinitely Confined Voters Are Not Indefinitely Confined."
23. *Paul Andrew Boland v. Brad Raffensperger*, Superior Court of Fulton County, State of Georgia, November 30, 2020, https://www.democracydocket.com/wp-content/uploads/sites/45/2020/11/2020-11-30-Verified-Complaint-1.pdf.
24. "How Do Election Workers Match Signatures? (2020)," Ballotpedia, https://ballotpedia.org/How_do_election_workers_match_signatures%3F_(2020).
25. Rowan Scarborough, "Georgia Election Law Replaces Verifying Ballot Signatures with Checking ID Numbers," *Washington Times*, March 30, 2021, https://www.washingtontimes.com/news/2021/mar/30/georgia-election-law-replaces-verifying-ballot-sig/.
26. See, e.g., "Kathy Boockvar," Ballotpedia, https://ballotpedia.org/Kathy_Boockvar. See also Chris Ullery, "Pa. Secretary of State Kathy Boockvar Had a Big Job Overseeing Election Reform in Pa. Then COVID Hit," *Courier Times* (Bucks County, PA), October 28, 2020, https://www.buckscountycouriertimes.com/story/news/2020/10/28/pennsylvania-sec-kathy-boockvar-secure-2020-election/3728060001/; "Advancement Project," Influence Watch, https://www.influencewatch.org/non-profit/advancement-project/.
27. *Donald J. Trump for President et al. v. Kathy Boockvar et al.*, United States District Court for the Middle District of Pennsylvania, November 18, 2020, https://www.courtlistener.com/recap/gov.uscourts.pamd.127057/gov.uscourts.pamd.127057.169.0.pdf.

28. *State of Texas v. Commonwealth of Pennsylvania, State of Georgia, State of Michigan, and State of Wisconsin*, Supreme Court of the United States, December 7, 2020, https://www.texasattorneygeneral.gov/sites/default/files/images/admin/2020/Press/SCOTUSFiling.pdf.
29. "USPS Contractor: 'Something Profoundly Wrong Occurred in Wisconsin During the Presidential Election,'" December 1, 2020, https://www.youtube.com/watch?v=hRUvP6cbtZk&feature=youtu.be&t=69. See also Isabel Van Brugen, "Wisconsin USPS Subcontractor Alleges Backdating of Tens of Thousands of Mail-in Ballots," The Epoch Times, December 2, 2020. https://www.theepochtimes.com/wisconsin-usps-subcontractor-alleges-backdating-of-tens-of-thousands-of-mail-in-ballots_3601580.html.
30. https://www.bizpacreview.com/2020/11/05/let-us-in-michigan-voter-counters-cover-up-windows-amid-accusations-of-violations-992983/.
31. Declaration of Gregory Stenstrom, *State of Texas v. Commonwealth of Pennsylvania, State of Georgia, State of Michigan, and State of Wisconsin*, Supreme Court of the United States, December 7, 2020, https://www.supremecourt.gov/DocketPDF/22/22O155/163048/20201208132827887_TX-v-State-ExpedMot%202020-12-07%20FINAL.pdf.

TWENTY-ONE: THE DEMOCRATS' UNRESTRICTED LAWFARE AND ART OF THE STEAL

1. "Trump: If Pence 'Does the Right Thing, We Win,'" Yahoo! News, January 6, 2021, https://news.yahoo.com/trump-pence-does-thing-win-181802824.html.
2. Half of Koch Industries' employees may be found offshore, and a third of the company's offshore serfs are low-wage Chinese nationals. See "Driving Change Around the World," Koch Industries, https://www.kochind.com/about/locations.
3. Eli Stokols and Noah Bierman, "Trump Lashes Out at Koch Brothers After Their Political Network Slams White House," *Los Angeles Times*, July 31, 2018, https://www.latimes.com/politics/la-na-pol-trump-koch-brothers-20180731-story.html.
4. Richard Eskow, "Marc Short: Koch Dark-Money Operative Is Trump's Liaison to Congress," PR Watch, January 23, 2017, https://www.prwatch.org/news/2017/01/13204/marc-short-koch-dark-money-operative-trump-legislative-director. See also "Short, Marc, Open-Secrets.org, https://www.opensecrets.org/revolving/rev_summary.php?id=80237.
5. Peter Navarro, The Art of the Steal, p. 2. Volume 2 of the Navarro Report, https://peternavarro.com/the-navarro-report/.
6. Jimmy Carter and James Baker, "Building Confidence in U.S. Elections," September 2005. https://www.legislationline.org/download/id/1472/file/3b50795b2d0374cbef5c29766256.pdf,p. iii.
7. Peter Navarro, The Art of the Steal, p. 2. Volume 2 of the Navarro Report, https://peternavarro.com/the-navarro-report/.

8. Bart Jansen, "Former Trump Campaign Manager Corey Lewandowski Proves to Be an Uncooperative Witness for House Democrats in Hearing," *USA Today*, September 17, 2019, https://www.usatoday.com/story/news/politics/2019/09/17/corey-lewandowski-testify-president-trump-house-judiciary-impeachment-investigation/2313866001/.
9. Molly Ball, "The Secret History of the Shadow Campaign That Saved the 2020 Election," *Time*, February 4, 2021, https://time.com/5936036/secret-2020-election-campaign/.
10. Ibid.
11. Kelly Mena, "'Naked' Ballot Rules Put Thousands of Pennsylvania Mail-in Votes at Risk, Philadelphia Official Warns," CNN, September 22, 2020. https://edition.cnn.com/2020/09/22/politics/pennsylvania-warning-secrecy-envelope-2020-election/index.html. See also Angela Couloumbis and Jamie Martines, "Republicans Seek to Sideline Pa. Mail Ballots That Voters Were Allowed to Fix," Spotlight PA, November 3, 2020, https://www.spotlightpa.org/news/2020/11/pennsylvania-mail-ballots-republican-legal-challenge-naked-ballots-fixed-cured/.
12. "Agency capture" is a well-recognized phenomenon in economics and politics. Traditionally, the term refers to the capture of regulatory agencies by the industries being regulated. Soros put a new twist on the term capture by putting in place people who would serve the interests of the Democrats rather than the public interest. See, for example, Regulatory Capture Definition (investopedia.com).
13. Shipwreckedcrew, "In 2006 George Soros Funded a Project to Elect Progressive Liberals to Secretary of State Offices—Now You Know Why," RedState, November 6, 2020, https://redstate.com/shipwreckedcrew/2020/11/06/in-2006-george-soros-funded-a-project-to-elect-progressive-liberals-to-secretary-of-state-offices-now-you-know-why-n276082. See also "Secretary of State Project," Wikipedia, https://en.wikipedia.org/wiki/Secretary_of_State_Project.
14. Avi Zenilman, "Secretaries of State Give Dem Firewall," Politico, November 2, 2008, https://www.politico.com/story/2008/11/secretaries-of-state-give-dem-firewall-015105.
15. "Guidance Concerning Examination of Absentee and Mail-in Ballot Return Envelopes," Pennsylvania Department of State, September 11, 2020, https://www.dos.pa.gov/VotingElections/OtherServicesEvents/Documents/Examination%20of%20Absentee%20and%20Mail-In%20Ballot%20Return%20Envelopes.pdf.
16. Ibid.
17. Ronn Blitzer, "Pennsylvania court: Secretary of state lacked authority to change deadline 2 days before Election Day," Fox News, November 12, 2020, https://www.foxnews.com/politics/pennsylvania-court- secretary-of-state-changed-deadline.
18. Brianna Lyman, "Michigan Court Rules Secretary of State Violated Law with Absentee Ballot Signatures," Daily Caller, March 17, 2021. https://

dailycaller.com/2021/03/17/michigan-court-claims-christopher-murray-jocelyn-benson-violated-administrative-procedure-act-absentee-ballot/.

19. Beth LeBlanc, "Judge Rules Benson's Ballot Signature Verification Guidance 'Invalid,'" *Detroit News*, March 17, 2021, https://www.detroitnews.com/story/news/politics/2021/03/15/judge-rules-secretary-state-bensons-ballot-signature-verification-guidance-invalid/4699927001/.
20. Michael Patrick Leahy, "About 73% Biden Vote Martin Gain in PA from Areas Given $18 Million by Zuckerberg-Funded 'Safe Elections' Project," Breitbart, November 19, 2020, https://www.breitbart.com/politics/2020/11/19/about-73-biden-vote-margin-gain-in-pa-from-areas-given-18-million-by-zuckerberg-funded-safe-elections-project/.
21. Michelle Malkin, "Who's Funding Shady Ballot Harvesting Schemes?," Rasmussen Reports, September 30, 2020, https://www.rasmussenreports.com/public_content/political_commentary/commentary_by_michelle_malkin/who_s_funding_shady_ballot_harvesting_schemes.
22. Saphora Smith, "China Forcefully Harvests Organs from Detainees, Tribunal Concludes," NBC News, June 18, 2019, https://www.nbcnews.com/news/world/china-forcefully-harvests-organs-detainees-tribunal-concludes-n1018646.
23. Mike Isaac, "Facebook Said to Create Censorship Tool to Get Back into China," *New York Times*, November 22, 2016, https://www.nytimes.com/2016/11/22/technology/facebook-censorship-tool-china.html.
24. George Petras and Javier Zarracina, "How It Works: What GOP Allies Can Do to Challenge Trump's Loss," *USA Today, January 6, 2021,* https://www.usatoday.com/in-depth/news/2021/01/06/electoral-college-certification-trump-voter-fraud-congress-electoral-vote-count-republican-challenge/6555229002/. See also "Counting Electoral Votes: An Overview of Procedures at the Joint Session, Including Objections by Members of Congress," Congressional Research Service, December 8, 2020, https://crsreports.congress.gov/product/pdf/RL/RL32717/13; Scott Bomboy, "Explaining How Congress Settles Electoral College Disputes," Constitution Daily, National Constitution Center, December 15, 2020, https://constitutioncenter.org/blog/explaining-how-congress-settles-electoral-college-disputes. Two hours of debate is the current interpretation of the Electoral Count Act of 1887 by the Congressional Research Service.
25. *New Day*, transcript, CNN, August 16, 2019, http://transcripts.cnn.com/TRANSCRIPTS/1908/16/nday.05.html.
26. https://cookpolitical.com/2020-national-popular-vote-tracker.
27. Brian Naylor, "Arizona Is 1st State for Republican Elector Challenge," NPR, January 6, 2021, https://www.npr.org/sections/congress-electoral-college-tally-live-updates/2021/01/06/953931288/arizona-is-1st-state-for-republican-elector-challenge.

28. Matthew Miller, "Timeline Reveals Capitol Hill Riot Began 20 Mins Before End of Trump's Speech," The Post Millennial, January 12, 2021, https://thepostmillennial.com/timeline-reveals-capitol-hill-riot-began-20-mins-before-end-of-trumps-speech/.
29. Jim Hoft, "35 Capitol Police Officers Under Investigation, 6 Suspended for Letting Protesters Inside US Capitol—the Same Protesters Who Were Later Arrested for Entering US Capitol," The Gateway Pundit, February 19, 2021, https://www.thegatewaypundit.com/2021/02/35-capitol-police-officers-investigation-6-suspended-letting-protesters-inside-us-capitol-protesters-later-arrested-entering-us-capitol/.
30. Domenico Montanaro, "Timeline: How One of the Darkest Days in American History Unfolded," NPR, January 7, 2021. https://www.npr.org/2021/01/07/954384999/timeline-how-one-of-the-darkest-days-in-american-history-unfolded. See also "Timeline of the United States Capitol Attack," Wikipedia, https://en.wikipedia.org/wiki/Timeline_of_the_2021_storming_of_the_United_States_Capitol.
31. Qiao Liang and Wang Xiangsui, *Unrestricted Warfare: China's Master Plan to Destroy America* (Beijing: China's People's Liberation Army, 1999).
32. Jimmy Carter and James Baker, "Building Confidence in U.S. Elections," September 2005. https://www.legislationline.org/download/id/1472/ file /3b50795b2d0374cbef5c29766256.pdf,p. iii.

EPILOGUE: SOLDIERING ON

1. Andrew Stanton, "Biden's Approval Drops in Latest Poll as Post-Inauguration Honeymoon 'Officially Over,'" *Newsweek*, August 2, 2021, https://www.newsweek.com/bidens-approval-drops-latest-poll-post-inauguration-honeymoon-officially-over-1615495.
2. Ryan Devereaux, "Storming of the Capitol Was Openly Planned but Ignored by Law Enforcement," The Intercept, January 7, 2021, https://theintercept.com/2021/01/07/capitol-trump-violence-law-enforcement/.
3. Gary J. Schmitt, "January 6: An Intelligence Failure?," American Enterprise Institute, June 27, 2021, https://www.aei.org/foreign-and-defense-policy/intelligence/january-6-an-intelligence-failure/.
4. Vivek Saxena, "FBI Evidence Changes Dems' Capitol Riot Storyline: 'What Did Pelosi Know, When Did She Know It?,'" BizPac Review, February 11, 2021, https://www.bizpacreview.com/2021/02/11/fbi-evidence-changes-dems-capitol-riot-storyline-what-did-pelosi-know-when-did-she-know-it-1028419/.
5. Raymond Wolfe, "Arizona Republican Calls for New Election After Audit Flags Tens of Thousands of Ballots," LifeSiteNews.com, July 16, 2021, https://www.lifesitenews.com/news/arizona-republican-calls-for-new-election-after-audit-flags-tens-of-thousands-of-ballots/.
6. "Huge Victory in Georgia for Forensic Election Audit," Citizens of the American Republic, June 25, 2021, https://citizensoftheamericanrepublic.

org/2021/06/25/huge-victory-in-georgia-for-forensic-election-audit/.

7. Thomas Lifson, "AG Merrick Garland Threatens 2020 Ballot Audits," American Thinker, June 12, 2021, https://www.americanthinker.com/blog/2021/06/ag_merrick_garland_threatens_2020_ballot_audits.html.
8. Julian Conradson, "Breaking: Twitter Suspends All Election Audit 'War Room' Accounts; Senator Wendy Rogers Predicts She Will Be Next," Gateway Pundit, July 27, 2021, https://www.thegatewaypundit.com/2021/07/breaking-twitter-suspends-election-audit-war-room-accounts-senator-wendy-rogers-predicts-will-next/.
9. Caitlin Dickson, "Poll: Two-thirds of Republicans still think the 2020 election was rigged," Yahoo News, August 4, 2020. https://www.aol.com/poll-two-thirds-republicans-still-165934571.html
10. The Editors, "Welcome to the Party, Dr. Fauci," *National Review*, May 25, 2021, https://www.nationalreview.com/2021/05/welcome-to-the-party-dr-fauci/.
11. Ryan Foley, "Sen. Rand Paul Pushes for Criminal Investigation into Anthony Fauci: He 'Lied to Congress,'" *Christian Post*, July 26, 2021, https://www.christianpost.com/news/rand-paul-pushes-criminal-probe-into-fauci-he-lied-to-congress.html.
12. Samuel Chamberlain, "Fauci Admits 'Modest' NIH Funding of Wuhan Lab but Denies 'Gain of Function,'" *New York Post*, May 25, 2021, https://nypost.com/2021/05/25/fauci-admits-nih-funding-of-wuhan-lab-denies-gain-of-function/.
13. "Fauci-Funded Researchers Headlined Wuhan Lab 'Gain-of-Function' Conference," The Thinking Conservative, May 12, 2021, https://www.thethinkingconservative.com/fauci-funded-researchers-headlined-wuhan-lab-gain-of-function-conference/.
14. "Rand Paul Sends Criminal Referral to DOJ Saying Fauci Lied About Gain-of-Function Research Funding," *Washington Examiner*, July 24, 2021, https://www.washingtonexaminer.com/news/rand-paul-sends-criminal-referral-doj-fauci-lied-gain-of-function-research.
15. Section 1001 of the U.S. Code indicates that any government official who makes "materially false, fictitious, or fraudulent" statements could face up to five years in prison. See "18 U.S. Code § 1001—Statements of Entries Generally," Legal Information Institute, Cornell Law School, https://www.law.cornell.edu/uscode/text/18/1001.
16. Alex Eliot Hayes, "The Culture of the Disappeared in Latin America," The St Andrews Economist, October 11, 2018, https://thestandrewseconomist.com/2018/10/11/the-culture-of-the-disappeared-in-latin-america/.
17. Dr. Robert Malone and Peter Navarro, "Vaccine inventor questions mandatory shot push, Biden's Covid-19 strategy," *Washington Times*, August 5, 2021. https://www.washingtontimes.com/news/2021/aug/5/biden-teams-misguided-and-deadly-covid-19-vaccine-/

INDEX